Travels into the Heart of Egypt

MEMOIRS AND OCCASIONAL PAPERS SERIES
ASSOCIATION FOR DIPLOMATIC STUDIES
AND TRAINING

Series Editor: MARGERY BOICHEL THOMPSON

In 2003, the Association for Diplomatic Studies and Training (ADST) created the Memoirs and Occasional Papers Series to preserve firsthand accounts and other informed observations on foreign affairs for scholars, journalists, and the general public. Sponsoring publication of book series is one of numerous ways in which ADST, a nonprofit organization founded in 1986, seeks to promote understanding of American diplomacy and those who conduct it. Together with the Foreign Affairs Oral History program and ADST's support for the training of foreign affairs personnel at the State Department's Foreign Service Institute, these efforts constitute the Association's fundamental purposes. Lillian Craig Harris's evocative essays comprise the twenty-ninth volume in the series.

RELATED SERIES TITLES

Claudia Anyaso, ed., *Fifty Years of US Africa Policy*
Herman J. Cohen, *The Mind of the African Strongman: Conversations with Dictators, Statesmen, and Father Figures*
Thompson Buchanan, *Mossy Memoir of a Rolling Stone*
Christopher Goldthwait, *Ambassador to a Small World: Letters from Chad*
John Gunther Dean, *Danger Zones: A Diplomat's Fight for America's Interests*
Robert E. Gribbin, *In the Aftermath of Genocide: The US Role in Rwanda*
Allen C. Hansen, *Nine Lives: A Foreign Service Odyssey*
W. Nathaniel Howell, *Strangers When We Met: A Century of American Community in Kuwait*
John G. Kormann, *Echoes of a Distant Clarion: Recollections of a Diplomat and Soldier*
Nicole Prévost Logan, *Forever on the Road: A Franco-American Family's Thirty Years in the Foreign Service*
Armin Meyer, *Quiet Diplomacy: From Cairo to Tokyo in the Twilight of Imperialism*
William Morgan and Charles Stuart Kennedy, eds., *American Diplomats: The Foreign Service at Work*
Howard Steele, *Bushels and Bales: A Food Soldier in the Cold War*
Theresa Tull, *A Long Way from Runnemede: One Woman's Foreign Service Journey*
Susan Wyatt, *Arabian Nights and Daze: Living in Yemen with the Foreign Service*
Virginia Carson Young, *Peregrina: Unexpected Adventures of an American Consul*

For a complete list of series titles, visit *adst.org/publications*

Travels into the Heart of Egypt

Lillian Craig Harris

MEMOIRS AND OCCASIONAL PAPERS SERIES
ASSOCIATION FOR DIPLOMATIC STUDIES AND TRAINING

Washington, DC

Copyright © 2016 by Lillian Craig Harris

New Academia Publishing/VELLUM Books, 2016

The views and opinions in this book are solely those of the author and not necessarily those of the Government of the United States or the Association for Diplomatic Studies and Training.

All rights reserved. No part of this book may be reproduced or transmitted in any form or by any means, electronic or mechanical, including photocopying, recording, or by any information storage and retrieval system.

Printed in the United States of America

Library of Congress Control Number: 2016941796
ISBN 978-0-9974962-5-3 paperback (alk. paper)

 An imprint of New Academia Publishing

 New Academia Publishing
4401-A Connecticut Ave. NW, #236, Washington DC 20008
info@newacademia.com - www.newacademia.com

Unless otherwise indicated, the photographs in this book were taken by the author or her husband.

Contents

Foreword, by Wesley Egan	viii
Preface	xi
Maps	xv
1. Fortress of the Soldier	1
2. The Ladies of Abu Zabaal	5
3. To Saqqara with Sadika	9
4. Death and Love in the Eastern Desert	13
5. Pyramiding in the Fayoum	17
6. With St. Catherine in Sinai	25
7. Praising God in the City of the Dead	31
8. Raising Dry Bones at Saqqara	39
9. Pagan Revival at Qasr Ibrim	45
10. Conspiracy of Silence at Jebel Asfar	53
11. Shooters in Zamalek	59
12. Susie and Diana at Heliopolis	63
13. In the Wadi of the King	67
14. The Mango Season	71
15. Ordeal by Fire at Abu Sultan	77
16. With Florence Nightingale in Upper Egypt	81
17. Qanatar Prison	87
18. A Shabti Takes the Photographer to Ismailia	93
19. Of Jesuits, Copts, and the Virgin Mary	99
20. Faith and Solitude at the Monasteries of St. Anthony and St. Paul	105
21. Crossing the Delta to Alexandria	109
22. Remembering the Battle of El Alamein Fifty Years On	113
23. Aswan without Tourists	119

24. Monkey Business in Wadi Natrun	125
25. From Cairo to Kharga	131
26. Around Kharga	135
27. South to Dush	139
28. In Dakhla Oasis	145
29. On Tour from Liberation Square	149
30. On to Baharia	153
31. A Gift at Dimeh	159
32. Port Call with the Honorary Consul	163
33. Consultation in Zagazig	169
34. Alifa Rifaat's Vision	175
35. Restoring Icons at Abu Seifein in Old Cairo	181
36. For the Love of Camels	187
37. Watching on Sham-e-Nessim	195
38. Tourist Trash in Sinai	199
39. Following Jehovah through Sinai	203
40. Befriending Cairo	207
41. Birding at the Barrages	211
42. Mena House and Minor Pyramids	215
43. Spiritual Journey on the River	223
44. Looking for Michael in Middle Egypt	231
45. Siwa: Escape from a Dying Oasis	239
46. Sorting It Out with the Zebaleen	247
47. Of Mud, Walls, and Women	251
48. Serabit—the Place Where Moses Dwelt	255
49. St Catherine's Mountain	259
50. Questions on the River	265
51. Along North Road	271
52. Missionaries in Minya	275
53. Humming from Western Desert to Eastern Desert	281
54. In Search of an Angel	287

55. Moulid of Al-Sayeda Zeinab	293
56. A Monastery Too Far	297
57. Trouble at Abu Seifein	301
Notes	307
Glossary	312

Foreword

Egypt reveals itself slowly and partially to even the most patient and sympathetic observer. In these fifty-seven essays, written between 1990 and 1995, Dr. Lillian Craig Harris takes us from Cairo to the monasteries of the Eastern Desert and the hurriedly built resorts of the Red Sea coast, westward to the vast near emptiness of the desert stretching beyond the Libyan border, south toward Nubia, and deep into the Sinai. Some places are familiar, but many will be new to you. Unlike most of her published work, this is not a scholarly consideration of Egypt's long sedimentary past or of its unpredictable present and future. Instead, it is a chronicle of her occasionally rueful, often joyful effort and need to connect with humanity outside the diplomatic routine of the modern capital. Sometimes she traveled with others, "male and female, foreign and Egyptian, diplomat and businessman, Christian and Muslim, and three minority conditions: agnostic, homosexual, and spy." Mostly she traveled with her British husband Alan Goulty, her kindred spirit, "the Diplomat." But in the end, at a turning point in her life, she traveled alone.

Her account of these adventures is disarmingly personal and minutely observed. She is a bird watcher (a twitcher in her adopted vernacular), but she finds people more interesting than birds. With her you will sit with old men in whose eyes you may see wisdom, tranquility, or at least trust. You'll watch passersby "who wave to us out of courtesy, not interest." You will hug lepers, console women in prison, counsel the suicidal, comfort a drug trafficker turned evangelical preacher, mediate for a dissident Coptic priest, tolerate honorary consuls and louts, adopt stray dogs, pray with mystics, support activists for women's rights, and argue with misogynists. You will find something sinister in Port Said, something which "sits quietly and with folded wing but clearly waiting." And you'll join in her disappointment during some ceremonial duties with Princess Diana in a Heliopolis cemetery.

During the springtime Sham-e-Nessim holiday you can "sniff the breezes" with city dwellers who since pharaonic times have gone to the country to renew the unity of man and nature. You will sense "a power of the sort that stalks" at Alexander's dilapidated oasis at Siwa and witness a "most unsuitable" death on the Nile. You will find her worrying about what sort of fathers the young garbage-collecting Christian men of the Moqattam Hills, overlooking the City of the Dead, will become and smile at her guess that, for the young guard recruits of Qanatar Prison, "learning to wear trousers is not easy for a man of eighteen." In the Sinai she learns why no man wants to be master of a castrated camel from a Bedu who asks out loud why foreigners want to know so much but learn so little?

It is difficult to imagine wandering around like this today in the aftermath of September 11. Dr. Harris's official status was senior enough that she had, or could cajole, access to areas and sites off-limits to most, but not so senior as to require the tiresome escort of her own security detail or of the local police and security forces. Her best advice when confronted with a police or military roadblock in the outskirts of town or in the wilds of the Western desert is to keep talking and keep the motor running. As her time in Egypt lengthened, the frequency of attacks on foreigners in Upper Egypt and along the Red Sea coast increased but not to the extent that her travel was ever much curtailed.

I lived around the corner for much of her time in Egypt and envied her determination to escape the diplomatic routine in Cairo. I also came to know well how important these journeys were in her personal search for renewal. I can imagine her striding across the sand to the monasteries of Wadi Natrun or climbing the rough path to the monastery of St. Paul the Anchorite, the first Christian hermit, and the monastery of St. Anthony, the first monk south of Suez. No doubt she would be humming, or perhaps shouting, the words of the old hymn Walking Across Egypt: "My stride will not be broken, my heart shall see the way." There it was that she debated the hierarchy of the cherubim and the seraphim and pondered the three archangels of the Coptic pantheon.

There are hints throughout these very personal and intimate essays of the author's slightly Faulkneresque family history. It seems that for at least some of the Harris family diplomacy could be an acceptable substitute for missionary service. You can hear the footfalls of her uncles and parents and grandparents and siblings, who wrestled with life's disappointments and triumphs and who swayed between their extremes. She herself describes these Egyptian travels as cathartic, and in the end she succeeds.

A regular visitor to the Church of Abu Seifein (St. Mercurios) in Cairo, she was one day asked to mediate a dispute between the resident priest and the Coptic Pope Shenouda. The priest, who had spent many years supervising the architectural and artistic restoration of the church, had refused the pope's order to leave and return to monastic life in the desert. "He had lost his temper in a debate with authority—how often had I done that?" She failed at her mediation; but in that place, she "had, after long loneliness, heard again the Voice which calls us to love God and to sacrifice for the sake of others."

We are lucky to be able to accompany her on her journey, for she succeeds in taking us more deeply into the mysteries of a people and of a timeless culture than we might ever have managed on our own.

WESLEY EGAN, U.S. *Ambassador (retired)*
Washington 2013

Preface

While living in Egypt in the early 1990s, I took every opportunity to travel in country, as a way to better understand the Egyptian people and their fascinating history but also, truth be told, to avoid when possible the monotonous round of diplomatic receptions and dinners. Accompanying me on most of these excursions was my husband, Alan Goulty, a British diplomat and himself the reason for my presence in Egypt. But my first visit to Egypt had been in the 1960s, when I was teaching at an Armenian college in Beirut, Lebanon. Then in 1985 I spent two months in Cairo as an American Foreign Service officer. Egypt fascinated me, and although I was a China specialist, I had hoped to return.

Alan and I met in 1981, when he was a first secretary at the British Embassy in Washington. We married in 1983. The difficulties in running diplomatic careers for two different governments —we were the first American/British diplomatic tandem—led to my resignation from the State Department not long after Alan was posted back to London in 1986. When Alan was nominated for Cairo as deputy head of mission, we were delighted.

The travel essays included in this book were written while we lived in Egypt from late 1990 to early 1995. Alan's position at British Embassy Cairo provided access to government officials and, when needed, official permission to travel in country. Ours was, in fact, the perfect travel position. If Alan had already been an ambassador, protocol would have prevented independent exploration. If he had been of lower rank than the number two in the British mission, we would probably not have received local Egyptian government facilitation when required. Instead, somewhat in the manner of ghosts, we were able, usually entirely on our own, to flitter through deserts, cities, and archaeological sites, trusting in the legendary hospitality and guidance of the Egyptian people—to whom this book is gratefully dedicated.

At the time of writing, the essays included here were not intended for publication. I wrote simply to record what we had experienced and to capture my emotions of wonder, frustration, and joy as well as the gratitude I felt in travelling among Egypt's diverse people and both ancient and modern treasures. Some twenty years later, these reflections may also provide useful reflection on the widespread unrest that eventually expressed itself in the Arab Spring.

The early 1990s were a time of general but usually hidden unhappiness under dictatorship, cronyism, nepotism, corruption, and the arrogance of the ruling authorities. Lack of concern for the needs of the majority of Egyptians, in particular those who were impoverished, led to bread riots and other forms of protest, most brutally squelched and kept out of the media. Although the country was rapidly modernizing, this was almost entirely to the benefit of the wealthy, while the plight of the poor was essentially ignored. Millions of people lived in enormous poverty; there was widespread lack of jobs, a very high rate of illiteracy, and, of course, inadequate education.

Egyptians of all sorts were ready to explain that the day of change would certainly come and the Mubarak regime would fall. But most Egyptians professed inability to do anything but wait. Although stoutly patriotic, many Egyptians had no hesitation in describing former British colonial rule as "the good days," when justice was more likely to be applied in response to any number of difficulties and problems.

But the early 1990s were also years of peace with Israel as a result of the Camp David agreements and of growing business opportunities for the middle classes. These advances helped to hide other difficult issues at home such as encroachment on desert land traditionally held by tribes, ingrained prejudice against Christians and Jews on the part of many Egyptians, and racism against darker fellow countrymen from higher up the Nile.

Fascinating as it was, living in Egypt faced me with difficulties.

Although diplomatic life looks glamorous from the outside, those thus engaged often find themselves attending seemingly endless receptions and other official functions and entertainments, their own and those of other diplomats and local government officials. During my first two years in Cairo, I balanced this by writing a book and teaching part-time at the American University in Cairo. The second two years brought opportunity—with the support of Egyptian and foreign volunteers as well as Egyptian psychiatrists—to set up a free listening service for despairing and suicidal people, work for which I had been trained in London. (Befrienders Cairo, affiliated to Befrienders International, which is itself now defunct, continued for several years after we left Egypt.) Cathartic trips outside Cairo were enormously helpful during what was one of the most active periods of my life. But our ability to travel in country was enhanced by other events as well.

From 1990 through early 1995 Egypt played a key role in the coalition to rid Kuwait of its Iraqi occupiers. This led to a stream of high-level British visitors to Cairo and a noticeable warming of official Anglo-Egyptian relations. Meanwhile, fear of the possible consequences of the 1991 Gulf War severely curtailed tourism to Egypt. These circumstances enabled us to visit many popular sites in relative peace and tranquility. Later during our time in Egypt, an outbreak of extremist attacks on tourists gave foreign heads of mission diplomatic headaches but provided Alan and me with travel opportunities less encumbered by hordes of tourists. When released from official life in Cairo, we took every available opportunity to slip off into the Egyptian deserts, frontiers, and ancient sites. In retrospect some of this traveling was quite dangerous; and we remain deeply grateful to the Egyptian people—friends, acquaintances, and passersby—for the kindness they showed us during our years "up the Nile." Four subsequent years in Khartoum while Alan was British ambassador to Sudan allowed me to return frequently to Cairo.

In the two decades since I lived in Egypt, an ancient country with kind and generous people, much has changed. My prayer for them is that the Arab Spring will eventually lead the Egyptian people towards true democracy.

xv

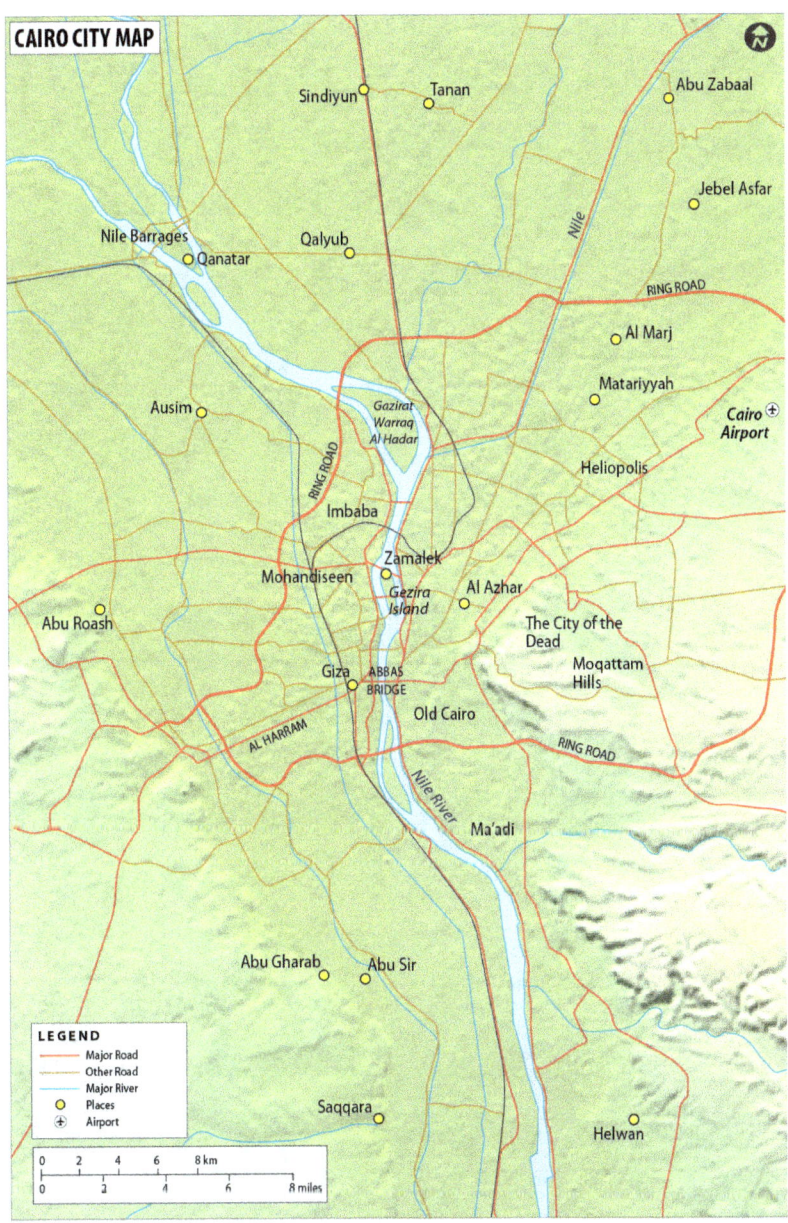

Greater Cairo.
Maps of World, Compare Infobase Limited, New Delhi

The Nile Valley and Eastern Desert of Egypt.
Maps of World, Compare Infobase Limited, New Delhi

xvii

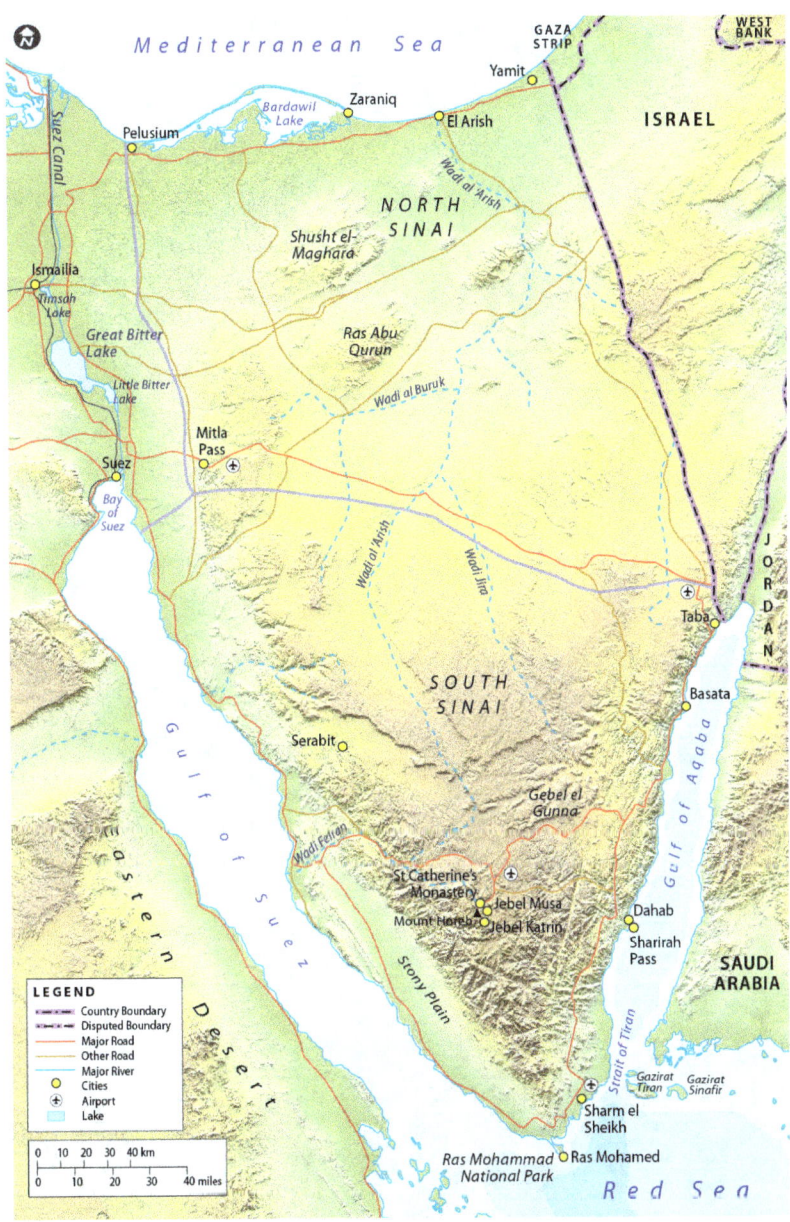

The Sinai Peninsula.
Maps of World, Compare Infobase Limited, New Delhi

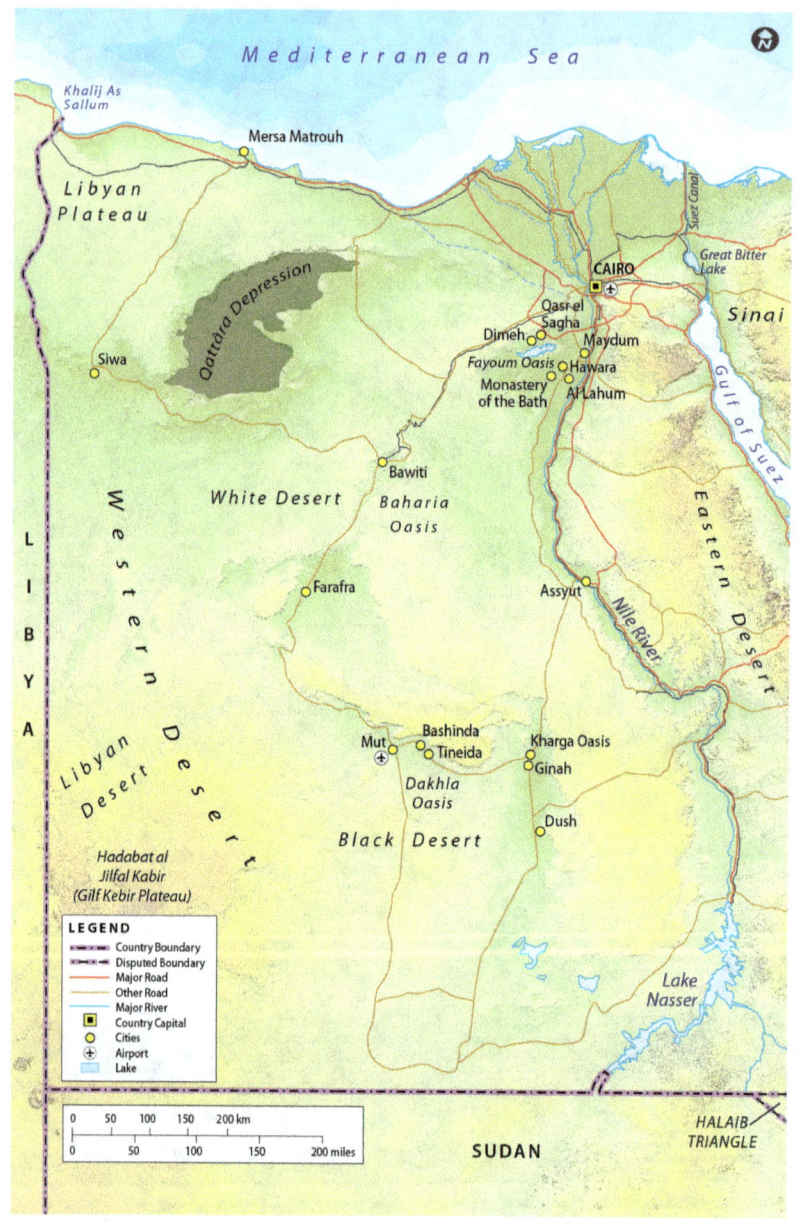

Egypt's Western Desert.
Maps of World, Compare Infobase Limited, New Delhi

1

Fortress of the Soldier

October 1991

The fortress of Qal'at al-Gundi rises to the left of the paved road. So perfectly does it blend with the desert hilltop that sun-dazzled travelers might even pass it unnoticed unless they chanced to look back from the east upon its yawning, broken walls. Why did Saladin build here? And which forgotten soldier does the name commemorate other than that great warrior himself? Far from Cairo, far from Palestine, surrounded by the silence and space of the Sinai desert, this once fearsome stronghold guards its secrets well. Only a few young soldiers from a nearby camp break the silence with their shouting. Like young men everywhere, they seem to have little respect for history.

"Have you any magazines?" one soldier asks hopefully when we stop. Sadly, we do not. Day trippers from Cairo seldom carry such luxuries. But the soldier's plaintive request calls up other questions. A thwarted intellectual outcast in the desert? A sex-starved young man hoping for a girlie magazine? A misfit who shuns the ribald talk around the evening fire? Or just a bored teenager longing for his family in Cairo? No matter, the moment has passed. The soldier tells us where to begin the ascent and then disappears. We have failed him and are of no further interest.

The track bucks and fishtails under the Range Rover's steady grip. Below are crevices and boulders. Eventually, we reach a level area bordered by deep sand and get out on a plateau less than half a mile from the road. Technology has its limits. Anyway, like Allenby entering Jerusalem, we prefer to ascend onto holy ground on foot.

The air is still and heavy with heat and silence. A broken track climbs steeply from the east towards a gap in the great walls whose giant dressed stones litter the wadis. The heat is scalding pitch and flaming arrows. We climb steadily, pausing once to pant under pretext of admiring the view. The Labrador retriever in her heavy coat is overheating and must be watered. We reach a level path and, after another steep scramble, the gate is ours.

"In the Name of God, the Merciful, the Compassionate." We rest in shade beneath the inscribed arch. Who were these men who built here, and where are the bones of their enemies who died on the ascent? Appropriately we bow to pass through the arch and enter their sanctuary. Built in the 1170s, the *Blue Guide* says, Qal'at al-Gundi was destroyed in the thirteenth century. Yes, but why? And by whom?

The remains of a small fire, an owl feather, a few small bones are the only signs of recent visitation. Two soldiers appear, laughing after their rapid climb, then disappear again and silence returns. Subterranean chambers reach to entrap the unwary, and we explore cautiously. Reverently, we peer into half-covered storerooms, broken-vaulted chambers, and then an enormous, dark cistern. A small stone falls a long way before thudding on the bottom. Empty. Did the last defenders give in at last with glazed eyes and broken lips, their surrender slurred through swollen tongues?

The small mosque that adorns the summit is also ruined. But its broken walls retain evidence of careful workmanship. The Labrador follows the tantalizing smell of fox onto holy ground and we call her back. Who last prayed here and for what hopeless cause? The towers on the eastern wall have fallen outward. Surely the work of an earthquake?

A light breeze finds us on the western wall as we survey the miles commanded by Qal'at al-Gundi. No arrogant crusaders or night creeping bedu could have pulled off a surprise here. It had to be siege. When the last defenders stood here longing for help, did they shade their eyes towards the Nile as we do now? For how long did they hold on after accepting that help would not come, that defeat was inevitable?

The desert seldom reveals its secrets, and, meanwhile, the night would surely come. To remain here after dark would be folly. We descend towards the desert floor, towards the road winding far below. Like jinn, the soldiers appear once again. No, we have no cigarettes. And once more we feel miserable to have let them down. Tourism, it seems, does not extend its benefits to all Egyptians.

Later, picnicking near the Cairo road at the foot of the only tree in sight, we look back and wonder. Did we really climb up there? A brown-necked raven, disgruntled by our presence under his tree, lurks in the shrubs that march across the sand. It is written, "By their works, ye shall know them." But we do not know, for the guidebooks are almost as mute about the origins of this desert fortress as the fortress itself. Even Steven Runciman's three-volume study of the Crusades fails to mention Qal'at al-Gundi.

The tree, long roots arching above ground by wind erosion and reaching far in search of water, provides the only shade for miles. How old is this tree and how did it get here? Likely the raven knows this, as well as who has partially burned one of the tree's still living roots. The tree sighs as a slight breeze arrives to caress it.

Lunch over, we collect a large sack of empty tins and other rubbish left by earlier visitors. Feeling righteous for having done this, we consider emptying a jerry can of water at the base of the tree. No, better not raise the tree's expectations. Beside, relief from siege is all too infrequent in the desert, and we ourselves have miles to go.

As we rejoin the main road that crosses the Mitla Pass to Suez, the raven resettles himself on the tree, the better to keep an eye on Tree and Fortress to which he has been appointed Guardian.

Qal'at al Gundi—the Fortress of the Soldier, Sinai, October 1991

2

The Ladies of Abu Zabaal

12 November 1991

I remembered a line from Max Boyce's account of his trip to a brothel: "I didn't wanna go!" Perhaps. Nor did I, particularly. But philanthropy is often the way affluence excuses its voyeurism. As a new, albeit reluctant, member of the British Embassy Garden Fete Disbursement Committee, I had little choice. At 8 a.m. Cairo time––I don't know what time it was in hell—we set out by car on the road towards Ismailia. With delays to meet the nuns and to check on a gift of wood, it would be two hours before we arrived at Abu Zabaal.

That was this morning. It's now 3:30 in the afternoon, and I'm back in the city doing what I do when greatly disturbed: listening to Bach, too loud, with an ache inside that feels like hunger but is probably a combination of fear, sorrow, and regret.

The Abu Zabaal hospital is in a military zone, the better to restrict access. Medical students are not taken to Abu Zabaal, a Cairo surgeon told me, and even many Egyptian doctors do not know the secret which confines some 650 sufferers there. A few foreigners are allowed in because three or four western embassies take an interest and to deny access might cause publicity. But, really, it is best not to speak of it. The disease represents backwardness, people say, so best not mention it. The afflicted are the poor. Best not to tally them—although they number more than 24,000 and are found throughout Egypt.

I've often noticed that most of the most difficult jobs, other than war and coal mining, are assigned to women. In the entrance courtyard, a nun had offered to shake our hands. Somehow I hadn't expected that—or the "characteristic" leonine faces, the sightless eyes, the stumps of eroded flesh. With a panoply of antibiotics, including Ramphasin, which I had taken myself for the related tuberculosis bacillus, this disease is controllable, even curable. But only if the patient takes the full treatment. Only if care and preventive measures are adequate. Only if the bacillus is caught before nerve damage has occurred. And only if others provide adequate help and support. All this I learned today.

In a low, rundown building put up in the 1930s, twisted and grotesque old men sit silently waiting. I like very old men. Often you can hold their hands and look into their eyes and see wisdom, tranquility or at least trust. But most of these untouchable creatures are ageless, blind, all hope erased from ravished faces. One man toasts bread over bricks at the foot of his bed, lifting and turning the loaf with stumps that can feel neither heat nor pain. Each patient prepares his own food, we are told, but the inadequate government rations have a way of disappearing before they reach the lepers. This is part of the reason our delegation of diplomatic wives has come here today.

"Leper!" Horrible label, written in decaying flesh. "Unclean! Unclean!" The ancient sufferers ring their bells down through history and decent, healthy folk banish them into the desert of Abu Zabaal. "Leper colony," the place where lepers are warehoused, is the last refuge of the damned, a place of the crawling wounded and the walking dead. Is there anything worse than this? Yes.

In the contagious ward, someone has broken all the chairs and young men crowd onto sagging beds set high on bricks. A body-building poster of a man rippling his well-oiled back muscles dominates one corner, and a fellow voyeur, who claims to know, whispers to me that leprosy, by some obscene parody, augments the victim's sex drive. I also learn that five years ago all floors here were earthen.

But now a hostile youth (who wants to be on exhibit?) sweeps the concrete floor. The sweeper, outwardly unmarked, tosses some solid object into a corner with a loud clang and gets on savagely with his work. The Italian nun is angry about the broken chairs but banks her frustration. No prize for guessing "who dunnit."

We ladies from Zamalek, Maadi, and Heliopolis gather our skirts and peer into the watery depths of a bathroom, awash with filth, broken toilet seats, and wastewater. There had been a plan last year to refurbish but someone was on the take and only two of six bathrooms were renovated. Someone has traced artistic lines in excrement on the entrance wall. When winter comes, I think, this place will be very cold.

"No games today!" an old dragon chortles as we exit back toward the courtyard. His eye sockets are screwed shut with scar tissue but a beatific smile flashes across his collapsed face. Two young men flank him on the bench, one snuggled close. The small circle of men around the blind buffoon laugh and wave at us. Perhaps they are wondering if even being a woman would be preferable to this life. And how long since any of them touched a woman, and what is going on here with the old dragon? A memory sings across the taut wires of my mind: Papillon taking the half-smoked cigar offered by a leper and so building the confidence that bought him a boat to freedom.

At the Caritas Center, rows of strangely subdued children are eating sandwiches. Prompted, they thank us for the chocolate bars. No snatching, no cries of "Ana! Ana!" Proudly, a worker announces, "Only three or four of the lepers' children contracted the disease here last year." But these are contaminated children. Who, except a leper, would want them?

A ten-year-old named Wasila gently takes my hand. We walk in silence past our gift of wood, now being carefully stowed for use as roofing material. The living conditions are no worse here than in many rural villages, I tell myself. And besides, we are told, "There is a strong social support network among the lepers." Wasila is small for her age and the scaly white patches on her face are, I hope, due only to Vitamin B deficiency. Her resistance, then, is low.

"We all have the plague within us," Camus said. I see that in the tale told by a pretty teenager, the mother of two, who was "married in" to Abu Zabaal from Upper Egypt when she was fifteen. What sort of family sends its daughter to be the third wife to a leper? She takes the medicine regularly, of course. But still, a volunteer worker mutters, "She shouldn't be sleeping with him." One of the grand ladies slips the young wife some cash, and we pass out of her life. Wasila squeezes my hand.

The chickens in the women's compound are as exotic as the patients, each chicken marked by ownership on wing or leg by colored yarn. We are greeted by a wizened woman, teeth grimacing from a gaping, noseless face, her voice throaty and obscure. Abu Zabaal has been her home since she was eighteen, nearly forty years ago. She grins hideously at her grand friend from Heliopolis, and the two women hug one another.

What do lepers die from, someone wants to know, since the bacilli attack extremities only? But the question is irrelevant: these are the Living Dead. In the dispensary, a mother displays her beautiful baby girl and other women clap their stumps in admiration. Their earrings, gypsy-bright scarves, and kohl-lined eyes emphasize their twisted facial features. Child of leper, wife of leper, leper.

Best to try to forget what I have seen. Wasila, to ensure that I do not, presses her tiny face against the car window. But though she asks politely, I do not give her my ring. Probably, I excuse myself, she will one day have no fingers on which to wear it. Besides, irrational but terrifying thought, what has she given me?

In the car on the long drive back to Cairo, I sit in silence as others cope with what we have seen by discussing servants, dressmakers, persistent fatigue from long nights at endless dinner parties. I wish they would stop talking. I need Bach and a bath. I need to be alone.

For some reason I keep seeing the way the cheerful, snaggle-toothed government dentist plopped a set of new dentures into a destroyed face. The dentures didn't make the man handsome, but at least he could chew again. And keep on waiting for Godot.

It is late afternoon in Cairo. I turn up the Bach, thinking about Wasila, suspecting that even if I tried to extricate her, they wouldn't let her go. She is a Muslim and I am a Christian, a leper. Best not to mention it.

3

To Saqqara with Sadika

5 December 1991

For twenty years, I have wanted to ride from Giza to Saqqara, over the desert in shining moonlight, every rock sheltering a fox, every dark wadi holding a chained demon. But that was a fantasy born in Beirut, city of dreams later turned into nightmares. In 1970, an American friend told me of her midnight ride to Saqqara in the 1960s, and since then I'd cherished the idea. Now, rather like the man who spent his life pursuing a rare warbler, my desire has been attained, although something important was missing—night travel on horseback in that area is no longer allowed. Nor would it be safe.

Three weeks ago, *Al Ahram Weekly* carried an article about the horse ride from Giza to Saqqara in daylight, making it sound an event of wonder—as indeed it ought to be. The stopping at the pyramid complexes of Abu Gharab and Abu Sir, the brilliant sunlight washing down the sides of dune and ruin—these catch the heart as they have for ages. But something the writer failed to mention was out there as well. Egypt's population has grown enormously in twenty years, and the backwash of civilization encroaches on the desert, its splendor, its wild life, its monuments, and its dead.

We gathered at 8:30 in the morning, fifteen riders on sturdy but underfed Arabian horses, who seemed to sense the pyramids from afar and pranced to be on their way. The day began windless, and we rode quickly, cantering for long stretches along a route that alternated canal and desert. Military zones and forlorn archaeological sites enclosed in barbed wire hung with windblown plastic bags make it no longer possible to cover the twenty kilometers from Giza to Saqqara in desert alone. The Cairo ring road, under construction at the edge of the town, is scheduled to cut through the plateau in a year or two, and after that, direct access to Saqqara from Giza on horseback may no longer be possible.

The elder of our two grooms rode a mare I know well, a slender red flame, which he stoked relentlessly, balancing his weight against her mouth in the way of careless riders, his feet sticking out before her withers. Her name, he told me, was Jamila. But I know her as Sadika, and though I had not ridden her for three months, she recognized my voice, signaling with her ears as I cantered, singing to her as so often before.

Someday, I know, perhaps even soon, Sadika will end on the rubbish heap near the stables with the other used up stable horses. The baladi dogs will devour her, bones and all. But today there were fewer carcasses in the smoldering dump, and the abandoned dogs expressed their resentment by pursuing our cavalcade a short distance through the sand. There is not much hope in these wadis for people or for animals. And that, of course, was why I had stopped coming here, I reminded myself—except for today.

A relatively clear day cheered us through the plantations where sorrowful donkeys turned the creaking norias, and filthy children shouted greetings and demands for baksheesh. From her perch in a palm tree, a lesser kestrel watched us pass and, once, a flash of electric blue announced a kingfisher over the canal.

Abdul Nabi, who owns possibly the largest Arabian stud in Egypt, had set the fee at 35 LE [*livres égyptiennes,* French for Egyptian pounds] each plus five for the two grooms. It isn't as though he needs the money. En route we stopped to admire his farm, which stiffened our resistance to an expected price hike at day's end. Lines of box stalls filled the vast barn, each containing a beauty with artistic neck tattoos attesting pure Arabian ancestry. Most of them seemed to be pregnant. Riding through Abdul Nabi's orchards, we helped ourselves to his tangerines and further fortified our resolve.

One of our company, an Englishman in a red shirt and out of place cowboy boots, told me that he was riding his "usual" horse. Someone else told me that the macho Englishman works for the Arab Organization for Industrialization, an improbable euphemism for arms manufacturing. He ought, I grumped to myself, to have replaced the Crocodile Dundee knife, carefully strapped to his waist, with a miniature missile. All such devices are, after all, just phallic symbols.

Red Shirt did not return the greetings offered by the old men and laughing young soldiers whom we passed. Foreign oddities who allow women in tight trousers to ride stallions, we passed quickly through their lives and they returned to their shishas and small plates of beans and bread spread before them on the sun baked Nile mud.

At Abu Gharab, we found the large stone vessels described by Al Ahram Weekly as blood basins. If the tomb wall paintings at Saqqara are accurate, the ancients slaughtered their bulls by tying them up and simply hacking off limb after limb. Not, I suppose, for purposeful cruelty but perhaps simply because that was the way it had always been done. So much of life seems to go on like that. Then, as today along the canal paths, peasant women carry loads of berseem home to feed the water buffalo. The women's kohl-rimmed eyes stared from wrinkled faces, which creased further in acknowledgment when I said to them, "As salaam aleikum."

At Saqqara, we ate an early lunch near the step pyramid. Once, a few years ago, I was able to enter Zoser's tomb in the train of the wife of a visiting British politician. The British archaeologist who accompanied us said that during his ten years in Egypt, this was the first time he had been allowed to enter the fragile step pyramid. The interior was a scene from Raiders of the Lost Ark, with large slanting beams, some collapsing, holding up the pyramid from within. The air inside the pyramid was dead. We spoke softly and moved quickly, to see and return to safety.

But today, there was no question of entry or even of getting close to the step pyramid. Too many tourists, too many horses, too many hands outstretched for permits and yet more baksheesh. I threw bread at an inquisitive hoopoe lark as the arms dealer, sitting near me in the sand, uncorked a bottle of well-shaken white wine. It's 10:30 a.m. Time for a drink in the desert. A tiny sand-colored spider climbed my right boot, going about its business in near to-tal camouflage among the human beings, whose large eyes were not large enough to see the surrounding dunes and ridges as living communities.

Our leader changed the route on the return, skirting a modern cemetery. The desert has always received the dead, preserving their bones in clean sand and thereby promoting the notion that because it is a place of death it is also a place of no life. Sadika's eyes narrowed, and her ears twitched as she trotted past the small black mare on which I rode. Perhaps, I thought, Sadika, too, knows that there is an end to living desert. But what if she does? Few people care what she feels or what she knows.

Large trucks carrying sand out of the desert and replacing it with Cairo's rubbish joined us on a stretch of road beside a major canal. Cheerful and thoughtless, the drivers usually waited until parallel with the line of horses before blasting their horns in greeting. Or perhaps, it was, after all, simply a warning that there is not room here for all of us.

"Unworthy custodians," I muttered self-righteously, although I was among the offenders. Or perhaps I was speaking for Sadika. But the little mare was already far up the line and no doubt preoccupied with the need to get back to where there was berseem, and water, and where the heavy-handed man in flip-flops would get off her back and stop trying to mutilate her mouth. But before eating, she would hope to have a quick roll in the sand.

Horses and barely surviving people are often dismissed as unable to think about tomorrow. But I begin to wonder whether they may be thinking of it more than we do.

Postscript re why I was no longer often riding with the stable where Sadika lived: overuse of animals, particularly by cruel riders; and groups of abandoned dogs in the desert where the horses were taken, making riding there a sad and sometimes dangerous ordeal.

4

Death and Love in the Eastern Desert

December 1991

Mons Porphyrites, the Jebel Dukhan, can be reached from Cairo in a seven-hour drive. But you can't get back that night and will have the choice of camping by the Roman fort in Wadi el-Ma'mal or near the ruined monastery of Wadi Umm Sidra, the mother of cherries. Rocks interspersed with clean sand cover the wadi floors and the purple, green, and brown jebel walls surround the wadis like cupped hands. The way in from the main Hurghada highway by four-wheel drive takes three hours along a route almost too filled with boulders to be declared a track. But intruders are drawn on through the wadis by views of distant peaks, which resemble a Chinese landscape.

The monastery site seems the end of the earth and for many it was. Most of those hundreds or perhaps thousands of unwilling travelers to the rock mines of Mons Prophyrites never returned. Their discarded bones lie in back wadis away from the rock quarries or, perhaps, like the former owner of the remnant of winding cloth I found at the nearby quarry of Mons Claudianus, were for love or pity's sake tucked into a crevice by a fellow slave.

The Roman appetite for purple porphyry and diorite sparkling with mica died with the empire, but Roman Egypt survives in the jebels and wadis of the Eastern Desert. The site of the slaves' years of anguished labor amidst intolerable heat and thirst remains almost untouched. It is as though just yesterday an order came to lay down tools and abandon the half-chiseled blocks, the low stone huts, and the long earthen loading ramps.

Did an exhausted messenger vomit out the word that Rome had fallen? Was work stopped by a Bedouin raid, a slaves' revolt, the stealthy attack of plague? On this the desert has nothing to say, its silence broken only by the distant sound of falling rock at night and the strident daytime cry of brown-necked ravens. The typical square Roman forts, the ruined temples to Serapis and Isis and their broken columns are all there, but the people have been released.

In a hermit's hole not far from here as the raven flies, one of these black creatures fed St. Anthony half a loaf of bread each day until St. Paul came seeking him and then—sign of divine approval—doubled the ration. So say the monks. But not far to the south of where the Christian monastic tradition began and only a few years earlier, at Mons Porphyrites and Mons Claudianus, the enslaved Christians seemed abandoned by their Lord. And so perished.

On Jebel Dukhan, purple chips, pebbles, and lumps of porphyry litter the wadis, carried by infrequent torrents for several kilometers out onto the plain that stretches to the Red Sea. The first modern explorers "discovered" the site by following these porphyry chips. Jebel Dukhan itself is scarred by ancient chisel marks and bore holes. Italian visitors of the 1930s, perhaps dreaming of renewed empire, carved their names into the living rock. But few transient visitors have ever come here. The ascent from the valley floor to the mine face rises two thousand feet in less than a mile, and the heat is near overwhelming.

Further south, high in the ridges of Mons Claudianus, two enormous slabs of diorite, signed XIII and XIV with a careful chisel, were one day propped up on small rocks. The intention was to allow access to the ropes and tree trunks that would ease their passage onto the ramp. Some seventeen hundred years have passed, and still they do not follow XII down to the plain for the hundred-mile journey by oxcart to the Nile and then by boat on the Mediterranean and across to Rome. A sand partridge cries harshly to its mate and scuttles off among the rocks.

There are also gold and emerald mines in the Eastern Desert. But modern Egyptians are mainly content thus far to exploit the coast, leaving the interior to its holy, majestic silence. Someday, tourists will come in droves to this place of spiritual power and will carve modern names. Already it has begun. Some fool named "Sabry, Misr Travel" signed in on "21-11-91" with bold letters on the ancient plaster of the pillars at the dry well in Wadi Ma'mal. Thus do we modern people diminish our future by mutilating our past.

At Mons Claudianus, more accessible along a semi-paved road, we are surprised by an odd high-wheeled truck, with seats that, having announced its approach with loud noise over great distance, finally arrived and disgorged twelve fat Germans and a slim guide named Adel. Claiming to be "half Bedouin," Adel laments the number of visitors who have begun to arrive unsupervised, partying by moonlight and littering the desert with plastic rubbish and tins. Guardian of the holy places of history, he looked sharply at our group of five with no guide.

We five left the Germans staggering up into the rocks and returned to our musings and wanderings. I rejoiced by day in the seeming emptiness of the desert and its glorious silence and by night in full moon on purple jebel and the peace of sleeping under the Big Dipper, awakening often to watch it march across the sky. Early on the third morning, a black and white wagtail and a mourning wheatear visited our camp. Footprints and scat of small mammals also appeared, but we never saw any of these silent watchers.

I rejoiced, as well, in the growing attraction between our shy young English friend and the lovely woman he had brought in his Land Rover. On the first night, beside the fire, their hands strayed together. And when we three others retired to our camp beds, they continued to gaze into the flames. Each day thereafter, their desire mounted, fed by wild beauty, youth, and the brilliant stars.

On the third night, they padded silently away into the moon-washed desert carrying a blanket. And in the morning their faces shone. Driving behind them on the desert highway back to the Nile, we saw them close, and our hearts, too, sang.

Driving in the Eastern Desert, December 1991

5

Pyramiding in the Fayoum

December 1991

There is something surreal about the Fayoum Oasis. You get lured in and end up staying longer than planned, even if you've made the mistake of booking at the frigid Panorama Hotel on Lake Qarun. The lake exudes a very unpleasant smell even in winter and the Fayoum hasn't been an oasis since the pharaohs built an irrigation channel from the Nile. Wolves are sometimes still seen, but the sacred crocodiles that once made Fayoum a place of pilgrimage can no longer be found. Still, the spirit of the crocodile god Sobek lives in a multitude of temples and carvings.

That's all part of the charm and the frustration of the Fayoum; it is, and it isn't. The lake is lovely but drying up and too salty for most freshwater fish. The hotel is a tourist resort but far too expensive even for middle income Egyptians and, as it's only an hour from Cairo, not many visitors stay there. Shooting birds is prohibited across the Fayoum, but men waving shotguns offer to take you out in boats.

We stayed three nights at the Panorama, and each time we drove back, the gateman refused to open up until we stated our nationality. We were, therefore, British on the first day, Russians the next, and thereafter Chinese. Never mind. He was always satisfied with our answer, any answer, just so we actually chose a country. Regulations must be obeyed.

We walked, that first evening, Alan, his visiting parents and me, along a nearby farm lane as the sky turned from flame to burnt orange. Bulbuls cried their plaintive evening hymn from palms silhouetted against the darkening sky. Flights of cattle egrets headed from the lakeshore to their dormitories. A heavily laden donkey plodded across a fallow field, tired head nearly reaching the ground. Not far ahead a fox crossed the road. We could have been hundreds of miles and hundreds of years from the nightmare of human activity along Cairo's 26 July Street.

It was dark by the time we returned to the hotel, and, chilled through, we decided to begin supper with soup. The waiter who served us babaghanouj instead of soup was indignant when we asked about the soup we had ordered. Yes, of course, there is soup, he said. See! Right here on the menu it says soup. Later in that first evening, we held another animated discussion with the hotel management concerning blankets. How many did we actually want if each of four persons needed three but all already had one—or did some of us have two? Raised eyebrows, a head count, and the bargaining started all over.

There is an undercurrent of suspicion in the Fayoum that must, I suppose, be connected to the Bedouin heritage. People have been ripping off the people of the Fayoum for so long that they feel a need to be on guard and, if possible, get even. On the following morning the guards at the Lahum pyramid were convinced that we were up to no good, which was, in fact, at least partly true. We had approached the pyramid from the desert side, hoping to avoid their attention until after we'd eaten our picnic lunch. This done, we were only just packing up when we saw a small but quite agitated group, galabiyahs flapping, rushing up the winding road that ends at a crumbling brick pyramid. It was unconscionable, even forbidden, they let us know breathlessly, that we had not passed by the gatehouse. The second, and greater problem was our pass from the Ministry of Antiquities in Cairo. According to the pass, five persons would be admitted free, but here were only four of us.

"Where is the fifth man?" the chief guard asked severely. He looked around apprehensively as though number five might even now be carrying off the enormous pile of bricks and rubble that rose behind him. (Or more likely, back at the hotel hiding from the December cold under a mountain of blankets). The Diplomat tried to explain the long-term nature of the pass, the fact that it was valid for many sites, the transitory nature of embassy guest lists, and the fact that the Cairo government agency from which we received it would not provide less than five passes at a time. This was neither convincing nor comprehensible to the chief guard, and suddenly, we were at stalemate although all he wanted was to keep to the regulations, and all we wanted was to get into the site and out of the icy wind. The Diplomat recognized the dilemma and figured a way out.

"Okay," he said. "I need to tell you about number five. Actually, he was unable to come today." This reply was satisfactory. Mankind does not live theoretically, and who, after all, would miss the chance to travel in a larger rather than smaller group? Suddenly all was understood.

"Malesh," said the chief guard, as though consoling us for a death in the family. His literate assistant wrote carefully on the pass in large Arabic script. We were free to visit, although we would, of course, be escorted by a guard who would probably know very little about the site, which would not inhibit his ability to pontificate in a broken version of just about any language the visitor professed to speak. This seemed reasonable to all concerned, as the real reason for a guide was to provide income for the local people and prevent the theft which visitors have engaged in for centuries. There was the added attraction that a guide might be able to prevent us getting lost in a tunnel. We set off behind our guide.

At Hawara pyramid near the guard hut, a tiny puppy struggled against a very short lead. This was necessary, we were told, or he would wander into the open tomb shafts and be eaten by jackals. Ptolemaic tombs call the visitor to dalliance, and so we lingered a few minutes fussing over the puppy. Here in this very place, we tell one another, Sir Flinders Petrie found the Fayoum portraits, enchanting likenesses of the deceased, which adorn those wooden coffins that remain, most now in museums. Of course, I do have an Egyptian friend who has one Fayoum portrait hanging in her Cairo living room. Why should she not have purchased it and prevented yet another Egyptian treasure being sold abroad?

If I had to put a value on coffin lids, I'd choose those lovely faces of real people over the solid gold triple caskets which ancient Egyptian kings took into their tombs. The paradox at Hawara is that while portraits of the ancient inhabitants of Fayoum have been shipped off to museums, bits of their bodies, sometimes rather large pieces, are still hanging around.

"No digging," our guide said sternly when I stoop to dislodge a human lower mandible half-buried in the sand. The scattered bones were evidence that others, including the jackals, rejected the order. However, the guide seemed particularly fond of this part of the tour and suddenly picked up a mummified arm, apparently kept "to hand" as a visual aid.

"Welcome! Welcome!" he intoned, making clawing motions at us with the leathery arm of his ancestor. The guide at Lahum, despite the unfortunate direction of our arrival, also turned out to have a strong dose of zany Egyptian humor. Later, behind the pyramid, he came into his own.

"My wife," he said, "is extremely big. Fat. Very fat. Ugly, too. And she eats constantly. Ala toul. Despite the fact that she is ugly, I have many children. They eat a lot, too. All this eating is terribly expensive, and I am a poor man. How am I to get all this bread which they require?" He looked expectant, then joined in our laughter. Why *ask* for a good tip when you can earn it? Then, to thank us, he announced that at Hawara pyramid local girls walk to the top with mud bricks on their heads and also dance around the pyramid, both of which in order to "make babies." We greeted this information with sobriety lest our guide himself was a believer in this ancient rite.

We left the pyramids by the way we had come, on the desert track which passes the Monastery of the Bath, recently reclaimed by the Coptic Church after many years desolation. The single monk in residence assured us that reconstruction was being carried out with the divinely provided assistance of the local insects. The place, it seemed, is visited each spring by a species of wasp that, for three months, labors feverishly to enlarge the thick walls, now cement-like and riddled with holes. This insect work must, however, be augmented by teams of laborers which were even then removing large blocks, rather dangerously it seemed, from the base of an unsteady ancient wall.

"God used the wasps to build for us in the years we were not here," the monk said. "This is a sign from the Lord to continue the work. But"—his brow furrowed, and the sky seemed to darken—

"there are no Copts in a five-kilometer radius. The faithful must come from afar to build, and they are poor, each with a large family that must have bread."

Again, this fixation on bread. Actually Egypt has so much bread, made from donated American wheat and heavily subsidized by the government, that it is commonly used as cattle fodder. The monk gave us each a swig of holy water and then an enormous round of bread imprinted with a cross. Holy Communion on the run, I thought, and being hungry, I pulled off several bites as the tour continued.

"No, we have no engineers," the monk said, standing near another teetering wall. "But God will provide." As God did, of course, we being on this occasion the Lord's chosen instruments.

At Maydum, the gateman was unpleasant, putting aside his lunch reluctantly and grunting through a mouthful of bread that, okay, the site was open. But the guide was jolly and led us happily into narrow passages filled with foul air and ancient cedar beams. In a nearby mastaba we crawled down a steep dark passage and through a hole the size of an oven door to inspect great slabs of granite.

"From Aswan," cried the guide joyfully. "And carved all of one piece." A cache of jewelry and the famous panel of Maydum geese had, he said, long since been transferred to the museum in Cairo. When we emerged breathless into the sunlight, the guide displayed a bloody finger—his own—and asked for a plaster. We failed him there, but sympathy and ample baksheesh restored his good humor.

Before we left Maydum, I sought a place to relieve myself behind the pyramid but was interrupted by two girls who leaped from behind a rock. Suddenly, I understood one more reason for the guide.

"Money! Money!" the girls screeched. "Baksheesh!" My pockets were empty save for a few tissues, which I showed to the girls to their disgust. But I could make up for the inconvenience, they told me confidently, by just giving them my watch. Nothing doing, I said, backing away while fiddling with my belt buckle. The two girls hooted in derision at my inhumanity and dashed away, bare feet making small patterns in the sand. Watching a stingy foreigner watering the desert was not *their* idea of fun.

We took the canal road back to Cairo, avoiding the main Fayoum highway, which seems to be some Cairo bureaucrats' answer to the population explosion. From nowhere, children leapt to mid-highway, swinging flapping ducks aloft by one wing. The distress of seeing birds thus abused mesmerized me, and I'll never know whether, had Alan not shouted, I would have braked in time.

The return to Cairo along the canal was slow and, after dark, as dangerous as any Fayoum road. We pressed on past heavy vehicles, plodding camels, and homeward-bound people, cattle, and dogs. Then, with the Dahshur pyramids as backdrop and just as rain began to fall, the Range Rover's fan belt broke. A passing trucker stopped to give advice and then, seeing we had a spare, swiftly changed the belt. But although we pressed him, he would take no payment.

As we drove back to Cairo, I remembered my first visit to the Fayoum. It was 1985. In Egypt for two months on behalf of the State Department, I was taken to the oasis by an American embassy driver who kept double tipping in my wake. Back in Cairo, I finally asked the driver why, all day, he had added to the money I left at every monastery and pyramid. His response was simple, heartfelt, and very Egyptian. "Madam," he said, "these people are *so* poor." That lesson I hope to have learned by now.

Travels into the Heart of Egypt　　23

Ruins east of Fayoum., December 1991

Mastaba at Meydoum, December 1991

6

With St. Catherine in Sinai

21 December 1991

The morning broke through frozen mist on the slopes of the holy mountains, throwing long shafts of light across the pink, green, and gray granite. A light snow, just ending, had dusted the sharp contours of Jebel Katrin and Jebel Musa, which rise behind the historically impregnable walls of St. Catherine's Monastery.

"The Lord is my Rock," said the Psalmist, "Of whom shall I be afraid?" St. Catherine's, visible through white haze, portrays the austere side of faith, the realms of contradiction and judgment. Here, it is difficult to miss the point that where man meets God, both suffer.

Misr Sinai's Cairo office had dithered about reservations at St. Catherine's tourist village, claiming full occupancy. This turned out far from true. We were relieved when we arrived and found shelter, but also because pilgrimages (even those that are only "sort of" pilgrimages) are best done in silence and solitude—perhaps even more so during Advent.

"Who shall ascend unto the hill of the Lord and who shall stand in his holy place?" the Psalmist asks and then answers: "He who has clean hands and a pure heart." Unworthy, we set out on the long path towards the summit of Mount Sinai where a simple chapel commemorates God's gift of divine law to Moses. "Lord, I believe. Help Thou my unbelief." I wore my silver Coptic cross, a talisman of faith to come.

A few backpackers, hearty youths, who had spent the night on the mountain, passed us on their descent to the comparative warmth of the monastery. They seemed somewhat surprised to have survived the bitterly cold night and amused themselves telling us how long and difficult the climb would be. We laughed with them for we already knew these things, having visited St. Catherine's before and having no desire on this visit to climb to the top.

Suffering, endurance and being able to claim "I climbed Jebel Musaor Mount Shasta or Ben Nevis or Fujiyama" were not our goals today. God rewards the "also-rans" with rare gifts: the warmth of our own companionship, the joy of cold air in brilliant sunlight, the mystery of shadow on rock, the inner voice that whispers "I AM"—these would more than satisfy us. And, to be honest, collecting a few more rare birds for our "life list" was also a possibility.

For an hour, we mounted slowly, reaching barely a third of the way to the top, before stopping for tea outside a stone hut. The tea vendor told us that the cold prevented his sleeping on the mountain, save in summer. But he was disinclined to conversation, served the tea and retired into his hut. Tourists are his business, but, probably, he despised our affluence, litter, and intrusive ways. We understood and sympathized that only economic necessity forced this modern hermit to share his holy place.

By nine o'clock, the sun had warmed the western slopes of Jebel Katrin, at the summit of which Catherine's body once lay, transported there by God after her martyrdom in Alexandria. The monks say they keep the remains in a very small casket because Catherine was hacked to pieces. Historians tell of lucrative and politically beneficial transfers of Catherine's fingers and other bones to Europe during the Middle Ages. ("Lord, I believe! Help Thou my unbelief.")

Across the rugged slopes birds awakened rejoicing in the growing warmth and the banquet that awaits them in fresh donkey droppings left by mounted pilgrims. We rejoiced in flocks of chukars, calling across the wadis between the holy mountains. Wheatears flashed bright black and white patterns, a scrub warbler skulked in a thorn bush and, finally, when we were back at the monastery, we saw Tristram's grackle, which only survives at two other places on earth.

At the gate into the monastery, the Muslim gatekeeper, an old man in a ragged greatcoat and tattered galabiyah ordered several reluctant backpackers to leave their gear outside. They suspected his honesty, but he made clear that he would not allow them to enter unless they left their kit with him. When the Diplomat greeted him in Arabic, the old man's manner softened, and he made us welcome. Though his task was cold and thankless, the monks trusted him, and that was that. Almost certainly, he could not read the Ottoman order posted inside the gate. (Neither could we, for that matter, although we learned later that it granted eternal temporal protection to the Greek Orthodox monks.) But the Ottoman firman was undoubtedly blazoned on the gatekeeper's heart. He would protect these holy men and their holy place as best he could. But why they put up with this constant stream of riffraff was beyond him, especially as the holy men charged no admission fees.

The monk who showed us around the basilica, a gallery of sparkling and immensely beautiful icons, was simply dressed in black. His heavy beard, like the hills outside, was frosted, and he, too, looked somewhat ragged. But his eyes were kind, and he apologized for not being able to allow women into the Chapel of the Burning Bush. This, it seemed, was due to my trousers. On an earlier visit, a shirt had been provided to cover my unholy costume, but not this time. God, perhaps, had changed his requirements for womankind?

Later, when the monk moved me away from standing directly in front of an altar ("Only a priest…"), I received grace to return his gentle smile. Like the Muslims and the Baptists, I know that every individual is his—and her—own priest before God. Doubtless St. Catherine will reveal this to the monks in good time. Meanwhile, I needed to ponder as to why I am so easily offended by other people's "mistaken" religious beliefs and practices.

But now was not the time to ruminate as one young visitor seemed to be having a very bad day indeed. Perhaps already wounded by some other dogmatic encounter with human interpretations of God's dealings with mankind—or maybe because his religious beliefs require that he cover his head in a holy place—this visitor rudely resisted the order that he remove his hat while inside the church. He'd already been forced to leave his backpack outside and now they wanted his hat as well! Angrily, he pointed back at the black pillbox worn by the monk.

"That," said the monk with a superior air "is different." Case closed. The monk had neither time nor inclination to say more, and the young traveler turned and stalked out. I wanted to go after him but decided not to do so. He was wrong, of course, but so was the monk. Why must religion erect barriers between mankind and a God who reaches out? And what could I have said? Perhaps "The Lord looks on a man's heart" (no mention of hats)? But that seemed to take sides and I didn't want to stoke the fire.

Meanwhile, it was clear that St. Catherine's mountain is not where one goes to find demonstrations of God's gentleness—at least overtly. Here the granite of divine law strikes the flint of human hearts, and we respond with awe and, sometimes, anger. Loving-kindness seems far removed from the spectacular mosaic of the transfigured Christ rising triumphant above the apse of the great church. But is not the resurrection itself a statement of loving acceptance of us as well as of Christ? The mosaic portrays grace, certainly, but no "gentle Jesus meek and mild." Embattled monks may perhaps be excused for becoming as righteous as the image of the God they worship.

Because it was almost Christmas—or perhaps I would have done so anyway—I lit candles before an icon. I don't remember the face of the icon. Maybe I didn't even look. Perhaps it was Catherine herself, but that didn't matter for clearly grace and love abound in the monastery. An icon is, after all, only an aide memoire meant to turn our thoughts to God's reality and presence. The names I mentioned, of two people living and one dead, are what counted. Those who have loved, suffered, and endured will not be forgotten so long as the miracle of prayer itself continues.

Through fifteen hundred years of suffering, the monks of St. Catherine's monastery have held on to their rocky sanctuary. Today they face the gravest crisis in their difficult history, as tourism threatens to turn the holy refuge into just one more attraction—"If it's Thursday, this must be Sinai"—and busloads of loud and often irreligious tourists "do" the monastery in record time and record numbers. In 1990 (shades of the missing Codex Sinaiticus), someone walked off with an icon. Now the Egyptian government, over the protest of the monks and international supporters, is talking about building a cable car to the top of Jebel Musa.

Do all these people really need to visit St. Catherine's Monastery, I asked myself. But how do you separate pilgrims from day-trippers and, after all, who can know who needs God more? Which group has greater need of a glimpse of the reality behind the icons? And if the monks refused entry, how valid would the Ottoman firman remain?

"The Lord is my rock." Jews, Christians, Muslims, and many others still believe this. At St. Catherine's monastery, lonely bastion of early Christianity, the choices are unbearably difficult. But that's as it has always been for those who seek God. Perhaps even the hard-eyed young man in the wooly hat received a gift we don't know about. Out of the rock, living water still flows.

We are received by the monks at St Catherine's Monastery, Sinai, December 1991

Lillian with cross at St. Catherine's Monastery, December 1991

7

Praising God in the City of the Dead

14 January 1992

Slender wedding-cake minarets and contrasting sturdy domes swirl out of the morning smog at the edges of the City of the Dead, giving Cairo's most famous cemetery a ghostly appearance. Since before the fourteenth century, the living and the dead have shared this area in symbiotic harmony. I was early for an appointment at the Islamic Mission on Paradise Street, a wide road that leads down into the City of the Dead. Happy for an excuse to visit this extraordinary place once again, I turned right into the Northern Cemetery.

The contrast to Cairo's overcrowded streets is remarkable. Few of the tomb dwellers can afford cars and the streets were built wide to honor the great whose eternal abodes now molder around us. But the poor are sensitive to interlopers, foreigners in particular, and young boys kicking an almost entirely deflated football between the ruts saw me drive slowly by and shouted, "How are YOU?" in tones both inquisitive and aggressive. The little car purred along, just back from the garage and eager to please. Off the broad avenues are narrow lanes between the mausoleums, and there women, children, and starving dogs vie for existence. The men were gone, looking for work or perhaps smoking shisha at some nearby tomb cafe.

I stopped in the empty road some yards back from the splendid tomb of Asfur (1506) near the cemetery entrance. The pleasing symmetry of simple lines and ornate calligraphy seem the work of an artist not a draftsman. Had I been an artist I would have sketched the lovely scene. Instead I had few thoughts except for the coming interview with Chinese Muslims at the Islamic Mission off Paradise Street. I feared that my Mandarin would be inadequate but knew it was the only way to avoid an Egyptian translator who would surely try to dominate the interview.

A young woman sat on a mat near the entrance of an alley surrounded by children and feeding bread to a seemingly catatonic old man. All but the old man stared silently as I turned the car around. The sunlight, growing stronger on the wall behind, makes them look picturesque, even content. I wanted to stay and sit a while against the warm wall, saying little while the children fingered my clothing. But I had neither the time nor the courage to do so. The young woman returned my smile as I drove away. All of us except the old man waved. I saw then that the man wasn't really old, just dying. Would they simply dig a hole in the floor and put him through to paradise or are there regulations governing immigration to the lower levels of the city? I had no doubt that the Egyptian bureaucracy would have found a way to involve itself.

Back to the underpass, then, and into Paradise Street. Second turning on the left, my instructions said. I signaled left, slowed, stopped, and was thrown forward several feet by an overloaded orange minibus, which—with a great crump—slammed into the back of the little car. I sat for a moment, head in hands, thinking about the young wife next to the sunny wall. When I looked up, the orange minibus had gone and traffic was piling up, horns wailing indignantly. Two policemen watched indifferently from the crowd which, apparently disappointed not to see blood, began to drift away.

My right knee ached, and I felt a tingling along the fault line of an old whiplash up the left side of my neck. Somewhat apprehensively I got out and regarded the little car. It was in much worse shape than I but looked as though it might still be drivable.

A man came up helpfully with the number of the orange minibus, and I told him I had an appointment, over there, in the Islamic Mission. He looked mystified. Several other people offered advice about car removal, hospitals, policemen, the price of cabbages—I love the Egyptians for their community spirit. But because there wasn't even any shouting, most people left, and I began to feel lonely, standing in the middle of the road with my insulted car, as a river of traffic parted and rejoined around me.

"Get your car out of the road," one of the policemen shouted, in what I took to be an unhelpful manner. But he dealt with security, not traffic, and it wasn't his business.

"Can't do that," I said. "I have an appointment with the sheikh and, besides, don't we have to make a report first?"

No one knew, or at least wasn't saying, so I crossed to the gatehouse, dodging another bus driven by a maniac, and demanded that my host be advised. No one had ever heard of him. My head began to hurt. I put on my obligatory scarf, covered it with a large hat to keep the scarf in place and tried to look like a demure Muslim female in distress. This failed, perhaps because of the hat. I reverted to being an American.

"Is there anyone here who speaks English?" I shouted to the hangers-on around the gate. Which is how I came to be rescued by a young Nigerian and another African in lovely robes, who advised me not to move the car, found a telephone, and renewed my faith in Islamic theological students, at least those from south of the Sahara.

The sheikh was, in fact, waiting for me with the promised Chinese imam in tow. He had rounded up a second Chinese imam as well whose job was to translate into Arabic whatever the first imam and I said to one another in Mandarin. Worse, he had been in contact with the office of the Sheikh of Al Azhar. Foiled, I found myself staring into the prevaricating eyes of the Grand Secretary, who rather reminded me of an imperial eunuch guarding the Ottoman era entrance to the inner court.

If the Grand Secretary is venal and once extorted 100 LE from me, I can let it pass. That he wastes my time and hinders my work is more difficult to ignore. Remembering the need to forgive seventy times seven, I forced a smile.

"Welcome, Doctora!" The Grand Secretary beamed his mercenary smile. Still feeling shaken, I muttered about an accident and apologized for being late.

"Malesh!" cried the Grand Secretary. "Alhamdulillah!" Behind his smile, as we used to say, there was nothing but teeth. I could tell he didn't much like me either, and that cheered me considerably. Perhaps I had even ruined his morning. I began to feel much better.

We rejected the outside table next to a dead cat, though no one mentioned that as a reason, went into the library, and got down to work, two Egyptians, two Chinese, and one American in a ridiculous and very large black hat with a head scarf under it. Several Muslims of assorted African and eastern European appearance were trying to read at tables in the background. It must have been difficult due to our loud conversation in three languages, sometimes simultaneous, with the Egyptians talking to one another above the Chinese and me. You could tell it worried the Chinese interpreter when he was shoved aside.

In a way I'd scored an end run by getting this interview at all. When, after I'd pestered him for four months, the Grand Secretary called me in to meet Azhar's "China specialist," this worthy told me that "definitely there are no Chinese at Al Azhar University," even denying any contacts at all between Al Azhar and Chinese Muslims. So I'd made an "inside contact," as the Chinese say, and here I was at last hoping for information to put into the book I was writing. The gentlemen facing me were undoubtedly Chinese, and this was certainly a branch of Al Azhar. However the Grand Secretary wasn't through yet.

It was a remarkable exercise from which I learned a lot. Who would have thought that conservative Islam and communism have so much in common? No one, it seemed, has greater admiration for the Chinese government than the sheikhs of Al Azhar. And, of course, no one had greater admiration for the sheikhs of Al Azhar than China's grateful Muslims. It was all a bit alarming until I realized that the Chinese were actually less defensive than the Egyptians and that, for some reason, both sides were afraid. That meant politics and I hoped to find a wedge in.

"We have no criticism of China's treatment of its Muslim citizens. Alhamdulillah!" said the Grand Secretary. "Haven't they themselves just told your Excellency that they have no complaints?" He pointed at the two Chinese who obediently said, "Alhamdulillah" fervently and in unison.

The Grand Secretary was vague about what the Chinese imams were studying and unhelpful about how Al Azhar could be of service to Chinese Muslims. The Chinese imam pushed away specific questions and returned to stories of his previous visits to Egypt, emphasizing how grateful he was. This I believed but kept probing for more specifics.

How many Chinese students are there now at Al Azhar? The imam said thirty and the Egyptian said ten. I rechecked with the imam and the interpreter, face impervious, left the request for verification unconveyed. He may have been rankled by the Egyptian mode of shouting conversation or perhaps still miffed by the Grand Secretary's statement that Egypt has an embassy in Taipei that handles relations with Taiwanese Muslims.

"Most of them are hui jen, my people," the old Chinese imam said of Taiwan's Muslims. "And you are quite right that we believe there is only one China and that there should be only one Chinese government." He was happy to be back on safe ground, but the Grand Secretary backed down ungracefully, insisting that he was certain Egypt must have at least a chargé d'affaires in Taiwan. The Chinese and I looked at one another wordlessly. The interview might, after all, go better than I feared.

But in the end neither side would give any information on differences of faith and practice or confess to a fatwa issued by Al Azhar for Chinese believers. No one seemed to know or remember if the Egyptian government had ever criticized China's treatment of its Muslim citizens. In fact, there is no special department for Chinese affairs at Al Azhar, although the Islamic Mission seemed to function as a sort of foreign ministry. There are no Sufi orders with members in both countries, the Grand Secretary said, guessing the direction in which I was headed.

"Nor are there any secret contacts between Muslims in China and Egypt," he said with great authority, then tripped himself up by adding, "We know nothing about that." The Chinese kept their faces blank. I already knew the answers to most of my questions as much of the information is in the public domain. But the Sufi connection was largely unexplored territory and the Grand Secretary might just as well have shouted "Bingo!" But here we stalled once again.

In the late 1950s and early '60s, the mainland Chinese had developed a close relationship with Al Azhar through the Chinese Islamic Association. Moreover, the world in general knows that the Chinese are very faithful to old friends. Yet since the early sixties, when the Chinese imam visited twice, he had not returned to Cairo until this year. In fact, he stressed these early dates, and I realized that he was telling me something I needed to know.

The newly reestablished Chinese relationship with Al Azhar was of course still on trial. The Chinese government, always wary of its own several million Muslim citizens, was suspicious of Al Azhar but saw it as an entry to the Islamic world. But why were the Egyptians so uptight? Perhaps those persistent rumors about the Sufis? Perhaps China's persecution of Chinese Muslims during the Great Proletarian Cultural Revolution? Certainly ongoing difficulties for Chinese Muslims in Xinjiang, Ningsha, and elsewhere in eastern China? Always wary of its own Muslim citizens, the Chinese government was suspicious of Al Azhar, but now apparently willing to consider a truce.

All four men who faced me were trusted representatives of their governments' positions—at least publicly - or they would not have remained in the positions they were in. But if it came to a choice, which loyalty would come first? I suspected that the Grand Secretary would do the will of the government, but I felt more kindly about the Chinese. Perhaps neither of their governments, both of which used its religious people in political ways, understood the gravity of the situation—or at least they thought they could contain the difficulties which would continue to arise.

Although my own fears of religious extremism made this difficult, I felt sorry for them all, in need as they were of religious liberty. Then the old Chinese imam told me that during the Cultural Revolution all religions in China had been poa weile (torn apart). I knew something of what had happened in China during that era and recognized the anguish behind his simple statement. Then he asked me to contact him during my upcoming visit to Beijing, and the Chinese interpreter smoothly neglected to translate this into Arabic.

We ended with pleasantries all round, the Chinese took several photographs of us together, and I thanked everyone profusely. As I was leaving, the Chinese imam told me, his eyes twinkling, that I would not be required to wear my "very strange hat" when I called on him in China. Then I returned to the ruined car in Paradise Street, where I found that the Diplomat had come to rescue me. Meanwhile, the Nigerian student had refused a "gift" for his kindness to me and pronounced, "One Muslim must help another." Surely it was the scarf under my hat that had convinced him.

Escorting me to curbside, the Grand Secretary expressed his gratitude for God's mercy: "Look at your car, Excellency!" he cried. "But you are untouched. Alhamdulillah!" Yes, I said, praise God. We had that, at least, in common.

As we drove away in the Diplomat's reliable Range Rover, I decided that Paradise Street is too close to the City of the Dead. What the Chinese call "spiritual pollution" risks spilling out from Paradise Street. Meanwhile among the tombs in the City of the Dead life goes on for there are still children playing in the sunlight, men struggling to feed their families and women caring for the ill and dying. Life there is possible. Paradise Street, by contrast, seems a pathway for self-righteous liars in skullcaps and maniacs in orange minibuses.

Inshallah, (if God wills) I vowed silently, next time I come this way I shall spend the morning with the women and children who live among the tombs. They, at least, will tell me the truth.

Lillian with Chinese Imams at Al Azhar, Cairo, January 1992

8

Raising Dry Bones at Saqqara

22 January 1992

On the canal road from Cairo to Saqqara, "the scenic route" someone called it, man is losing the war against machines. The road is for the most part a busy dual carriageway through what was recently farmland but has become a patchwork of fields and factories, palm groves and unfinished low-rise buildings. January is the time of cauliflower harvest, and vast mounds of white and green are carefully and artistically arranged at roadside and on donkey carts heading north to Cairo. A man passes on a bicycle peddling hard against the weight of enormous cauliflowers in two panniers. He, apparently, is too poor even to own one of the soul-drained gray donkeys.

The bus, hired by the Egyptian Exploration Society, passes through a vanishing world of peddlers, shisha smokers and curbside (if there were such things) letter-writers at small tables. Here scribes await the fare of rural illiterates who must deal with urban bureaucratic intrusion into their already endangered lives. Behind me in the bus, two older expats exclaim in dismay over the encroachments of civilization.

They point out a once magnificent villa now surrounded by ugly modern housing and mutter mournfully about Hassan Fathy, the great architect who designed dwellings in keeping with Egypt's spirit and culture—and was ostracized for his pains. The curious indoor/outdoor living style of the semi-rural poor is evident in makeshift shelters and wares spread at roadside.

Ten years ago, the jangling bells of donkey carts and the shouts of hawkers would have predominated. Today all other sound is smothered by car horns and the roar of sugar refinery and brickyard. The battle of farmland against industry is being lost here. Where will the cauliflower and cane grow when the topsoil has been stripped to produce bricks for Cairo's insatiable maw?

"Egypt's culture respects the right of women not to work," a high-ranking Egyptian civil servant told me last week. She patted her silk dress. "We are much better off than Western women!" I think about that on the canal road to Saqqara where poor women in worn black robes offer cauliflowers, mirrors, socks and shiny cooking pots while struggling to keep small children out of the roadway and hoping to sell a few items in time to pack up and cook the main meal of the day. Before jostling for space at roadside, they will have risen well before dawn to pick, sort, and arrange their wares. Other women bend to the age-old chore of washing clothes in a canal, which every year becomes more fetid. They are watched over by cattle egrets that line the banks at decent intervals, spaced like British anglers and just as uncommunicative.

At Badrashin Village the road narrows to a bumpy lane, and the bus jostles slowly around mounds of rubbish and swarms of people. Hundreds of children shriek and push in a schoolyard, their play area inadequate for ball games. "What *does* Egypt plan to do with all these people?" someone in our group asks rhetorically. We turn right over a bridge and drive slowly past sedate plantations of date palms. Gaunt, rangy water buffalos slobber over their berseem and packs of dogs scavenge for the droppings of humanity. People wave plastic sacks of tangerines at the bus, and we know we have reached the tourist zone.

The entrance to Saqqara, necropolis of ancient Memphis, marks the division between desert and sown. At the gate is a prominent British professor who has worked here for thirty years. It is his job to reconstruct the glorious past from the slim pickings left after centuries of reusing stone and brick. He wears leather shoes and a jean jacket that says "graffiti" on the back and the way in which he refers to "our Egyptian colleagues" suggests frustration over interference and delay.

Once, the Nile lapped gently here during each annual inundation. Now all is regulated: water, rebuilding, people, grave-robbing. We leave the bus and head across the sand along the partially reconstructed causeway that leads up to the mortuary temple of King Unas. Over the hill are the remains of an early Coptic monastery, which we will not visit today. Today the "Christian era" is too modern to interest us. For the Professor, the ancient Egyptians and their cult of the living dead are what Saqqara is all about.

The causeway alternates sand and dressed stones, and we are warned not to pick up any of the innumerable potsherds least authority take offense. No chance now for the modern villagers who live at the end of the desert to creep in here and select a few building blocks. Those days are gone forever. We tread carefully upwards towards the tomb of Khnoum-Hetep, churlishly buried by Unas in the Fifth-Dynasty building of his causeway. "The Great Destroyer," our Professor says of Unas, although he admits that by hiding the tomb, Unas preserved its reliefs against the arrival of those custodians of time, the modern archaeologists.

Unusually, the tomb is open today, and we crowd in. Here are gentle scenes of two brothers, sharers of the tomb, embracing one another in life and in death. But are they brothers or lovers? No one dares question the Professor. On this visit I do not go to see the mummies laid casually in an outbuilding. Probably they date from the destructive, and some say loathsome, Christian era when people went about irreligiously stuffing cadavers into other people's tombs. But perhaps I am afraid that, having seen the portraits inside the tomb, I just might recognize someone?

The Professor walks quickly, hurrying our straggling mob of voyeurs. We include a very pretty young woman with long black hair, heavy eye makeup, chewed fingernails, and a Maltese terrier—a breed she insists was known in pharaonic times. Clearly annoyed at our collective ignorance and disruption of his working day, the Professor disclaims any knowledge of longhaired dogs on tomb reliefs. The slender young woman's eyes flash, and she bides her time.

Still the causeway mounts and so do we, stopping to admire the unpublished reliefs of gazelle, gerboa, birds and hounds (all with short hair). One portion of the causeway has been reroofed with stone slabs, which once covered the entire passageway, allowing only a central beam of light to penetrate to the priests below. I recall the explanation of an historian who recently took me along this way, demonstrating how the priests must have shuffled through the above ground tunnel, carrying offerings and chanting prayers in unison.

"Hum, hum, hum, hum," the Historian sang, lurching from one large foot to another. "The light shot down upon them, sparkling off gold ornaments. They carried the drink offerings carefully so as not to spill. No commoner came here under pain of death. No one saw the priests save the ka spirit of Unas who waited impatiently to slake his thirst.

"Hum, hum, hum, hum," I maneuver my way through the crowd in the tunnel. The Maltese terrier lifts a leg against the wall, and the Professor looks at us both with obvious pain. Past the royal court tombs, past the solar boat pits, we mount towards the final resting place of the great king.

At the "Persian shafts," deep pits dug in Ptolemaic times, the Professor is distracted by a general cry for explanation. Reluctantly, he retraces his steps, as he has already made clear that the deep pits are "really not of interest to us." The shaft tombs were booby-trapped to smother tomb robbers with sand and thus their contents were recovered intact, he tells us. The Historian, however, claims that they were opened in the modern era and found to be empty. Members of our group began to debate with one another.

From atop the ruined pyramid of Unas two feral dogs try to set up dialog with the Maltese terrier. The canine aristocrat disdains to respond, and other dogs, drawn from the surrounding desert, join the discussion, keeping up a chorus of wailing and shouting which threatens the eternal sleep of those buried here. Several guides with other groups look with irritation at our group for having brought about this blasphemous situation. Rocks are hurled, and the Anubis chorus grows fainter.

An ancient and bronzed Egyptian guard divides us into two groups for entry to the pyramid, but refuses to let the Maltese terrier have a look although he displays great eagerness to do so. Someone with no stomach for close spaces and bad air volunteers to hold the Maltese while the advance party scrambles down the gangplank into the funeral chamber. At the end of the corridor and assisted by a kerosene lantern, we are told that we are looking at "the world's oldest extant religious text."

"The text is much older than the pyramid, which itself dates from about 2300 B.C." the Professor tells us. "It's so old, in fact, that much of it is unintelligible, though we can read the symbols." Here, perhaps is the furthermost door to the past that Saqqara has to offer. But no one has pushed through and the Professor himself stays outside in the sunlight where the guard hammers on the gangplank to tell us to hurry up as others are waiting to enter.

Egyptian schoolgirls cluster around the Maltese terrier, who, to his great indignation, is then picked up and cuddled. He sniffs suspiciously at their radio, which blasts romantic songs in French. The girls giggle and ask us where we come from and if we can speak Arabic while the Professor moves us on to prevent "waste of time."

The pace quickens after that and the Professor's temper grows more strained as we are now ready to visit his dig. The site, higher up on the plateau, was looted of reliefs in the last century and then lost again under the sand. Now, the graves of several kings of the Tutankhamen era are slowly coming to light once more. This is an area of great archaeological importance, the Professor tells us, but as it is not yet open to the public, special permission has been necessary for our visit. We, of course, are profuse in our gratitude. Best not to mention that I visited this dig a month ago with the Diplomat—who gave the guard 10 LE and told him mum's the word.

Inside the tomb complex of Horemheb, we gawp at dancing friezes of newly captured slaves, scribes tallying tax, men begging mercy of God and the King, the latter with upstretched arms. The walls are lined with open wicker baskets that contain collected shards and bones, to some of which mummified flesh and grave clothes still cling. When I ask whose bones these are, the Professor snaps that I am not to touch them. Alarmed, I look around to see if one of my companions has stuffed a skull into a back pocket or hidden a thighbone in his jacket. But everyone looks as apprehensive as I am and even the Maltese terrier doesn't look tempted.

We leave Miya and Horemheb to their sand and cataloguers and walk back along the plateau. High on the pyramid of Unas, the two white dogs—perhaps the ba and ka of Unas—keep up a running commentary on the likely fighting capabilities of the Maltese. But I have stopped listening to formal commentary either canine or human. The sun is very hot, and it should be time for lunch.

Following the crowd around Zozer's step pyramid, I discuss with a librarian what people actually learn from history. He admits great skepticism that we learn anything at all and says that although he does, of course, find all this pharaonic stuff very interesting, what does it really matter anyway? He concludes that all we have learned here is how the ancient ruling elites felt about death, nothing about the common man. This sounds familiar, I tell him, and parrot a heresy heard recently from another friend: "Where are the tomb scenes of children studying, men building houses, women washing clothes in the river, people making love? It's all about the souls of the aristocratic departed!"

But we speak in hushed tones, and soon I divert to question a sculptor who is visiting Egypt on a Fulbright. A day earlier, he had gone to the camel market and was still feeling overwhelmed by the animal suffering he saw there. The sculptor has sad eyes and wears his hair in a ponytail like a hippy of the sixties, which he probably was. Somehow I feel more comfortable talking to him and to the librarian than I do listening to the Professor. There is something of life and its problems with them, not just fascination with exotic ancient ways of treating death.

By now it really is past lunchtime. I come around the step pyramid and reach the Professor and a small huddle of hard line listeners just in time to hear the owner of the Maltese terrier ask the question she has been saving up. The Professor is eloquent on the ancient funerary use of stone and mortar but she stops him in mid-sentence.

"But how," she asks earnestly, "did they get the air out from between the bricks?" The Professor appears to reel mentally while asking himself how he can be expected to deal with people who neither listen nor use their brains. Recovering himself, he tries to answer her, insisting that both mortar and bricks displace air and so forth.

Perhaps I am the only one who sees the look of triumph in the young woman's eyes. And only then do I recognize how closely she resembles the court ladies in the tomb paintings.

9

Pagan Revival at Qasr Ibrim

13 January–2 February 1992

You get to Qasr Ibrim by taking Misr Air's 6:30 a.m. shuttle from Cairo to Abu Simbel and then travelling for three and a half hours across Lake Nasser amid the floating pelicans. The pelicans lumber into flight like 747s, running awkwardly across the water surface as the boat approaches, too bemused to realize they ought not to keep landing just in front of our oncoming boat. Perhaps you could also get to Qasr Ibrim by driving from the Dakhla oasis in the Western Desert and then somehow fording the Nile. But negotiating the jagged mountains that guard the site would be an achievement even more noteworthy than obtaining the military permits needed for embarking on Lake Nasser.

Our party of eight swelled to eleven at Abu Simbel where the Leader of the Egyptian Exploration Society expedition met us with a tug hired from the Lake Authority. The Leader has arranged to include a travelling archaeologist and girlfriend, both recently from Sudan, as the archaeologist is an expert on the Meroitic civilization that defined Nubia before the Christian era. Both archaeologist and girlfriend are extraordinarily thin.

The Nubian crew shout above the din in their incomprehensible language as our tug roars past the Abu Simbel temples. According to an onsite plaque, these temples were raised above the waterline "with the cooperation of UNESCO." This is Nubia, land of drowned culture and displaced thousands, whose ancient cultural records and modern lifestyle perished in 1962 beneath the rising waters of Lake Nasser. The Leader refers to Egypt as though it is a foreign country.

Our Japanese fellow travelers from the Misr Air flight file down the slope towards the temple in a long crocodile as we chug by, waving and loaded to the wheelhouse with full crates of vegetables and frozen chickens and empty crates for carting away the material remains of Nubian history. These will mostly be warehoused by the Egyptian authorities, as there is no room and relatively little interest to display them. But the tourists are engrossed with their cameras and the majesty of Abu Simbel and do not wave back. The Starving Archeologist and girlfriend find a seat atop an empty crate and sit stiffly in the sunlight looking gaunt. The Diplomat and I pass sandwiches up to them.

The Leader begins our education with a lament, belied by his jolly manner. The loss, the inestimable loss, he says. The drowned papyrus documents contained records of the Meroitic civilization, of early Egyptian Christianity, of the brief Roman occupation, perhaps even the lost works of Livy. All these are irretrievably gon, while Ramses II's megalomanic celebration of his victory over the Hittites was saved for Japanese tourists. The Leader, it seems, has controversial opinions.

The Starving Archaeologist helps himself to another of our sandwiches and a piece of our cook Nabawy's excellent quiche, saying nothing. In fact, for the next three days he will say little as the Leader relentlessly invites his opinion as to which side of the Christian/Pagan divide claims his loyalty.

We leave Abu Simbel behind. Egyptian Nubia seems today a world of water-washed beauty but in reality it is a graveyard. The first thing you notice is that there are almost no people here and, with the exception of our boat, no noise. Barren hummocks of mountains reach out of the blue lake. Ledges once the aeries of eagles have turned green with moss. Far above the drowned cities, navigation buoys have become lookouts for ospreys. The only sign of human habitation is the occasional rowboat with a solitary fisherman casting his net.

Eventually, on a lonely outcropping, the ruins of Qasr Ibrim appear, crowned by the remains of a tenth century cathedral, probably the most important surviving Christian Nubian monument. The British Priest, who lives in Cairo but is a spiritual exile from Sudan, sucks in his breath with a soft hiss of delight and devotion. The Leader is alert to such signs.

"Ibrim," he wrote recently, "may have been the last place where true paganism could be practiced unhindered beyond the imperial frontier." In fact, in the late Roman era, Ibrim even "enjoyed a major revival of paganism." On the plane the Priest had read these phrases to me with profound disapproval that words such as "enjoyed" and "true" had been used with reference to paganism. Now we had the author of those shocking phrases before us and can better understand: the Leader himself seems to be a pagan revival. Black curls dance above a round cherub's face and his bacchant belly is barely covered by grubby trousers. In fact, his entire body dances with exuberant energy as he continues his lecture.

Archaeological work didn't begin at Qasr Ibrim until 1961. Too late the city, which had been inhabited continuously from about 1000 B.C. until the early 19th century, was recognized as a unique mine of information. Both the site of early excavation and the ancient cemeteries are now underwater and today Qasr Ibrim, despite a short causeway, is in effect a tiny island.

Yet this small site, some forty kilometers from Abu Simbel, is the only remaining monument of Northern Nubian culture. Here paganism and Christianity vied for control until the seventh century when Qasr Ibrim became a bishopric. Here the religion of the pharaohs made its last stand under the watchful care of Isis until the cult of the Virgin Mary consumed her. But here paganism still has its defenders for archaeologists are at war with one another over priority and interpretation, some of which is clearly infused with theology.

"A lot of Christian buggery went on up there!" The Leader's arm flails towards the high plateau overlooking the dig. The Egyptian Exploration Society survey, using a photography kite, shows a thousand Meroitic minisites: cairns, stone circles, and broken dry stone structures. Footprints, carved along a pilgrim way, extend across the plateau and up into the cathedral. Who were these people, where did they come from and how did they combine Christian and pagan rites? The Nubians kill the tug engine and a holy silence envelopes us.

We are alongside one of the two houseboats that lodge the expedition members. Guftis, traditional diggers from Middle Egypt, sleep on mats in the adjoining barge. At night, jackals and the odd hyena prowl for food. We climb onto the decrepit hulk of the first houseboat as the guftis begin to unload the frozen chicken.

In the wardroom, the fifteen or so members of the Team, engrossed with themselves and their work, have gathered for lunch around a long makeshift trestle table. They are exhausted people, unaware that we come determined to buy their time with bags full of whisky, wine, beer, and chocolates. They tuck into their letters from home and, for the most part, ignore us. This will not continue for long. Both Christians and pagans love company. Fellowship over wine and bread is part of a common tradition.

The Leader is obsessed by the evolution of one religion into another and in the afternoon leads us in joyful celebration around Qasr Ibrim's Byblos-like jumble of walls and pillars. His lecture is a litany of continuity, hope and pagan footprints. Above us, the cathedral walls rise crookedly, whitewashed by snowy egrets and black kites. The Leader descends into the baptistery next to the crypt where the bones of at least two bishops and a camel have been identified. Earlier archaeologists dug and confused, cluttered and laid waste, dumped items now deemed of major value. The Leader is vigorous in his denunciation of them and all their works.

On the hillside below the cathedral, mud brick walls are emerging under the careful work of the Team who cannot yet tell if these structures are houses or part of the same religious institution. Oddly, there are almost no kitchens. They have gone through the levels of Nubian and Meroitic cultures into something they call "the X-group" because they know so little about it. It is a mystery they can understand anything at all as they spend only two months here every other year, and while they are away, the fishermen visit to rummage and spoil.

Here a Scottish dentist and a British doctoral candidate, both thickly coated in dirt, survey and scrape, extracting small items of cloth, papyrus, metal, wood, and clay and occasionally allowing the guftis to throw baskets of black earth off site into the lake. A German doctor hired to treat the Team seems to be following the Dentist into a second career. He, too, has plunged into the hunt, his soiled white shirt and tie offset by a mud streaked face. A few days ago, he proved his worth by identifying a small skeleton as a stillbirth. Why the infant had been buried under the floor remains a mystery, but the theories are as dense and pervasive as the dust.

The Priest arises with the Team at first light. Actually, he has no choice for he has slept on the floor of the wardroom anti-room, used in daylight for sorting. As the Team scatters to dig, piece together broken pots, catalog and photograph, the Priest climbs to prayer in the small church overlooking the cathedral. An arm of the lake separates this place from the main dig, and the completion of work there a few days before our arrival took men and expertise away from Qasr Ibrim itself. This assertion of Christian power has not been fully forgiven.

"The Biddlery," the Team calls this church after the famous professor who, completing work on schedule, packed off, leaving them to their pagan pursuits. In Cairo, the famous professor had told us that the Team was suffering an epidemic of gastro-intestinal disease brought on by lack of discipline and poor hygiene. Almost we sensed this as suggested evidence of God's disapproval. But now the professor is gone and tacked to the wardroom walls are irreverent poems about the Biddlery. The Leader attempts to explain this away in terms of generation gap, but we are catching on quickly.

"Archaeologists spend their days digging up centuries-old rubbish and concocting fanciful theories about what it all means," the Diplomat suggested to me privately. But we cannot doubt their expertise: specialists on baskets, textiles, potsherds, and ancient languages appear around every corner. Some of them seem weak on broader historical understanding and current events, but they can read Coptic and Greek, Latin and ancient Arabic and long for the discovery of a bilingual text which will open the secret of Meroitic to them.

"Ah, the bisexual text!" the Leader cries. "Perhaps today or tomorrow." Meanwhile, the experts deliver themselves to the task while daylight lasts, turn off the generator at 9 p.m., and dream that their fingers, groping carefully through the earth, have at last touched that sacred fragment of papyrus. Someday, the lake may rise again, just as it has fallen during recent years of drought, and will it be that long sought text, hidden still in the rubbish heap of history, which perishes? May the gods forbid! On then! Delve the ramparts!

On the second day, the Priest surveys the cathedral once again and sees that it is good, "almost complete enough for celebration of the Eucharist." Whether he does so or not, I can't say, for when I climb to the summit he has gone. A little owl perches primly over the altar and there is a mihrab against the eastern wall. Qasr Ibrim's cathedral has been "a place of prayer for many nations" but has now become "a place of desolation and a habitation for owls." Christians destroyed Temple six, behind the cathedral, the Leader says; and when excavators disturbed the soil in 1986, the smell of pagan incense rose again from the site.

But all is not lost. On the second day, too, the Priest accurately spots that the textile experts are resistant to calling a piece of fabric "Christian" despite the presence of crosses, which they—also accurately—describe as being a pre-Christian symbol. The Priest laments that he has by only a few days missed the Famous Professor, a man he perceives as of like mind and spirit.

We return that evening just at sundown from a walk over the high plateau. The pottery specialist has repaired a number of broken pagan pots and returned them to their places on the plateau. I ponder that no one knows what scenes occurred there, whether demonic rites, funeral ceremony, or healing ritual. I ask myself whether anyone considered whether those pots were intentionally smashed by the priests who used them. If so, what might happen now? We descend mystified and fearful towards the darkening river. The plateau is left to the hyenas and the night.

A lone figure toils in the last embers of light against a mud wall on "South Rampart Street." That the Dentist is ill we know, for at meals he is grim, and the Doctor keeps feeding him rehydration solution. But gastro-enteritis has become the hair shirt of his devotion. The Dentist knows that faith is well rewarded at Qasr Ibrim.

Two years ago, Qasr Ibrim yielded up a poem written by the Roman Governor Gallus to his mistress. Apparently, Gallus himself thought the poem too awful to send and so threw it out with the rubbish. But the classicists rejoiced in some sixty learned articles about discovery of the work of a contemporary of Virgil and clamored for more papyrus texts from Qasr Ibrim. All clamored, that is, except one scholar who had based his doctoral thesis on Gallus as a great writer and was, of course, forced to debunk the discovery as fraud.

On the third day, we are resurrected from this dead city towards what is called civilization. None of us is happy to leave. The bilingual text had yet to appear, and though we saw a herd of gazelle on their morning expedition across the jebel to another arm of the lake, the anticipated gigantic crocodiles have failed to show. I said goodbye to the Starving Archaeologist who, engrossed in a map of his next stopping place in the Eastern Desert, did not bother to respond.

As the tug moved past the cathedral, I realize that since Friday morning I have not heard the call to prayer—except in the cathedral and now in my own heart for the recovery and success of the Dentist.

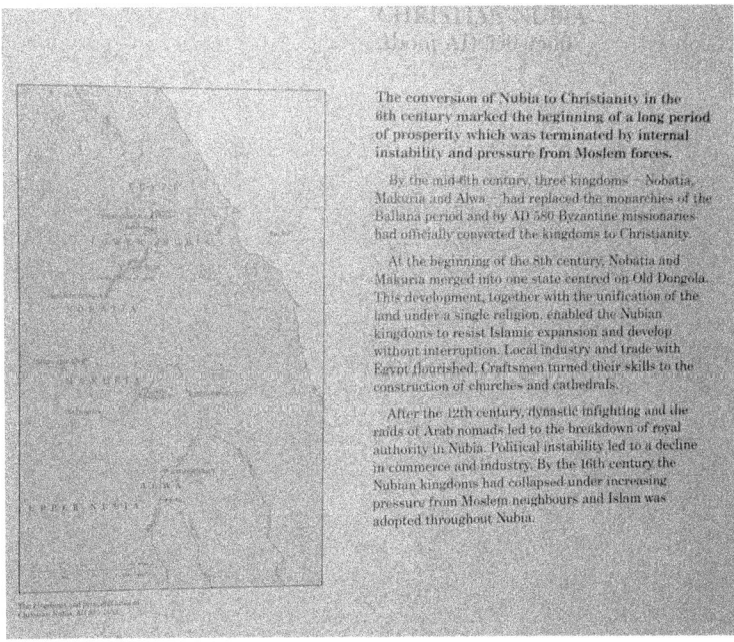

Christian Nubia—panel at Sudan Museum, 1992

10

Conspiracy of Silence at Jebel Asfar

21 February 1992

It was evening, and the day had begun inauspiciously. Never betray an owl's roost. That much I know. But Big Bird is, I persuaded myself, among the foremost advocates of Egyptian wildlife preservation. That's how, after a year of treasuring the long-eared owls, visiting their roost on daily dog walks, breaking open their casts, and mulling over what they had eaten the day before, I betrayed them. The moment I mentioned long-eared owls, Bird Watcher Jekyll was transformed into Twitcher Hyde. Long-eared owls had, it seemed, eluded Big Bird on three continents, and she "needed" one for her life list.

We must get on the hot line, Big Bird said, inform the world, bully the authorities into safeguards, organize tours. Though I recoiled, I had already given the general location of the roost and feared that, now in full cry, Big Bird would alert any number of voyeurs. Unless I could extract a promise of containment, in a few weeks we might even see long-eared owls for sale on 26 July Street alongside Egyptian hedgehogs and green sea turtles.

The Naturalist became an ally. It isn't a matter of "needing" birds, he said emphatically, but whether they need us. He and I entered into a conspiracy of silence and laid plans for the containment of Big Bird. First, however, there was today's bird watching expedition—which soon confronted me with a much more painful choice.

Our group of twelve was mixed: male and female, foreign and Egyptian, diplomat and businessman, Christian and Muslim, and (people being even more interesting to me than birds) representatives of three minority conditions: agnostic, homosexual, and spy. An interest in birds provided a bond when we met, most of the group for the first time, at 8 a.m. in the parking lot of the Heliopolis Sheraton. Two hours later, we would discover that when it came to conspiracy, there was little difference among us.

Take the road through Ismailia, turn right into the desert about thirty minutes from Cairo, drive on for another ten minutes, and stop in the "reclamation" area. The site is totally unmarked by village, sign, or natural features and few visitors, other than the rare goatherd leading his flock through the sparse new growth, would be likely to find the same wadi twice. Big Bird, who spends a lot of time in the area, could probably find it blindfolded.

"That's a human skull," the Development Expert said. We'd left the vehicles on the road, walked about 200 yards into the desert and were looking down into a shallow depression when he and I saw it. But skulls are not a particularly unusual discovery in Egypt. The deserts are full of bodies and body parts, many at least 2,000 years old. Besides, someone had seen a raptor go to ground and the group was determined to have a closer look. The column moved on in the stealthy gait of veteran stalkers. Only the Development Expert and I hung back. Something here looked peculiar.

Loose sand accompanied me as I slid down the side of the depression. A skull all right. But a brown dress, a red scarf in two pieces and a mass of black hair, tangled like the ruined remains of a tire left too long in the desert sun, showed that this was no mummy. The Expert joined me in the shallow wadi.

The skull, when I lifted it, was heavy with its contents. A few scraps of flesh clung to the fissured cranium and a beetle perched in an empty eye socket. The teeth were perfect. No dentist had been at work here. A young person, we told one another, and certainly a woman, given the hair, the dress and the small size of the skull. Surely a very young woman, a teenager. Oddly, despite the dress, there was no body and no bones other than the lower jaw, which rested on the sand a few feet away, licked clean by a jackal or a fox. The object of our attention stank in the still morning air, and I replaced it carefully on the sand.

"Beetles work fast," the Development Expert said in a knowledgeable, faraway voice. "And the foxes." He nudged the jawbone with his boot as the others in our group returned to watch us from the lip of the depression. Heaviness like the pressure of a fist settled into my gut. Perhaps a shallow burial, someone suggested. But there was no sign of digging, only the brown dress laid out with a mass of black hair upon it. There was no need to say what suddenly we all knew, but still I tried.

"Her family..." I began, thinking of the penalty of even supposed infidelity to traditional behavior. But the face of the young Egyptian civil servant stopped me.

"These things happen," I said lamely, embarrassed for him, the only Egyptian in our group. Stricken, the young man stood silent as though we had unmasked him in a personal crime.

"*I knew* this would happen to me some day!" Big Bird wailed. "I knew I'd run into a body sooner or later." Here, definitely, was something she did not "need." A body meant trouble, inconvenience and intolerable delay. Most of what Big Bird wanted to show us awaited, and now *this*. Nonetheless, she maintained her commitment to democracy. We would vote on the matter, she said, and decide whether to file a police report. Not immediately, of course, as that would spoil the day's intended purpose, but later, at an appropriate time.

The fist turned in my stomach as though I, too, had suddenly become implicated in the murder of this young woman. Time to watch birds, time to betray owls, no time to die. But I kept quiet.

"Best to forget this entirely," the young Egyptian said. He turned away, anguished. Certainly the brunt of investigation, if we betrayed our find, would fall on him. There was no need for a vote. The only Egyptian in the group had spoken. The Ambassador, the Naturalist, even the Spy and the Development Expert, concurred. Because we had found nothing, seen nothing, knew nothing, we left the place, quickly climbing out of the offending wadi and back into our three Range Rovers. We didn't even put sand over the skull, I realized later, just left her there with her perfect teeth and the feasting beetles.

"There's a likely place for stone curlews, just down the road," Big Bird said as we drove on.

The weather was magnificent. Spring had come after an unusually dull and cold winter and the desert rejoiced. We parked our cars and spread out. Tiny insects and giant dung beetles strutted across the sand between flowering bushes where we identified bar-tailed and hoopoe larks, spectacled warblers, brown-necked ravens, and the coveted stone curlew. We drove on to Tenth of Ramadan City, taking a back road in to avoid a recently reoccupied military outpost. Big Bird and the Young Egyptian, riding with me and the Diplomat, told of being detained at other such outposts, once for six hours and once for eight, by illiterate soldiers who thought they understood the motives of skulking outsiders armed with binoculars.

"It's a wonder we weren't shot," Big Bird said. "If we're stopped today, we'll just say that we have come to investigate the sewage problem." The sewage oxidation ponds, part of an experiment in natural sewage treatment, were, in fact, our destination. Here birds had gathered, colonizing the newly wet and almost entirely unvisited area. But here, too, death had arrived before us.

Sometime over the past several months, a point of pollution saturation had occurred. The soup of sewage had been poisoned by industrial waste, the project to create wetlands had come undone, and the area was dying back into desert. Marsh harriers still wheeled overhead and there were still common snipe, Kentish plover, ruff and little stint. But the geese, teal, and ducks had gone. Several hundred moorhens had died in the past year, and there were no more little grebes, painted snipes, or purple gallinules. The end approached. The desert returned, sucking in the fetid water and the earth bound birds and, sometime later, releasing all, purified and broken down into their elements.

The Ambassador's wife, being pregnant, was nauseated by the smell, and so we put away our telescopes and moved on to Jebel Asfar. But at the Yellow Mountain, man's effluence had again brought only temporary benefit. A canal carrying raw sewage from Cairo had irrigated the orange groves and made the trees along its edge a haven for rare Smyrna kingfishers. But these trees were being inexplicably cut down and the kingfishers seemed to have gone. Further back from the canal, large stands of trees where black kites nested were also being removed. Mewing, the kites circled above us.

"Does anyone need a Senegal thick knee?" Big Bird cried. But the Ambassador's wife longed for her Cairo villa, and so we turned towards home.

The Diplomat headed the Range Rover towards the Nile. I slept briefly, lulled by heat and the accumulated fatigue of life in Cairo as we hummed along the rutted tarmac. But in my dream a young woman watched me from empty eye sockets. She wore a brown dress and carried a faded red headscarf. Although she had no face, a few scraps of flesh clung to her skull, and her teeth were perfect. My own head lolled against the headrest, and dimly I heard Big Bird in diatribe from the back seat against people who trash their desert, their trees, and their common heritage of international birds. Several times she mentioned the need to save owls.

The Young Egyptian, who dropped by a few days later, told me that dismemberment is a common practice when Egyptian peasants attempt to conceal murder. Yes, he said, people do such things. But if you inform the authorities, you had best remain anonymous, or you could face several days of inconvenient interrogation.

My conscience was also calmed with the certain knowledge that I could not possibly find that wadi again. And also by resolving, whatever happened, to keep Big Bird from ratting on the long-eared owls. The girl in the brown dress is dead, and I do not know her killer. But the long-eared owls must be kept alive and unexploited. Sadly, however, within a short time, Big Bird had revealed the "find" in an international birding publication.

11

Shooters in Zamalek

13 May 1992

"It was one in the morning when the shooters came," the Car Washer said. His mouth curled up on both sides of the harelip in a grimace of embarrassment and fear. "He was very strong, and she was very big." He waved his hands over his thin belly, covered by a pair of ragged trousers rolled up to the knees.

"Baby," he said in English, making certain I knew what he meant, and his eyes hurt me.

"Someone called the police," he said in Arabic. He made dialing gestures, and then dropped his arms in despair. We stood in silence for a moment until I said the obligatory "*malesh*." But he was not able to give the usual response to condolence.

"But they were good," the Car Washer said defiantly. "They were not evil." His moral dilemma was painful. I hadn't known he'd loved them so much and, again, I felt ashamed of us all, myself in particular, for not having saved them.

"They died together," he said, "and afterwards there were cartouches in the street. Egypt is no good." Grieved and angry, the Car Washer turned away, stumbled, and slopped water on his feet. I suspected he had one of those shotgun shells in his pocket, a memento as well as a symbol of the tyranny that governed his life.

I, too, had heard the shots from three streets away and, jolted awake, sat upright to stare into the darkness. Five or six rapid reports and then the descent of greater silence. No shouting, no barking dogs. Just deep night. On the floor beside our bed our dogs, Megan and LBJ, the latter a rescued street puppy I brought home, sat stiffly erect, ears straining. Then we sighed, turned, and settled. There was nothing to be done. Whatever had occurred was over.

It took me four days to gather courage to face the Boab. As usual, he sat before the building on his small bench and respectfully uncrossed his legs in response to my greeting.

"They are dead," he said quietly. "They aren't here. She was very big, and he made too much noise at night. Someone called the police. Police!" He spat the word. "She was very good, and now she is dead." He pointed to the street and raised his eyes toward heaven. "Malesh. Malesh." Allah gives. The police take away. When the effendi speaks, there is nothing the powerless can do.

Marco and Satchico were littermates. A year or so ago, during the pogrom in which their mother disappeared, someone hid them—the Boab perhaps or the Car Washer or one of the young soldiers who guard the Korean embassy. After that the street people cared for the two puppies as best they could. The soldiers fed them from their meager morning meal, and in exchange for safe passage, the zabaleen threw a few tidbits off the rubbish wagon. Compassion bound together those at the bottom of the heap.

"The Koreans eat dogs," the Boab told me in whispers and it became his religious duty to protect the two succulent pups from such barbarian behavior. Months later when Satchico had her own puppies, the Boab gave her an old coat to lie on and showed off the puppies with pride. Reverence for the miracle of birth connected him to the wellsprings of life. But when he urged me to find homes for them, I tried but could not.

"No one wants Egyptian dogs," an Egyptian vet told me when, newly arrived and with courage intact, I collected another street dog's litter and delivered them to him. Though he said he would use chloroform, instead he injected them in the heart while I punished myself listening to their cries from the outer office. For weeks, those infant voices haunted me, and I had no strength to play God's role again. Let someone else take charge there, I said. Who am I to try to compensate for the Egyptian ability to appreciate the wonder without connecting with the agony to follow?

For a while, then, Satchico's puppies kept company to the Boab's lonely hours. Two were run over in the street, and I realized that privately I longed for parvovirus or even hungry Koreans to carry the others quietly away. Then one day the starvelings vanished, and I knew the Boab had finally been forced into action lest the presence of a pack bring down the shooters on his Satchico.

Killing is wrong, the Boab said firmly. But if you put dogs into the desert, perhaps they have a chance. I thought about the puppy-eating wild packs at Giza and asked no more questions. Instead, we all watched as Satchico rebounded from her ordeal. Even the hind leg, left hanging after she was hit by a car, filled out somewhat, and she and Marco played furiously in the street following their morning swim in the Nile. Every morning when I walked Megan, the littermates strode proudly with us to the edge of their territory.

In China, the papers claim, a decree has gone forth that all dogs must be destroyed. Dogs eat grain which people need, the Party says. But the Boab and I cannot imagine a world without dogs. Perhaps, if I could translate, he would agree with the anthropologist Loren Eisely, who described human beings as "earth eaters." In Egypt, at least, we still have bread. But life is in God's hands.

"Marco is foolish," the Boab told me two weeks ago, and I knew he referred to the midnight chorus. "Marco is very foolish, but Satchico is good." I walked home humming a line from a song of the Seventies: "God bless the beast and children. Keep them safe. Keep them warm. Give them shelter from the storm."

In the end the Boab was, of course, defeated. No one asked his opinion for it did not matter. Today the bored young guards at the Korean Embassy gate shuffle their boots, leer at passing women, and dream of Upper Egypt. The Car Washer bends his ruined face over the bucket of filthy water. The Boab sits staring into the distance.

Marco and Satchico are gone, but the poor we have always with us. At night, we who have lost those we love will listen for the return of the shooters.

Megan and LBJ awaiting their treat at home in Zamalek,
Cairo, February 1992

12

Susie and Diana at Heliopolis

14 May 1992

The Commonwealth cemetery in Heliopolis has been encroached on by urban sprawl, and some say really ought to be turned into a small public garden. This will not happen so long as the fierce young War Graves Representative in the kilt has anything to do with it. He had, moreover, placed the twenty or so journalists attending this event inside an enclosure referred to by free-range diplomats as "the reptile pen." Which just about shows how stuffy civil servants can be about people who photograph a princess in bathing costume from high-rise buildings overlooking the Ambassador's swimming pool.

But that was yesterday's news. Today Princess Diana would lay a wreath at the base of the large stone cross that dominates the Second World War Commonwealth cemetery. Hundreds had come to watch her honor men who died in the service of her husband's grandfather, King George the Sixth. Hundreds more hung out the windows of nearby buildings. Security guards scuttled back and forth.

The dead lay in neat rows: Scots, Welshmen, Indians, South Africans, with a few Sudanese and Free French tucked in among them. As always, family messages on the headstones mention "forever," "remembrance" and "the going down of the sun." Awaiting the sirens that would signal the arrival of the Princess, we strolled among the headstones with their painful professions of love and loss.

Near the cross, a wriggling mass of Brownies in yellow and

olive uniforms had formed an "honor guard." You needed to look carefully to see Susie. It was, in fact, the way she blended in so well which worried me.

"Look," Susie's mother told me last week as she pummeled my stiff shoulder. "I've never asked anything for my daughter. She doesn't want to be different. But, if the Princess stops to speak to any of the Brownies—oh, let it be Susie!"

It was almost a prayer, which, of course, none of us could answer. Princesses are clothed in layers of minders and advisers, guards and dignitaries. Still the word went out among the diplomats, courtiers, and military escorts. Susie. Susie. Make sure the Princess talks to Susie. Alan said he'd tell the Lady in Waiting. The Ambassador registered the request. The Colonel had it in hand. Bluntly, being an American, I mentioned Susie to Diana herself when I was presented. Now, three days later at the cemetery, several of us waited anxiously. What if Diana forgets?

The sirens wailed closer, the cavalcade stopped, the lovely young woman in blue and cream advanced up the center path towards the Cross of Remembrance. An enormous hat shaded her face and the Reptiles groaned but kept snapping. The Colonel in scarlet beret strode magnificently beside the Princess, his sword swinging grandly against his spurred boots.

The Australian Priest stood in brilliant robes beneath the Cross of Remembrance. The sun shone. The wreath was placed. The bugle sounded. The dead rejoiced in hope of resurrection. The Brownies waited tensely, their tiny flags held still at last.

The Princess passed along the row of Commonwealth attaches and their curtseying wives before presenting a medal to a retiring gardener. She greeted his wife, his children, his brothers, and, so it seemed, most of his cousins. Then she took a few minutes among the headstones, the Colonel resplendent at her side. It was, perhaps, his finest hour.

Finally, Princess Diana turned to walk through the arching trees, under which the Guides, the lesser dignitaries, and the Brownies had regrouped. The little girls were wide-eyed and silent, star-struck, open-mouthed. The Princess stopped and spoke to one of them only and then passed on beneath the trees. A groan arose from the back ranks where several of us paced. The Brownies' faces mirrored vast disappointment for the Princess had missed Susie.

"Quick," several people said at once. We moved swiftly to reposition the Brownies at the end of the arcade, Susie limping among them. But the crowd had thickened, and tiny people were pushed back. The Queen's Flight waited, and the Princess was leaving. I nearly wept in frustration.

But God often helps those who forget the rules. The policeman nudged a young diplomat, who turned, lifted tiny Susie, pushed through the crowd, jumped over the hedge, and set her down directly in the path of the Princess. Diana paused—there was a whispered conversation, a trembling attempt to curtsy. Then the Princess passed out the gate to her waiting escort. Sirens sounded, and she was gone. If they had been able, the dead men would have cheered. They had been honored by the presence of a brave little girl who, like many of them, has only one arm and one leg. On May 14, the Cairo Brownies will say, the Princess flicked a fly off Susie's nose.

Susie meets Princess Diana at the Commonwealth War Cemetery, Heliopolis, Cairo, May 1992

13

In the Wadi of the King

7 August 1992

Wadi Rishrash cuts through the desert furnace like a flue, its boulders, limestone walls, and occasional tamarisk trees offering scattered refuge in a weary land. Every few years, heavy rains fill the wadi with raging water which tosses the enormous rocks, obliterates the track and carries a few tamarisks down towards the Nile. But today the sky is brilliant and cloudless, and desert winds drink moisture from our bodies as thirstily as the few remaining ibex suck water from the hidden springs. When night falls, the traveler will feel he has been purified by passage through fire.

This is the land of the Ma'aza Bedouin, pastoral nomads whose domain extends from Nile to Red Sea and as far south as Wadi Qena. Or perhaps, as we are only two hours' drive from Cairo, Wadi Rishrash is still within 'Amarin tribal territory. Even Joseph Hobbs' book on the Egyptian wilderness does not pinpoint this place. And the guidebooks do not mention Wadi Rishrash at all.

Just as well. Irrigation and peoples of the river have crept into the wadi's mouth where it opens towards the Nile. Already the discarded tins, dead trucks, and plastic sacks of settled life have begun their march up the clean sand of the wadi. Not far north on the Nile road, the cement factories of aptly named Helwan also spew filth, and, although the government frequently promises to enforce restrictions, nothing yet stands in the way of "progress."

Earlier this week, I lunched with an Egyptian aristocrat who had known King Farouk. When news came that Egypt's last king had been deposed, the Aristocrat said, he was boating in Alexandria harbor "with one of the king's female cousins." Later, he and his fellow detainees wore their silk dressing gowns in prison and vied to see whose cook could send in the most delicious meal. They were so outrageous, the Aristocrat said, that in the end Nasser threw them all out of prison.

I forgot to ask the Aristocrat if he had ever been to Wadi Rishrash. Probably not. Most Egyptians cling to the Nile Valley. From their desert wadis and hilltops, the Bedouin watch "progress," including pollution from Helwan, spreading towards them like the ancient Nile in flood.

After losing our way several times in the newly cultivated area, mainly on the advice of farmers we asked for directions, we found our entrance at last and began a rock strewn drive up the wadi under a relentless sun. In some places deep sand sucked at the tires. We were nine, a small army in three off-road vehicles whose dust could be seen for miles. Most of us were connected to the "Britch Empassy," as a repairman recently wrote on my invoice. But although we joked about "Wadi Rifraf," it was because we felt ourselves to be strangers here. The Bedouin care nothing for diplomatic immunity.

A hunting lodge, built by Prince Kamal el-Din, looms at the head of the spectacular wadi. For forty years, it has stood isolated in heat and occasional torrent, empty save for shadows, and blowing sand. No need to come here anymore, it seems to say. The singer and the song, the king and the slaves who built the track, the slayer and the slain are no more. Almost all that remains, other than Bedouin memories, are several orange-colored buildings and a small green patch of trees and shrubs down near the well. There, a tank of scummy water provides life to scrub warblers, passing tribesmen, and a multitude of biting insects.

The multilayered yellow wadi walls rise up behind us as we unpack lunch in an ornate wooden gazebo. Firewood is precious, but the Bedouin have respected this royal playground so that even most of the window frames in the buildings remain in place. Three enormous conical dovecots, now empty, rise behind us. King Farouk, we decide, must have liked roast pigeon stuffed with rice and pine nuts. More likely, as game was increasingly scarce even in the 1940s, his retainers needed to provide at least something for the royal party to shoot at and thus revive their flagging spirits after the arduous journey up the wadi.

The British, Hobbs wrote, decided to protect wildlife and so prohibited hunting on the Ma'aza plateau. Even the Bedouin, who depend on game as a source of protein, were chastised for infringement and their dogs slaughtered least they be used in the hunt. Different rules, apparently, applied to "the Britch" themselves. Thomas Russell, a British inspector of interior, once killed thirty ibex after depriving them of water so that they gathered near the well in Wadi Rishrash.[1]

We saw no wild animals. The herds of oryx and of ostrich that roamed here early in the century are gone. The Barbary sheep is extinct in Egypt, and only a few ibex and gazelle remain. These are closely guarded—except, of course, from modern Gulf sheikhs who pay well and in advance.

"I feel certain there is something illegal about our presence here," said the young British friend whose pending departure from Egypt we had come to mourn. Nonetheless, he has been here several times before, once even spending the night. Because this wild place holds special meaning for him, we ignore the swarms of flies and feed ourselves richly on smoked salmon, quiche, chicken salad, fruits of the Nile Valley, fine wine, and chocolate cake.

Two men and three camels come down the wadi and pass within hailing distance. Their pace is slow, graceful, and rhythmic, at peace with the desert. The Bedouin water their beasts and themselves and return up the wadi, waving to us with courtesy rather than interest. One of them has left a sack hanging from a tree by the well. No one will remove it until the owner returns. This is the desert code. This is how it has always been.

Suddenly we are embarrassed for we recognize ourselves as intruders. As were King Farouk and Prince Kamal el-Din. As are the settlers, the modern Arab hunting parties, and the rapacious officials in the Valley. Though we wish to offer food to the Bedouin, we fear to wound their dignity. And we understand that we are barbarians, people who enter without asking and feast arrogantly before those who live on life's margin. We wave back to cover the moment.

Kings, British rulers, Nile dwellers come and go. The rocks, the heat, and the Bedouin remain. They want nothing from us and fear only that we have come to take away their gazelle and their freedom. It is five o'clock in the afternoon and darkness will not fall for another three and a half hours. But suddenly we wish to be gone from this forbidding and perhaps sacred place.

To spend the night would be to ask for trouble. At night the men of the desert might return, we tell ourselves. And then how could we not answer their questions?

14

The Mango Season

19 August 1992

We walked from the Indonesian national day reception at the Meridien Hotel along the corniche to the British Embassy. In the old days of Kitchener, Gorst, and Lampson the Residence gardens stretched down to the Nile. Several of the immense plane trees of that time remain outside the wall which embraces the British residence although the remaining mango trees of that era, still dropping ripe fruit like blessings at this time of year, are all inside the high gray walls. The wife of a former ambassador told me she used to worry about those "British trees" now exposed to the pulsating humanity that on August evenings seeks relief from the heat along the waterfront. But people do need fire to boil tea, and the base of a tree is a convenient grate.

Recently, one of the young soldiers on guard outside the British embassy shot himself. He was exhausted, people said, due to the heat and had been ordered to work a double shift through the night. So he went into his guardhouse, there at the end of the compound where the road turns, and some time in the black hours of night, during which people most often despair, he killed himself.

Several Egyptians at the Indonesian reception insisted that as suicide is a sin certainly the young man's death was accidental. But you don't shoot yourself in the head with a rifle by accident. I wondered what else had been going on in his life and why no one noticed the signs of depression that almost certainly had been there before the evening of his death. Why had no one noticed how close he was to the edge?

The Indonesian reception had been the usual scrum, to be dissected afterward with the usual care: the large ladies with bosoms like aircraft carrier flight decks holding up their heavy jewelry, the thin waiters stepping over wires laid carelessly over the carpet, enormous men pigging out at the too lavish buffet, hordes of little Indonesians no one had ever seen before scooting about doing we knew not what. The Diplomat, who was standing in for the British Ambassador, and I were accosted by an unknown man who shook our hands and announced himself "the Ambassador of Iraq to the Arab League." But as we had our orders about fraternizing with "the enemy," we were obliged to stiffen and move to a safer part of the great hall.

The Diplomat vanished into the crowd while I made conversation with the ambassadors of Guatemala and Uruguay just because we all happened to find ourselves together and then the wives of the Australian and American ambassadors came up one after another with pleasantries and thanks to God for the mango season. Next, I talked with a Turk I know, a lawyer slightly in his cups, who told me that the difference between Arabs and Turks is summed up by the word "discipline." Then while the Turk (shades of Ataturk) was trying to convince me that no "good" Muslim could be a modern person because Islam is "primitive," a Romanian journalist came and pulled him away. By then we had shown the flag for a decent interval, and it was possible to leave.

A British embassy car took us back to Gezira Island, past the place where a few days earlier in the week a man exposed himself while I was walking home from the Gezira Club with my dogs, Megan and LBJ. I suppose the fellow may originally have stopped his car on the corniche to take a pee. But although I gave him plenty of time to finish and tidy himself away, after he saw me round the corner, he preferred to prolong the moment, his back to the traffic and another of those enormous plane trees beside him.

The Flasher looked to be in his late twenties, with a vulnerable face and a long thin member like a piece of rope that he twirled rather sadly. He didn't look as though he was enjoying any of this, and afterwards, I felt sorry I had not handed him the dahlia I was carrying. After all, it takes a brave man to expose himself to a middle-aged woman in a Miss Marple hat who carries a walking stick and an enormous dahlia in one hand and a leash attached to a fat Labrador and an Egyptian street dog in the other. Compared to the Flasher I was downright dangerous.

The dahlia had been given to me at the Gezira club by one of the more ragged workers. My Retainer, I call him privately, because I am forever slipping him a few pounds, and he is forever calling down God's blessings upon me and my lineage for several generations in both directions—which seems a rather good bargain on my part. It was the Retainer who warned me that the Gezira club management planned to put out poison for the wild dog pack that lives in the central field. This information saved the lives of both my dogs a few days later when I saw the small packets, innocent looking but filled with poison, which had been placed where most Gezira Club members walk their dogs, several of whom subsequently died.

But on the morning I encountered the Flasher, my Retainer had simply given me a gorgeous dahlia from the bunch he was carrying behind an old woman as she made her way to the pet cemetery. So as not to hurt his feelings, I took what was not his to give or mine to accept. Egypt does this to people. Even flowers get recycled. But I digress.

In the aftermath of the Indonesian reception, as we were driven back to Zamalek, the Diplomat and I also discussed the sexual symbolism of garden produce as it had recently been brought to our attention by Farag Foda. This prominent Egyptian journalist wrote with disgust about religious extremists so preoccupied with sex that they refused even to speak the names aubergines and carrots. Mangos, I supposed, fall into the aubergine category and should also be forbidden in conversation, but we'll never know, as the extremists had assassinated Farag Foda some two months earlier. Surely, I should have given that dahlia to the Flasher, I told the Diplomat. Flashers, as I reminded him from my years as a befriender in both London and Cairo, are sad, needy people, not dangerous villains. But the Diplomat gave me that look which meant he would prefer to change the subject.

We got out at the Four Corners Italian restaurant where they serve lovely pasta au saumon fumé and unspeakable Omar Khayyam wine. Part of the charm of the Four Corners is the friendliness of the staff. The new hostess is a modern Egyptian working girl, not beautiful but neat, colorfully dressed and with that same look of hesitation, hopefulness, and vulnerability I had seen on the Flasher's face. When I smiled, her return smile registered the relief of one who anticipates condescension from foreigners and other members of the "upper classes" and usually gets it.

It was after 10:30 when we left the Four Corners. Out on the street cars were parked haphazardly on the pavement and groups of young, up-market Egyptians were chatting and gesturing, blocking the sidewalks and spilling over into the main street. Several of the young women were dressed in skimpy costumes, one even in shorts. You never see Egyptian women in shorts in daytime Cairo. But these were the night people, those with rich parents who allow them to stay up all night partying and watching videos and then sleep until early afternoon before preparing to start all over again. But since it's the mango season, why not?

Walking home along the dark streets over uneven pavement, I almost stepped on an enormous mango, only slightly bruised by its fall from a tree overhanging the road. We carried away this plumb, smooth treasure, slightly sticky and filled with flavor. On a corner three young soldiers in black uniforms and ill-fitting boots were sharing a cigarette.

Eleven o'clock and all is well, for there are no dangers here. Soldiers are on duty, the rich are at play, and the poor are asleep in stairwells and forgotten corners of our part of Cairo, any island world. The religious extremists are far away, unless, of course, one has disguised himself in a black uniform. No one but the street dogs watched as we approached the soldiers on the next corner.

"This descended from heaven and had your name on it," the Diplomat told the lucky fellows and handed over the mango.

Travels into the Heart of Egypt 75

The River Nile at Cairo, 1992

15

Ordeal by Fire at Abu Sultan

21 August 1992

The Sheikh is taller than average, over six feet, about forty but with dignity and presence more often seen in the elderly. A white mesh skullcap covers his head, and over the cap he has placed a long white shawl, which descends to the middle of his back. His face is alert but quiet and a paunch is just beginning to fill out his galabiyah. He sits barefoot on the grass mat, leaning on a large pillow propped against the outside wall of the ruinous house. Crowded under the reed matting of the shelter that extends from the shack, a group of supplicants watch the Sheikh intently, for his are the words and actions of divine judgment.

Our two-hour drive from Cairo to the Sheikh's majlis near Abu Sultan has left us thirsty. We sip sweet cardamom-flavored coffee while the Israeli anthropologist unpacks his video camera and trains it on two women seated on a mat across from the Sheikh. Between the two mats, a fire glows in an open pit. The heavy iron handle of a long coffee bean roasting spoon protrudes ominously from the fire.

"Do you pledge that you have done no sorcery against the outcome of this trial?" the Sheikh asks four young men seated on another mat to his right.

"We know nothing of such evil, O Hajj," they reply one by one. "We have come only to find truth." All peer anxiously at the coffee spoon and then at a middle-aged woman dressed in black who has righteous indignation written across her smooth features. Six thousand Egyptian pounds—her entire fortune—has been stolen and among the suspects is her own son. He, it seems, will lick the spoon on behalf of his sister as well as himself. The younger woman sits beside her mother with an expressionless face.

The facts, as known, have already been written and witnessed, each man signing a separate statement of innocence, the illiterate by affixing a thumbprint. All have thereby agreed to abide by the judgment of the bish'a. The older woman, responsible for the fee, now negotiates with the Sheikh. Finally, as she does not have the 165 Egyptian pounds that he asks, she pulls off her rings and hands them to him as security. The Sheikh weighs the rings in his hand before tucking them into his pocket.

Prayers follow, all lifting hands to Allah for justice. Then the four young men, faces tense and determined, kneel before the fire, and the Sheikh settles himself beside them, lifting his hands once more in prayer.

"I think she brought the son along to ensure that the man she thinks is the thief had no excuse not to attend," the Anthropologist whispers. He is writing a book about the use of ordeal in applying justice and has become a close friend of the Sheikh. The Anthropologist's Israeli bodyguard, seated on a mat nearby, cuddles the four-year-old daughter of the Sheikh's brother, keeping her quiet as the moment of ordeal approaches.

Masterfully, the Sheikh increases our suspense by demonstrating on the back of his hand how the spoon is to be licked: firmly, without hesitation, and three times. More prayers follow for God's approval and direction, and then there is a final retelling of the charges. On the wall of the house is a color photo of a man's gaping mouth, his swollen, protruding tongue covered by a raw burn. The Sheikh raises the spoon, pounds it three times on a rock, brushes away the sand three times and holds it out to the first man.

There is complete silence as each of the four licks in turn, their eyes staring. Tears run down the face of one but he makes no sound. Twice the spoon hisses on contact with a dry tongue. After all four have rinsed their mouths and spat into a square pit behind the fire, we begin the obligatory five-minute wait. It is a ritual that has been conducted thousands of times by the Sheikh and by his fathers before him. Baraka, divine favor, has rested upon his family for many generations.

We wait in continued silence. Nearby, a tethered water buffalo bellows and from across the courtyard come sounds of women tending their bread oven. Flies settle on us and creep into our mouths and the corners of our eyes. Under a tree next to the shelter, drinking water sweats through large clay zirs, one of which rests in a bomb casing, souvenir of the 1973 war between Egypt and Israel. The bodyguard kisses the child, and the Anthropologist continues his filming, murmuring commentary in Hebrew. That he is an Israeli here in this place seems even more extraordinary than the bish'a itself.

The Sheikh, however, is a man of justice whose business is to look into hearts, not nationalities. He is attracted by a man who speaks knowledgably to him in Arabic about blood feuds in the Negev. They are a symbiotic pair and have become such close friends that the Anthropologist has access to all the Sheikh's records in order that what he writes will make clear the ways of traditional Arab justice.

The five minutes is up, and the four men are ordered to extend their tongues. The Sheikh inspects each tongue carefully, rubbing it with his thumb as the rest of us shuffle about for a better view. The Sheikh asks the first man to rinse again, and the Anthropologist sighs. All of us see the large ragged blister before the guilty man lowers his head. The other three men begin loudly to praise God for justice.

Accused and accuser, guilty and vindicated, leave together as they came, in one car. The thief's family will be summoned to repay the stolen money. There will be no need for months in the courts, endless waiting, high legal fees, bribes, or torture of suspects. The police will not become involved, for, although the bish'a is not legally recognized, the thief cannot turn to the police for they, too, will now believe in his guilt. Nor will there be compensation for false accusations. This is allowed only when a woman's honor has been unjustly impugned. But in cases where a woman is found to be impure, she is taken away by her family, usually to be killed. This is the ancient law. No one is allowed to interfere with justice. All this the Anthropologist whispers to us.

Before leaving, we give the Sheikh a plastic carrier bag filled with cans of beer. This, the Anthropologist had advised us, would be a most welcome gift for, although the Sheikh is holy of course, he is not strait-laced. We leave the Anthropologist behind, watching as a car filled with men seeking consultation with the Sheikh approaches down the farmland's rutted road.

On the desert road back to Cairo, we see a flock of grounded birds in the distance around which seems to be a watering hole or small marsh. Driving off road for a better view, we come over a ridge and recognize migrating white storks, at least forty of them, with pink bills and long pink legs. A lone man carrying a hoe tops the ridge of sand from the other side, and the storks rise wearily, trailing their long legs and then landing nearby to await the intruder's departure.

We return to the road and drive on until an army truck suddenly lurches from a desert track and then comes to a halt broadside across the paved road. The two cars immediately ahead of us slow and then accelerate, swerving around the obstacles as several soldiers jump from the truck. I brake hard and prepare to turn onto the shoulder and keep moving, but then realize that the soldiers are unarmed and one of them is barely standing.

"He collapsed," the others say, supporting him and leaning into our windows. "The truck is slow and we must get him to the hospital." Their eyes plead. There is already one passenger in the back seat but somehow three soldiers, including the barely conscious man, manage to crowd in as well and we set off at high speed towards Cairo.

The injured youth moans, held upright by his comrades, his eyes vacant and his neck slack. Our offer of water is rejected by the others. No, it is not sunstroke. Was it an accident then? There is no response. Has he been shot? No, they reply, though one of them has blood on his clothing. They are frightened teenagers and do not wish to speak.

Twenty minutes later, we reach the military hospital, and the two soldiers half carry the third out of the Range Rover. We go on our way none the wiser.

Yes, but today we met a man who could have made them tell the truth.

16

With Florence Nightingale in Upper Egypt

August 1992

Florence Nightingale thought Dendera loathsome. She had just visited Thebes, Luxor, and Karnak and, sailing down river in February 1850, found Dendera "a vulgar temple, covered with acres of bas-reliefs, which one has no desire to examine." From art critic, she moved on to religious as well as architectural interests. The thick walls and passageways of the Temple of Hathor are "the very sanctuary of priest craft, a wonder of holy artifice." All here was derivative, tawdry, and, worst of all, "only Roman."[1]

Perhaps it was those enormous columns at the entrance supported by capitals with a woman's face and cows' ears that turned Florence against Dendera. Or perhaps it was her rebellion against male-dominated religion, which venerated a few women and enslaved the rest. Very likely her reactions also had something to do with the modern people she met. But this we cannot know for though *Letters from Egypt* contains copious lament over the "debasement and misery" which were the lot of most Egyptians of that era, it says little more specific about the people of Dendera.

Florence Nightingale was sincere, learned, and perhaps as fair as she could be given the circumstances and the era in which she wrote. But she was a tourist, carried about in that protective bubble of affluence and influence which allows persons of means and education to travel as though in a sealed capsule. And I disagree with her about the religious art. In a crypt beneath the Temple of Hathor is the most exquisite bas-relief of Horus I have seen, each feather a delicate grace note in alabaster. Perhaps sand fill or stale air kept

Florence out of the crypt. Or, more likely, she turned back nauseated by the stench of the antechambers, home to hundreds of witwat, bats that flee before intruders or hang trembling and chittering a few feet overhead.

The Diplomat and I left Cairo on the 7 a.m. Egypt Air flight to Luxor where Baha, his ruined face beaming, met us with a car. A neat moustache covers both sides of the riven lip through which crooked teeth protrude. Because Baha speaks normally, he cannot have a cleft palate, and his lip could probably have been repaired relatively easily in childhood. Instead, "God's will" has ruined his chances for marriage although his job in the tourist industry brings him far more than the average man's wages.

The road north from Luxor to Dendera crawls along the canals past village after village where people and animals live, eat, sleep, give birth, and die on the Nile mud. In 1968, the first time I visited Egypt, I went away dazed but more by the suffering of humanity than the splendors of history. So, too, it may have been for Florence. Shortly after her Egyptian sojourn she went to the Crimea where, administering to the broken bodies of British soldiers, she established modern nursing as a career and thus passed into history.

I knew that in over a century, especially during the past two decades, much had changed in Upper Egypt. There are better roads, water pumps, television sets, refrigerators, and antibiotics for those who can afford them. But the growing mass of humanity has increased pressure on available resources. Egypt is, after all, mainly a shoestring oasis. The landless and unemployed flee down river to Cairo in ever-greater numbers. Social tensions, including between Christians and Muslims, are increasing.

It takes an hour to reach Qena where the River performs a great bend. Dendera is just a bit further on and Florence came to it from the Nile, riding her donkey across fields of flowers and sorghum. These still surround the site, but our approach is along the canal where carts, tractors, trucks, and people career haphazardly into our path so that Baha frequently swerves the car violently while shouting "Donkey!" in a harsh bray.

Oil drums block the road just outside Qena. Baha stops the car and uniformed police and local "helpers" dressed in galabiyahs and carrying long rifles lean in and examine his papers. No one speaks to us or asks for our identification. As obvious tourists we are presumably harmless. A police officer decides to come with us and, not asking, simply gets in with us for a ride to Dendera. Whether he is a protector or an opportunist we do not know.

Why are there checkpoints here, we ask Baha when the policeman had left us. "In case a religious fanatic appears," Baha replies. "If one comes by, they arrest him and put him in prison." But how do they know he's a fanatic, we persist. "Oh," Baha laughs. "That's easy. They just know."

Already this year at least fifty Egyptians are known to have died in Muslim-Christian clashes, most of them in Upper Egypt. The underground Islamic League that killed the Speaker of the National Assembly in October 1990 now claims responsibility for the killing of prominent writer Farag Foda in June. But for the majority of Egyptians, who are peaceful people given more to fatalism than to activism, the greater threat is still police excess in coping with the growing danger of religious extremism.

Before us rises the enormous and well-preserved Temple of Hathor, cow-headed goddess of succor and protection. When modern temple guards enthusiastically describe how Coptic Christians had heavily damaged the temple, I sense that their disdain related more to their Christian neighbors than to those neighbors' ancestors. A fifth-century Coptic basilica, as yet incompletely excavated, fills the right temple forecourt just inside an enormous archway, which leads into a compound surrounded by mud brick walls. This looks like cohabitation, at least in the past. But all fanatics are brothers. Just a month earlier, an Islamic League spokesman proclaimed that, "The pharaonic statues and temples are pagan remains. They must be destroyed."[2]

Behind Hathor's temple is a much smaller temple to Isis, another mother figure sometimes considered a version of Hathor. This temple is in even more obvious competition with Mary, the mother of Jesus Christ, for Horus, son of Isis and Osiris, was also a divine representative of eternal life. Here the damage by early Christians to rows of beautiful wall carvings is more extensive. As we pause to reflect on history, hundreds of migrating white storks fly low above us, heading south to winter in the Sudan. Their wings beat softly, shushing in the still morning air, transfixing us in a moment of grace.

The day had become extraordinarily hot, and we think of cold beer, recalling that one of the most important annual events in ancient Dendera was the Festival of Drunkenness, celebrated on the twentieth day of Thoth, god of learning and of books. That tie between scholarship and drunkenness, which also crops up in Greek mythology, is intriguing. However, we respect modern mores by waiting until we are safely on the move towards Abydos to open the cooler and become, as the Diplomat puts it, "Lost in Thoth."

The road to Abydos from Dendera requires another hour and a half of fearless navigation by Baha. Black and white kingfishers and squacco herons search the canals for fish while small boys seek opportunity to destroy themselves under our wheels. We pass a dead water buffalo, victim of an encounter with metal moving at high speed. People stare as we rocket along in our metal canister, intruders on a slower world, which, caught by surprise, does not know how to respond.

Nightingale seems to have liked Abydos well enough, for she visited the home of one of her boatmen and marveled at the fine clothing of his principal wife. But we find no similar consolation. For us, Abydos seems a terrible place where ancient and modern ruins meld, rubbish lies everywhere, and children incessantly wheedle, whine, threaten, and even weep for baksheesh. Just as we arrive, the city's several mosques began their Friday duel of sermons from loud speakers, demonstrating that acrimony divides Muslim from Muslim as well as from Christian.

The immense sandstone and limestone Temple of Seti the First (1318–1304 B.C.) is the main attraction. But this has been so extensively rebuilt that the joy of discovery is diminished. Three guards sleeping through noon prayers rouse themselves to pester us for money as we pass into the massive forest of pillars in a great hall, which opens out into many side chambers. In the half-light are passageways and bas-reliefs, many still with vivid colors laid down over two thousand years ago. Here willful destruction predates the Christians: in several sections, the egomaniac Ramses II had erased his father's cartouche and inserted his own.

The Temple of Osiris, behind that of Seti I, was designed to be flooded by the Nile inundation but is now permanently swamped by rising ground water. A young man sidles over demanding that we take him on as a guide. When he will not go away, we finally agree to let him lead us to the Ramses Temple. Though this turns out to be locked, we pay so he will leave us alone. Next, three teenage boys hail us with news that the Keeper of the Keys is sleeping and it will cost us 5 LE, up front, for them to arouse him. We decline to bargain over this unreasonable price and decide we have had enough of Abydos and its parasites. But as we walk away the boys follow jeering, threatening, leaping. It takes mention of the police to persuade them to stop.

Our path back to the entrance leads through an arm of the village where small children attach themselves to our arms and legs, screaming for baksheesh, pens, and bonbons. A young woman, perhaps a descendant of Florence Nightingale's host, motions us to take refuge in her house. But she, too, is on the take and does nothing to rescue us from her voracious offspring. We pay to leave.

Dorothy Eady, an Englishwoman who believed herself the reincarnation of one of Seti I's concubines, died in Abydos in 1981 after living there for many years. During this time Umm Seti, as she proclaimed herself, seemed to have held her neighbors at bay with a mixture of friendship, ancient magic, and real scholarship. A friend recalled that the villagers didn't attack her "because they didn't know what powers she could call down on them."[3] Fervently, we wish for those powers.

Finally, we exit the temple site in a cloud of noise, heat, dust, and disgust. The ability of tourism to breed avarice and contempt is all too clear. And so, too, we grouch to one another, is the negative impact of young Egyptian boys on tourists. At the open-air restaurant in front of the site, we are informed that as foreigners we will have to pay 2 LE each for a Pepsi. Our western principles of "fairness" are once more offended, and we walk away, pausing only to visit the lavatory. There the young male attendant locked me in and, as soon as he hears the flush, confounds me by flinging wide the door, apparently fearing that somehow I might manage to escape without paying.

Baha, waiting by the car, is embarrassed by what we told him about his countrymen and takes us to a nearby restaurant, where he buys us a cold drink at Egyptian rates. The young proprietor tells us that the tourist business is "not too good" these days but cannot explain why. So we took his picture next to a sign in English: "Falafil sandwich: It smells good!" Florence Nightingale, it would seem, had Dendera and Abydos backwards.

You can start from Cairo, visit Dendera and Abydos, and return to Cairo on the 5 p.m. flight. But why would anyone want to do so? The Jolie Ville on Crocodile Island just outside Luxor is a Swiss cordon sanitaire in Upper Egypt, a place of iced drinks, delicious food, and a large clear swimming pool. There, though prices are low by European rates, one tourist spends more in a week than most Egyptians earn in five years.

Last week, according to the Arabic press, stone-throwing youths attacked a busload of French tourists in Luxor. But this could not have been very serious as the French embassy denied knowledge of the incident. Still, guards patrol around the fringes of Crocodile Island. And a muscular chap in a safari suit who sits alone scowling into his orange juice must surely be a member of the much feared security police, the mukhabarat.

The heaven of the religious fanatics, we decide over an exotic combination of fruit juice and rum, must be something like the Jolie Ville, a fantasy of naked bodies and fawning attendants. And the only children here, although this is surely against the law, are the two small boys who hold the door open and politely serve cold kerkadeh juice to new arrivals.

17

Qanatar Prison

5 September 1992

Qanatar prison is some twenty-five miles north of Cairo near the Nile barrages. The road along the river's west bank cuts through villages and fields that appear nearly as primitive as a century ago. Animals wander in and out of houses or are slaughtered at roadside, dog packs swarm over rubbish heaps, men with short-handled hoes bend and rise over the crops in ancient rhythm.

On weekends, the Imbaba markets on the outskirts of Cairo are in full swing. Mounds of lemons, onions, potatoes, cucumbers, and tomatoes decorate the roadside, each heap squatted over by a large woman in black who swats flies, makes change, sorts carrots, and breastfeeds her child simultaneously. Watermelons are less expensive here than in Cairo but affordable by few who live here. The foul seller dips his ladle into the neck of his great jar and scoops the beans onto a metal plate. Meat is a luxury, and the cuts on offer are the rich man's leavings: buffalo feet and sheep heads, tripe, and assorted other offal.

On weekends, Qanatar prison, more chaotic than grim, seems a continuation of the markets. Families bearing boxes of vegetables queue for entry, jostled and ogled by Saidi conscripts to the police service. Sometimes referred to as "the Baladi Boys," young men from upriver strut about in their ill-fitting uniforms trying to look important despite seemingly incessant scratching of their groins. Who can know whether they are oversexed or perhaps just tormented by fleas? Perhaps both. We remind ourselves that learning to wear trousers is not easy for a man of eighteen. A whistle blows, and the crowd surges into the compound of the men's prison.

The Evangelist lives in a private cell. He is English and was, by his own admission, a drugs courier. But that was before he was arrested and then "got saved." Since then, he tells us, he has been greatly persecuted for the Gospel's sake in this place of horrors. At night the Baladi Boys urinate outside his window, shouting to one another and burning plastic bottles to boil their tea water. Righteous wrath shakes the Evangelist's thin body and his blue eyes pierce us. There is no respect for law here, he tells us. How, then, can civilized nations deal with the Egyptians?

Nothing, he says, is being done to help him. Why hasn't the ambassador come to visit? Why did the stupid consular officer bring him an ice chest when there is no ice here? And when vegetables are sent they must be "very fresh" or they won't last. If he cannot see a non-Egyptian doctor, he "won't last much longer." Moreover, twenty-five years is a barbaric eternity! Cannot the Queen intercede on his behalf? Is Britain powerless?

Although it is stifling hot, the Evangelist wears his shirt buttoned up to his chin. He reads to us from the First Book of John, and his monologue alternates between praise for the love of Christ and seething hatred for all Egyptians. He speaks of Bible studies in his cell and the terrible beating administered to a young Somali who tried to escape Qanatar Prison. He himself was beaten by other prisoners when he tried to share the love of Christ by reading God's word to them as they ate their bread and beans.

"Never, never will I learn Arabic," the Evangelist declares, "lest I tell these Muslims what I feel about them. Surely then they would kill me and be done with it." Before coming to Egypt seven years earlier he'd had a vision of what was to be, the agony to which he would have to submit. Nonetheless, he reminded us, St. Paul wrote that, "It is not yet clear what we are to become." After two hours we embrace him, wish him well and hand over our gifts. He does not wish to let us go, but the Baladi Boys take him away anyway: a wild bird whose broken wings were probably broken long before he entered this place.

In the Prison Director's office across a narrow road, two female guards—stout, veiled and good natured—are filling the Director and his friends in on the local gossip, something about a bus, and a truck, and people shouting, cursing and leaping on and off. There is much laughter, a ringing telephone occasionally answered, and strident blasts on a whistle outside the open window. Occasionally a young woman guard wearing a uniform cap over her headscarf enters with a paper on which the Director affixes his signature with a flourish. His friends refer to him as "Pasha," and one of the group sips his Miranda with little finger crooked in the approved delicate manner. We wait in chairs along the wall.

The Girlfriend arrives, majestic in a long white prison dress, her nails beautifully manicured and gilt earrings framing a pretty, middle-aged face. The Director greets her warmly, she addresses him as Pasha, and they chat easily in Arabic after which he waves magnanimously for us to use his office for our visit. So down we sit with the Girlfriend and begin to shout to one another above the shrill uproar of whistles outside the window.

The Girlfriend is an English grandmother, but she, too, is serving twenty-five years. Six years ago, she arrived at Cairo airport with a wooden elephant filled with heroin in her suitcase. Everyone believes that her Egyptian lover, now doing life in the men's compound across the road, planted the goods on her. Everyone, even the Director, says she is apparently innocent. But until amnesty or a new trial can be arranged nothing will be done. Even though the lover has confessed, the Girlfriend must remain at Qanatar prison. It is good that her ability to cope seems to grow stronger as the years lengthen.

She begins by telling us stories about those who are worse off than she is, those who are imprisoned because they are pregnant and unmarried or because a family suspected that its daughter had an inappropriate boyfriend. Then she describes a well-connected woman awaiting trial in a private room in the crowded hospital, a room with video, refrigerator, and servants. This rich Egyptian woman tortured her Taiwanese maid to death but tells all who will listen that she won't be here for long. To sentence her would be illogical, she claims, for she is who she is, and "that Taiwanese was trash."

The rich woman does well to convince herself that she won't have to stay much longer, the Girlfriend says. The women on the killers' ward are peasants, servants, and third wives, and if they can get their hands on that rich woman they will tear her apart.

This will not be for the sake of the Taiwanese woman, of course, but because of her arrogance and for her jewelry. The Girlfriend speaks next of the Filipina maid who killed the Kuwaiti princess for whom she worked and now has more peace and security than she knew during five years of torment. The other women at Qanatar have opened their hearts to her, and she has started to speak again and has even gained a little weight—although God knows how, given the moldy bread filled with cigarette butts which is the stable diet here.

We move out to the courtyard to sit in the sun on stone benches surrounded by embracing families and broken boxes of food. Yes, the Girlfriend says, her health is much improved. The vegetables and vitamins have worked. But more books, please, and the sheets are in tatters although she keeps mending.

Across the courtyard filled with families, a teenager sits alone weeping the departure of her family. She clutches a plastic sack containing cooked spaghetti in tomato sauce, and her thin body heaves with grief. I move next to her on the stone bench and take her into my arms, rocking with the sobs and waiting for the sharp edge of her agony to dull. We say nothing for there is nothing to be said, and I would probably not understand anyway. Does she live on Ward 10 with the prostitutes or Ward 4 with the addicts and dealers? Is she a killer from "upstairs"? It doesn't matter.[1] She thanks me, we embrace again, and I feel as though a daughter has been wounded. The girl picks up her lumpy plastic sack and walks slowly away. She does not know that I will remember her for the rest of her life.

On the stone bench, the Girlfriend, too, is fighting tears. But though she fears to hope, she is very strong and knows that she must not despair. So she tells us another story, about the Fat Woman who rules Ward 4 and is feared by all, even the guards who sometimes appear at night, throw everyone's belongings onto the floor, and then pour the cooking oil on top. We laugh together at the foolishness of it all. The Girlfriend composes herself. "God forgive me," she says. "I never pray." But, I ask myself, is her very life not a prayer?[2]

We are unusually silent during our drive back to Cairo for there is little to be said in face of the wasted lives and human misery we have seen. On arrival home, we learn that Alan's new secretary, recently arrived from Scotland, had this day suffered a heart attack and died in the embassy swimming pool.

Lillian comforts a poor woman near Qanatar prison, September 1992

18

A Shabti Takes the Photographer to Ismailia

2 October 1992

The tiny museum in Ismailia contains a lovely granite bust of Isis and a marvelous painted shabti that awoke my avarice. I couldn't have imagined that shabti on my coffee table, but the idea of being able to give it to the Photographer took firm hold on me. She is old and no longer able to dash down the street or up a flight or two of stairs as she did when she was a professional. Nor can she any longer carry heavy cameras into mosques or other places of interest. That shabti, a miniature servant to carry out all commands for the dead, could perhaps just as well be put to work for the living—and what a great comfort it would be, too!

The Photographer's hands are knotted with veins and her skin is like Japanese rice paper. When she arrived three weeks ago, she already had a large abrasion on her leg where a careless fellow hit her with a suitcase getting off a ferry in Greece. Now her arms are covered with bruises put there by my affectionate dogs, and she clings to the porch when I open the door, and the canine girls run to greet her. Still, she comes to stay with us for a few weeks year after year.

Travel is a panacea for the old, lately become very old, and here in Egypt there is comfort. Is not this the land of eternal life, the Valley and the Delta where eons flow into eons and time is no more? Here, for some strange reason, the Photographer's chronic asthma is always much better despite Cairo's pollution. And here, she nestles into the space carved out long ago for her in my heart.

We are like two kindred spirits one month a year when she

comes to me. During this time, I become her shabti and she my ancient mentor. Together we laugh and wander the backstreets, and sometimes we wander gently onto the verges of the future. For despite Egyptian longevity, time grows short, and we both face the unknown, uncertain of her journey from here on.

Neither of us had visited the ancient sites of the eastern delta, most of them now severely encroached upon by urban sprawl, ruined by the lime kilns of the 19th century, or still largely unexcavated mounds of earth under which the rubble of history awaits. An Egyptian recently questioned a lecturer from the British Museum about Britain's role in "looting" Egypt of its treasures. Thinking no doubt of the woeful condition of much of what remains here, the lecturer sighed and carefully replied, "Certain items were removed in circumstances which do not now pertain."

So we went to Ismailia on the shore of Lake Timsah, the Diplomat driving, a good vantage to begin our delta exploration. There are no crocodiles left in Crocodile Lake, but the Etap Hotel is comfortable, except for sagging beds. The late summer air is filled with fragrance of jasmine and the cries of sea birds. With us came the whisky, necessary tonic for one with advanced osteoporosis. The heavy cameras we left behind, replaced by a new disobedient contraption, which whirs and confuses. But there is no longer any need for "professional quality." Nothing remains to be proven. The record of our passage is all that matters.

Daphnae eluded us. A two-hour search along farm lanes and through marsh lands being reclaimed for agriculture brought us back to our starting point near Ismailia. But although we passed quite near this town destroyed in the sixth century Persian invasion, we could not find the unmarked site. But driving along the Suez Canal, we saw ships passing beyond the dunes, just over the ridge, like ghosts sailing through the desert. Soldiers turned us back, and we struck out into the interior along bumpy roads that lead to everywhere. Villagers shouted greetings as the Photographer shot from her window.

The next morning, we managed to locate Tanis after a journey along canals where water wheels pump life, and small boys bathe with their enormous black buffalos. We crossed from town to desert and finally Tanis, San al Hagar, rose before us, a jumble of broken obelisks and fallen statues painstakingly pieced together, where possible, by generations of French archaeologists.

The Photographer puffed softly to herself and put on her "I love Egypt" hat at a jaunty angle. We hurried through the inadequate museum and out into the hot sun of the site. She took pictures of me next to a broken obelisk and, later, passing through the triumphal gateway.

"Fallen lady," declared the guide. "This is the queen." He pointed to yet another recumbent Ramses whose kilt and prominent breasts must have misled him. The Photographer and I chuckled over his ignorance and he at ours, and we marched on together through the necropolis, dangerous and newly opened to public view. Deep pits, broken stone slabs, hidden stairways, and drifting sand impeded us, and I scuttled up and down shouting advice on whether the climb was worth the effort she would have to make. The Photographer rested in the shade of a broken column puffing frequently on her medihaler. Once, two years ago in Russia, she left it in the hotel and nearly died. These days she always carries two.

A week ago, in the middle of Cairo, when she turned gray, and the medihaler did not help her breathing, I flagged down a passing car and managed to bring her home where a powerful stimulant was available. Ahmad was the name of our young rescuer. He works at Mr. Lizard in Zamalek and refused to take any payment. When the Photographer has returned to the United States, I told myself, I shall go to Mr. Lizard and buy something expensive.

After Tanis, we found our way to Tell Fara'un, partially cleared by Petrie in 1886 but now only mounds and pits in the middle of a busy town. Our car moved slowly between donkey carts and vegetable stalls. Occasionally a file of camels passed carrying dried stalks for roofing. We did not get out at Tell Fara'un for access was not evident and the Photographer had grown weary.

Back beside the canal we passed peculiar, multi-roomed mud dwellings surrounded by newer two-story buildings. Everywhere there was an atmosphere of crowded fertility. The fields were filled with cane and fruit trees, and people waved and shouted for foreigners are not common here. We drove carefully through heavy traffic behind pickup trucks overflowing with riders. The penalty for speed was apparent, including a truck with the entire engine of a passenger car fused into it. The broken hulk of the sedan perched uneasily above the canal.

The afternoon declined. It was time to turn towards Cairo along one of the rushing arteries that flow into Egypt's immense heart. We skirted the city of Zagazig with its rail lines, university, and masses of humanity. At the intersection south of town, we passed the ruins of Tell Basta, sacred to Bastet the cat goddess. But Basta would have to await another expedition. The Photographer nodded in the front passenger seat, her seat belt holding the small, frail body upright and her face suddenly smooth and almost youthful in sleep. The roof rack hummed, and the chain holding the spare wheel tapped in rhythm as we threaded through the delta and down to the Cairo suburb of Boulak on the Nile.

The next day we learned that our decision to pass through Zagazig instead of via Abu Hamad has saved us from involvement in an "incident." On that day people rioted following the death in custody of a local baker accused of some minor crime. For the Photographer, who recently suffered two broken ribs when an old friend hugged her enthusiastically, any rough handling is perilous. I breathed a grateful word to Bastet but said nothing of our escape to the Photographer.

Yesterday a shopkeeper in the Khan Khalili fixed me with an inquisitive stare and, demanded, indicating the browsing Photographer, "Your mama?"

"Yes," I said, grateful to admit to this piece of the truth. Yes, in a manner of speaking, a second Mama for over twenty years now.

Lillian, the Diplomat, and the Photographer on the Nile,
Cairo, October 1992

19

Of Jesuits, Copts, and the Virgin Mary

9 October 1992

There are no Jesuits left, living ones at least, at the Church of the Holy Family in Exile. But the Jesuits are well remembered in the small, ornate church in Cairo's Matariyyah district for in the garden behind the church the mortal remains of forty or more Jesuits rest in a grotto crypt. In Europe, church history is usually more interesting than church present, but the reverse is often true in Egypt. Nonetheless, the presence of so many dead Jesuits greatly overshadowed the words of the small Coptic Catholic priest who showed us around.

The Jesuits went away in 1959, he said definitively, favoring his lame leg. It was the one date about which he had no doubt. The building still belongs to them, he added, but Coptic Catholics pray here now, and we have 130 families. "We are trying to get possession," he said, hinting controversy but refusing further explanation. Limping down the aisle, the short, round figure in a gray cassock described each wall painting in detail.

We signed the guest book in the narthex, and the Priest pocketed our donation, murmuring that the poor box was locked. Back up the aisle then to the altar where we were informed that the Jesuits turned their backs to the congregation, but Coptic Catholics must have a free standing altar so they can circumambulate with incense. Still, he said, we recognize the authority of Rome for, "Our bishops are chosen in Egypt and approved by the Papa."

It was Friday morning and although the main service of the week had just finished, a sense of neglect filled the church—or perhaps it was only cultural difference. On the high altar was a vase full of dead flowers, and the altar was littered with used tissues, candle drippings and various liturgical paraphernalia. The beautifully embroidered altar cloth was dirty, and the Priest leaned on the altar, taking weight off his leg. As he explained "the differences between European and Egyptian Catholics," he toyed with a metal box of incense crystals on the cover of which were painted pictures of two European vaudeville characters of the forties. Then we went outside and descended into the crypt reserved for the Jesuits.

"They went away," the priest repeated, "but they come back." He chuckled. "When another one dies, they take the earliest dead one out and put him over there in the ossuary." On a double row of vaults were names of a few Egyptian Jesuits as well as those of European Jesuits of several nationalities. The latest Jesuit here had gone in 1990, two years earlier, the Coptic Catholic priest said. The floor was wet with rising ground water and above the crypt the old chapel was locked. Sensing unspoken controversy, we turned down a half-hearted offer to go find the key.

The site of the Church of the Holy Family in Exile in Egypt has held a church since ancient times, but the present building, in Spanish style, was built early this century. The Coptic priest seemed uncertain of the date of what had, he made clear, nothing to do with him. We declined his perfunctory offer of tea and left him puffing a cigarette and shouting directions to two workmen cutting fronds from the tall palms next to the church.

As we left the compound we came face to face, across a busy road, with several score Muslim worshippers who bowed in unison from mats spread out in an alley. The line of prayer extended directly through the church's high altar as it stood between them and Mecca, a situation that would certainly have delighted my Jesuit mentor at Georgetown University in Washington, D.C. But that dear man had joined the ranks of dead Jesuits buried in Rome. Outside the gate two unwanted kittens lay dying on a newspaper and three soldiers in white summer uniforms lounged, keeping the fragile—we surmised—peace.

The nearby "Tree of the Virgin" seemed to be an improbable monument. Great sun-bleached branches of a Sycamore fig that had died in 1906 are propped up around a young tree no less revered as the very tree under which Mary and Joseph rested on their flight into Egypt. Since medieval times countless pilgrims have come here and some still find their way through Matariyyah's crowded lanes. But save for the guard and one Egyptian family, we had the place to ourselves. We looked into the ancient well just outside the tree compound and saw that its arches are much lower than the area on which the tree stands, making it improbable that well and tree site date from the same era.

Earlier Raymond and Mina had directed us to the Tree of the Virgin from the Church of the Holy Family in Exile in Egypt, climbing joyfully into the Range Rover and shouting, "They are Christians" to inquiring onlookers. The two Good Samaritans refused payment for their service and waited for us to finish looking at the Tree so as to tell us how to get through the alleys and around the rubbish heaps to St. Mary's Church, next on our agenda. Cars hooting loudly hurtled through the narrow lanes and several times we leaped onto the rubbish the better to cling to the building walls and escape what seemed certain death at the hands of people on errands more pressing than ours.

At St. Mary's we found the missing vibrancy at the Tree and also at the Church of the Holy Family in Exile. Sunday is a working day in Egypt and thus the main Christian services of the week are held on Friday. Hundreds of Copts had filled the ugly lower level of the church. We had arrived during catechism class and rows and rows of children shouted responses in union under the orchestration of adults who leaped and gestured like cheerleaders. Grave black-robed priests wandered slowly among the believers who kissed their hands and poured forth grievances and requests for prayer. It seemed appropriate that an air traffic controller named Imad should come to our assistance.

"They are learning Coptic songs," he shouted above the roar of voices. "When they know the words, they will be taught the music." He then quoted the Lord's Prayer in Coptic as proof that the language still survives. We wondered at the harsh and strident intonations but Imad reassured us: "No, it is only about religion and, well yes, perhaps sometimes about history. But politics is left to the government schools."

In the new sanctuary of St. Mary's, reached by a long outside staircase, rows of older girls were singing in a melodious minor key. We stood behind them, taking secret nibbles from the rather tasty holy bread on sale outside at fifty piasters per circular loaf. On a scaffold high above the spacious basilica, workmen painted in bright colors. A large figure of Christ filled the dome, and there was no evidence of Mary, although we found Matthew and Mark staring at us further down. Luke and John had yet to appear but several many-winged seraphim had already uncovered their brilliant modern faces. Despite the name, we were in a very masculine, assertive church, the home of unfamiliar Christian relatives whose walls contained what seemed to us disturbing family portraits in strange poses. For this we somehow blamed ourselves.

"Contributions for the building works are all local," Imad said. "We needed more space and the old church had to be rebuilt."

Are there troubles here, we asked, as in Upper Egypt, between Muslims and Christians? And what about that new mosque almost next door which has a minaret every bit as tall—perhaps a bit taller—than the church tower?

"We don't have those troubles here," Imad said. "May God protect us." You trust in the government then, we asked, probing impolitely. He answered quickly and with conviction: "We trust in God." Imad's friend, whose English was less good, waited until we were about to leave, by which time he had worked out how to say what he wanted us to understand. Then he caught our arms and held us back to hear the truth we already knew.

"The Copts suffer," he said. "Very much we suffer."

Outside, the crowds in festive mood continued to shout and shove one another, cheerfully munching on holy bread and catching up on neighborly news. Religion is among other things a way of life, a mark of identity. Many of these Christians had small crosses tattooed on the inside of their wrists, a sign that, for some reason I have never understood, almost universally enrages Muslim Egyptians I have asked about it.

The Copts in the churchyard smiled on us as fellow Christians and gladly shared their bread in a sort of free for all Holy Communion. But though "all share in one body," they seemed as different from the Coptic Catholics as the Coptic Catholics are from the departed Jesuits.

Then from the tall minaret next door arose a frightful roaring, an amplified Muslim call to prayer, which drowned out the confusing Christian babble below. At least I thought, comforting myself, the Christians and Muslims in this area have noise in common.

Icon of the flight to Egypt, Al Muallaqa, Old Cairo.
Illustration supplied by the church authorities.

20

Faith and Solitude at the Monasteries of St. Anthony and St. Paul

17 October 1992

Two years ago on the road to St. Paul's monastery in the Eastern Desert, we picked up a young pilgrim who told us how on a previous visit he'd walked the last fourteen kilometers from the main road. When he finally arrived, the Coptic monks had washed his dusty feet. Today the holy men would have time for nothing else if they washed the feet of all their visitors. The same is true for the nearby fourth century monastery of St. Anthony. There, too, rows of stone guesthouses have been built to house the growing numbers of pilgrims and tourists.

No fee is charged either to visit the monasteries or to stay there briefly. However, a large sign on the outer wall of St. Paul's makes clear that guests are expected to leave after one night. But, this being Egypt, exceptions are always possible.

"Come for a week," said a cheerful brother who asked about scholarships for study in England and described the high level of education among the monks. He was, he said, a chemist and took his vows after a successful few years working in America.

St. Anthony and St. Paul each thought he was alone until, according to Coptic tradition, God brought them together in the desert shortly before Paul's death. In sign of divine approval, the raven that for years had supplied Paul his daily half loaf of bread flew in on the day of meeting with a whole loaf. And so the miracles continue to this day.

Visiting the monastery of St. Anthony, we were shown the bones of St. Yusuf who died in 1826, having through divine grace healed many supplicants. We were told that Father Tadros, also a healer, had died only a few days earlier. When the desert heat has sufficiently desiccated his body, perhaps he, too, will be put on display to continue his ministry.

The approach to St. Anthony's is along a straight new road which ends at towering mud brick walls built centuries earlier as protection against raids by those the modern monks carefully describe as "Bedouin," the desert nomads. A hoist used to admit visitors is no longer needed and the great door stands open, attended by a bandaged beggar who mutely raises his eyes as we arrive.

A pull on the bell cord and a soft-spoken, black-robed and black-bearded father appears, welcoming us despite this intrusion on his Sunday devotions. He wears a cowl on which are embroidered six crosses on each side, one for each disciple and one, representing Christ, at the back. We are led into the fourth century church of St. Anthony, restored in the twelfth century, frescoed in the thirteenth, and desecrated in 1482 when Bedouin occupied the monastery and slaughtered the monks.

An Egyptian family with noisy children joins us on our wandering behind the monk. Neat gardens are watered by a spring that flows from living rock. We drink at the spring and feast on dates thrust upon us by two novices. Today forty-five monks and fifteen novices live here, and new applicants must be turned away for lack of space. Above the monastery, a difficult half-hour climb leads to the cave where Anthony once lived and died. We are told of miracles of healing and of spiritual contests with the devil and before we continue on to St. Paul's the monks offer us tea.

It is after four by the time we reach the Monastery of St. Paul, connected by a modern road along the Red Sea coast but until a few years ago accessible only along a difficult mountain track. A young British friend in Cairo and two of his friends tried the track between the two monasteries last December but had been driven back by cold and darkness, having lost their way for several hours among unmarked precipices and enormous boulders. Even the monks no longer remember this track well and one who tried it recently was found near death after an absence of three days.

"Who is there?" a voice shouts after we ring the bell.

"Visitors," we cry.

"Where are you from?" the Voice queries.

"Cairo, I mean England. Is it possible to enter?" we shout back.

"Possible," the voice responds and after a ten-minute wait, another black-robed figure emerges, that of Father Agathon, a chemist.

"Two children recently saw St. Paul here in his chapel where he lived and beneath which he is buried," Father Agathon tells us. "When we rushed in to see him, he had vanished. But the children described him. He is still with us."

There are four churches within the great walls, and we visit all, stopping as well to see the garden where an old monk feeds his innumerable blue-eyed cats. We also visit the spring that has flowed constantly down the centuries. As at St. Anthony's, the few icons on display seem to be of little historical interest. Our questions about a library are politely turned aside as the monk continues his recital of the ravages of time and man, the difficulties in obtaining governmental permission to make repairs, the joys of living on the edge of existence and in the center of God's will.

Afterwards we are given a cold drink in the large guesthouse where on summer evenings up to seven hundred guests can be accommodated. But tonight there is almost no one here. A full moon turns the surrounding desert to gold and purple. The coolness is welcome after the fierce heat of the day.

Egypt is where Christian monasticism began. The concepts and practices derived from the experiences of the thousands of hermits and monks who strove with Satan in the fire of Egypt's deserts from the third century onwards changed the course of Christianity. Priestly celibacy, the concept that flesh and the material world are evil, physical privation to purify the soul, spiritual combat with the powers of darkness—all these grew out of early Egyptian Christianity. Eventually, the flame lit by the desert fathers was banked by the weight of history. An elderly monk at St. Paul's, now one of sixty-four plus seventeen novices, was a few years ago one of only two fathers whose task was primarily to maintain the crumbling and remote monastery. But today the flame has flared again.

Christian historian Kenneth Scott Latourette wrote that, "Political and economic disorders in Egypt in the third and fourth centuries may have bred a sense of insecurity which impelled many to seek escape from the world...Probably, too, monasteries arose in part from disgust with city life, with its dust, crowds, noise, and moral corruption."[1] All this sounds very much like modern Egypt and may help explain the flood of applicants to the monasteries and the construction of the new guesthouses.

On the road north to Suez, we are blinded by the lights of heavy trucks carrying building materials for more hotels in Hurghada and other Red Sea cities. But the roar of traffic is eaten by the desert silence. The desert fathers still retain something of their solitude.

"How can Christianity survive in Egypt when so many Copts continue to leave?" I once asked a monk at a monastery in the delta. His response was absolute. "We monks will never leave Egypt," he said. "The monasteries will always be here. We are not alone and we shall never leave."[2]

21

Crossing the Delta to Alexandria

24 October 1992

The 8:15 a.m. non-stop to Alexandria pulls out of Cairo's ornate Ramses station right on time. Though the man next to me reeks of garlic, the train windows are clean, the first-class ticket cost only 15 LE, and we will cover two hundred or so kilometers in less than two hours. I am on my way to the fiftieth anniversary of the battle of El Alamein and, as I have always thought of cemeteries as holy places where we may reflect and learn, I am eager to arrive. I settle back and relax thinking of Woody Guthrie's "magic carpet made of steel" carrying me "down through the delta to the sea."

Cairo's urban sprawl eats up the first few miles as ramshackle housing—mud bricks and patchwork low risers—encroach on agricultural land. Rich black earth is turned into red bricks in illegal kilns and used by "baladi engineers" who construct death traps. Two weeks ago, a relatively new fourteen-story building crushed forty-five people to death in the Cairo suburb of Heliopolis.

My fellow passengers are almost all men, commercial travelers and several military officers dressed in whites or well-pressed camouflage fatigues. The train is barely clear of the station before most of them are tucking into sandwiches, cakes, and scalding glasses of tea served from a trolley. The two attendants pay particularly solicitous attention to the military men. Leaving the flocks of thin goats picking over the rubbish of outer Cairo, we move into the delta where dirty brown sheep browse in green fields.

Soon we are passing green eucalyptus, palms, and banana trees. Then come bright green young corn and rice seedlings, tawdry green minarets and plastered tombs, and silver-green rows of mature cabbage. Shiny green water hyacinth clogs the canals. White donkeys punctuate the green and two red-brown bullocks plow sedately attached to a wide wooden yoke. Suddenly there is a camel train of at least twenty beasts and their riders, nodding in unison behind a gray donkey framed in bright red plastic panniers. I long to examine them closely but already they are gone.

Is Egypt a modern, or even a civilized, country? I have heard several diplomats in Cairo pose this question to one another. But what is civilization, and why do we equate it with machinery? And which Egypt do they mean? Are their generals who are traveling with me in the train civilized because they have been to Sandhurst and Fort Bragg and learned the arts of modern warfare? Who are these teenagers shortcutting through the train yard as we rocket through their town? Are they "civilized"? And why are there small children playing on the tracks next to ours? On a siding, a train stands alone, festooned with people who cling to the top and sides of the carriages like fleas on a street dog. Where are they hoping to go? Will they get there safely, and why must they risk their lives to do so?

Here in the delta, the simplicity, the direct reliance on nature, the primitiveness that marks the lives of most Egyptians are all apparent. Our fast moving train is out of place, inappropriate, ignored. People and animals have grown indifferent to the noisy metal monsters that roar through their fields, beside their canals and next to their mud houses. They try not to notice our alien eyes prying into all their affairs. A man baths naked in a canal; another urinates nearby. Women in robes and headscarves of many bright colors wash their family's clothes and scrub their silvery cooking pots. Most of them seem heavier and fairer than the darker-skinned women further up the Nile. We see their gray laundry hung behind the low houses. We count their geese, notice who is sleeping while others pick cotton, and wince when a vegetable seller boots a kitten out of his way. May Allah correct him!

The graveyards, too, are poor and crude, composed of closely packed blue and green plaster monoliths. A waiting procession moves slowly through the cemetery carrying a simple box without a lid. "Man is as grass: in the morning he flourishes and at noon is cut down," the Old Testament tells us. Before we, too, can mourn, the train has left the scene and swooped down to the main Cairo-Alexandria highway. "Alex. 115 kilometers," a road sign announced.

The land has become soggy. Flooded rice fields are presided over by masses of white egrets and a lovely wide canal carries barges filled with white stone. Smaller boats, colorfully painted, contain two standing men each. The men fling wide their nets. Willows weep into the canal and a peculiar vine drapes large purple flowers over all other vegetation. Then, within a few kilometers, this canal too narrows and becomes clogged with water hyacinth, beautiful, deadly Rose of the Nile.

Here in the train we are urban, modern, powerful, rushing to our business in Alexandria. Outside, in the real world the picture is of complacent poverty and great lethargy despite the well-tended fields. Everyone moves slowly, human and beast. There is no need to hurry for history goes on forever and, anyway, there is little energy to do so. Many here spend their lives being cured of bilharzia and then catching it again and again. The "land of menstruating men," the Romans called Egypt, seeing the men with blood in their urine. A European recently told me that Egyptian culture accommodated to the pace of bilharzia centuries ago and cannot now, even though a cure is available, rush the cadence. Can this be so? I sip my tea, and the military officers ask for more cheese sandwiches.

But soon the train brakes, slows dramatically, and we inch forward through the suburbs of Alexandria. The faces of people waiting passively beside the tracks are noticeably more European. We pass small factories, scrap yards, plantations and many new high-rise tenement buildings. But still there are palm trees loaded with bright red and orange dates and, on the balconies, gray laundry hangs amidst carpets, bird cages, and plastic sacks. Everywhere there are mosques, many new, and in all shapes and sizes. "Man does not live by bread alone" and, anyway, the military officers have finally finished all their sandwiches.

The call to prayer begins as I descend at Sidi Gaber, the first Alexandria stop. I cross the tracks carried along by the shoving mass and emerge into a square where taxis wait. One driver scoops me up and I, too, disappear into the maw of the ancient city of Alexandria.

22

Remembering the Battle of El Alamein Fifty Years On

25 October 1992

In the heat of an October morning, fifty years on, over two thousand people arranged themselves in ragged rows facing the orderly headstones of the Commonwealth war cemetery at El Alamein. Some of the pilgrims were elderly and bent, weighed down by war wounds and campaign medals. These were the ones I watched the most carefully. They were the only ones who could answer my questions.

In the row ahead of me, the New Zealand chief of staff gave up his seat to an old warrior who could barely stand, yet struggled to attention as the standards and wreaths were carried down towards the Stone of Remembrance. Sometimes tears ran down the faces of the old soldiers, especially when the Last Post sounded, and then again when the pipes swirled over the desert stillness.

"They shall grow not old," said the Duke of Kent. "We shall remember them," replied the multitude. Indeed. How could anyone who has heard the story forget that night of 23 October 1942 when the British Eighth Army, led by Scottish pipers, set out across the wire and mine fields to reach Rommel's Afrika Korps? And who, an old soldier told me, could forget the Germans who met them?

We had gathered in Alexandria some sixty kilometers from El Alamein, which was hardly more than a stop on the rail line in 1942 and even after fifty years not much bigger. It would be necessary to get everyone to the several ceremonies to be held at cemeteries in El Alamein and then back to Alexandria in one day, a formidable task but one carried out for the most part with military precision.

"They were very young," an ancient Australian said of the German troops as we sat around the hotel lobby waiting for transportation to El Alamein. "Those who survived put their hands on their heads and asked for water." He repeated this: "They were very young and so were we." His friend, another old soldier, nodded: "We had a fourteen-year-old with us. A big lad who'd lied about his age. But the Army wasn't careful in those days. If you were warm, they signed you up. He's buried at Tobruk." Then he smoothed his battered campaign hat and changed the subject.

"Know why we pin these up on one side?" he asked me, pointing to his hat, and then answering his own question. "To get a clear line of fire, especially when we want to attract the ladies." He grinned, and the other old men seated around him guffawed with delight.

But death could not remain far from their thoughts. "Old Toby died last week," someone said of a favorite officer. "Well, he had a good run," another replied. "Ninety-four years of age." I slipped away unnoticed as they returned to reminiscing.

In Alexandria on that first day a nervous young diplomat misplaced several room keys, among them that of the British Prime Minister. Then, the Duke of Kent's luggage was taken to the local hospital with his travelling blood supply. The Ramada Hotel angered some people by serving up canapés marked with flags which said "October 1942, El Alamein" on one side and "NO WAR!" on the other. And I committed a terrible faux pas by asking the Admiral of the Egyptian Navy, resplendent in white uniform, which delegation he represented. Still, given the number of visitors, the assembled dignitaries and the logistics needed to move them about, there was surprisingly little confusion during the two days of remembrance.

"The trouble is, they want us to do too much," one old soldier grumbled. "But we only want to visit the battlefield and the train station. It looks the same, you know. We just want to be here and remember. That's all." Instead, there were receptions and dinners in Alexandria and at Alamein itself an international service, a Commonwealth service, a Greek service, a French service, a Jewish service—all well attended.

In memory of a movie in which Spencer Tracy marched into

town after the battle of El Alamein and demanded a Carlsberg, the Carlsberg brewery company provided free beer to the seven hundred who attended the British consul general's reception. There the press crawled over British Prime Minister John Major and the Duke of Kent and photographed old boys wearing their hats and amazing arrays of campaign ribbons. Eventually the journalists discovered the old soldier who had lain wounded in the desert for four days after the battle rolled on towards the Libyan border.

On October 25, the main day of commemoration, the road between Alexandria and El Alamein was clogged with coaches and cars whose security escorts waved and hooted frantically at one another, driving like madmen to demonstrate the importance of their passengers.

"Well, I survived the battle," a retired British general said within my hearing. "But now please tell me when I can open my eyes."

As the minibus I was placed in left the hotel to drive the sixty or so kilometers to Al Alamein, a cry went up from several Members of Parliament: "Stop! We've lost Winston! That's him standing back by the door!" Our driver swiftly reversed to allow us to pull in Winston Churchill, Member of Parliament and grandson of the more famous Churchill, Prime Minister of Britain during the Second World War.

There are several World War II cemeteries at El Alamein and services were held at all, beginning at the German memorial with an international service. The stark German memorial rises like a fortress from the desert and on that day was particularly well guarded by German paratroopers seemingly selected for their height. Coaches to right of us, cars to left of us, disgorged their passengers while, evidently poorly briefed, the German paratroopers tried to prevent several official British cars driving up to the monument.

Three times the Prime Minister and the British Ambassador in the lead car, followed by the Duke of Kent and the Deputy Head of Mission, were ordered to halt and the Ambassador obliged to describe in German who they were. Tempers began to fray.

"Drive on!" the Duke of Kent ordered at last. "No wonder Monty had such trouble with these blighters!"

Eventually the column of dignitaries, diplomats, veterans, officials, attendants, and wives swept forward between flanking crowds of European, Egyptian, Australian, and other Commonwealth representatives. I touched my red felt hat and smiled at an old man in lederhosen who wore a green felt hat crowned with an enormous feather. No doubt he, too, was one of the survivors.

The German band struck up to announce the start of the international service. Officials mounted the dais and priests spoke in Italian, German, and English. Bugles played and wreaths were carried forward. I stood behind the Duke and admired the way the veins in his large ears picked up the red pinstripe in his suit. An Egyptian security officer pushed through the sweating multitude and positioned himself directly in front of the German ambassador's wife. In the interest of female solidarity, I tapped his shoulder and asked him to move—which to his credit he did.

The Church of England Archdeacon from Alexandria exhorted us to love our enemies and seek to understand one another, following which Winston Churchill, standing not far away, wondered aloud if "the blighter knows who won the war." Someone whispered to me that Rommel's son, although invited to today's remembrance service, had failed to accept. Meanwhile, standing shoulder to shoulder in the stifling heat, I wondered who would faint first, hoping not me. Then, during the interlude of silence, someone nearby farted. A Royal Green Jackets bugler pulled us out of our torpor and back to attention.

"Nobody plays it like the Green Jackets," a British veteran told me as we were leaving. "Did you hear that German try it on? And those Italians couldn't keep in step despite all their feathers!"

On then to the next events. In the vehicle I shared with members of parliament, one member declared, "The Church of England deacon was certainly speaking for a different constituency. But our own service will be better." Others grunted agreement, and we all drank Perrier water before we pulled up at the newly refurbished El Alamein War Museum. Here an Egyptian official lectured us on the critically important Egyptian contribution to Allied victory at Alamein, which he claimed had been overlooked.

"There is really nothing here for those who knew Alamein," the retired British general said to me after we had walked through the sparse museum. But the old soldiers inside were not listening. They had gathered with delight around a display that described the Italian flag "wavering" over the battlefield.

"Exactly," the ancient warriors cried, "Exactly."

It was time then for a standup buffet lunch hosted by the Duke. I left my red felt hat on the table at the door next to several French generals' hats and was horrified to find soon after that two African diplomats had discarded their greasy chicken bones onto my hat.

"Never mind," the British Secretary of Defense, a sensible man, told me. "These things are meant to try us. Have it dry cleaned."

Meanwhile, the Egyptians—whose President did not attend and whose news media played down the event—seemed bemused by all the fuss. The Battle of El Alamein may have changed the history of Europe but did not seem to relate to modern Egypt in any particular or useful way. Apparently, they had not been told that the cost of the war led into the demise of the British Empire including British withdrawal from Egypt.

A British diplomat, who had checked several members of the British delegation into a Cairo Hotel, later related how the clerk had asked her twice, "Winston…what did you say the second name is?" Later when the diplomat expressed outrage at the clerk's ignorance, a young British aide de camp came to the clerk's defense.

"Before I went to work for the Defense Secretary," he said, "I had never heard of the Battle of El Alamein." All Britons over forty who heard this sucked in their breath, but no one spoke. We were all learning the lessons of history, the greatest of which is, it seems, the obligation to remember.

The Egyptians wisely remembered to take the opportunity of the occasion to raise—for the first time in ten years—the issue of as yet uncleared British minefields in the Western Desert.

"These are not a problem when only the Bedouin live there," they said. "But when you are trying to develop resorts—well, you see the difficulty. "

During all the ceremonies, prayers, and eulogies at British, German, and Italian cemeteries, no spoken part was given to the veterans. Not that they cared, they told me. In effect, they left it to the rest of us to sing the hymns, to march smartly, wear strange clothing, and make fine speeches. They had already performed, and it was beyond anyone's power to add or to detract.

The veterans of the Battle of El Alamein laid their wreaths, saluted, and wept a little, mostly in private. The guns had gone silent but, fifty years on, they still remembered the fearful sounds of artillery, the terrifying encouragement of the bagpipes, the terrible explosions, and the horrors of the barbed wire, especially on the first night of advance. But most of all, I think, they remembered their fallen friends.

For the veterans of El Alamein, living and dead, being there and remembering fifty years on was what counted.

23

Aswan without Tourists

13 December 1992

Aswan is the loveliest spot on the Nile. There the river swirls around great rock islands called Elephantine, Kitchener, and Amun and rushes through the first cataract as the felucca tacks, and Captain Magdi shouts orders to his crew of one. The clear water is low, revealing waves of vegetation and enormous submerged boulders. Safely through the cataract, we ground on granite, pull in the centerboard, and have to be poled free.

"The Nile is working very strong," says Captain Magdi. Then, to divert us, "See! Chicken of the Nile." A flock of moorhens scuttles out of reach, and a squacco heron shouts a protest that we have approached too near. Granite walls surround us, many defaced by modern inscriptions in white paint.

The writer Amelia B. Edwards, travelling here in the 1870s, found this stretch of river altogether charming. But she came before the advent of the Cataract Hotel and well before the stark New Cataract which blocks the river view, the Oberoi whose air traffic control style tower desecrates Elephantine Island and the Isis which spreads a fungus of pink villas along the river bank.

Tourism is on the verge of swamping Aswan for it has rearranged the skyline, polluted the river with plastic waste, disrupted the tranquility of the area, and restricted access to the riverine islands for visitors and locals alike. Worse, it seems in process of sullying the thinking of local residents so that they move ever more firmly into the legendary, grasping manipulation of which they are often accused.

But there has been a reprieve. "The Party of the Beards," as the militant Islamists are known in Aswan, has carried out nine attacks on tourists and tourist facilities in Upper Egypt in recent weeks, causing one death and thirteen injuries. Therefore, the tourist hordes have been diverted elsewhere by American and European travel agents, and Egypt, which derives at least half its foreign exchange from tourists, is hurting badly.

Were we to listen carefully to the reasons given for attacks on tourism, I suspect we might find ourselves in agreement with many of the Islamists' complaints. Mass tourism *does* corrupt the local people. Moreover, it promotes xenophobia, avarice, and contempt on the part of both travelers and local suppliers. "If it's Tuesday, this must be Aswan" is not the way to know Egypt, even though many tourists don't want to know as they are mainly interested in sun, sex, and oddities wherever they can be found. Tourism has become the opportunity to pay outrageous prices, be hassled, and perhaps robbed, by aggressive touts, suffer severe stomach upset, and come away historically confused and culturally alienated.

But the Diplomat and I are near collapse from the work and social overload of Cairo. Moreover, we know that the international press has exaggerated the danger, fanning the flames of Europe's fear of militant Islam. With Aswan's foreign visitors at low tide, we seize the opportunity for a few days relaxation.

The fifteen-minute taxi ride from Aswan airport to the city center is far from relaxing. Our driver, seemingly high on hashish, drops us, shaken and willing to pay any price for deliverance, at the ferry that will carry us to the Club Med on Amun Island. On Amun, we believe, there will be tranquility because so many of the topless women and energetic young men have stayed in Paris, Bonn, and Geneva. On Amun there are no organized games to avoid, no joint excursions to escape. On Amun there are no dinner parties. We shall find peace there.

But nothing is perfect. In the Club Med way, we must share a table that evening with a sour German couple, who declaim in German to one another against our intrusion and in English about the usurious prices they have paid compared to local booking fees. In return for their rudeness, we let them in on how little we have paid to be at the Club Med. Other guests include yet more Europeans, two of them noisy, demanding children. There is as well a small group of Japanese. Although wine is "unlimited" at dinner, this turns out to apply only to Omar Khayyam rouge.

"Omar Khayyam," I whisper to the Diplomat in despair on that first night. "You'd have to be out of your mind."

"You will be when you have had some," he replies smoothly.

The food is good, however, and we have already found that the pool is usually empty and feluccas quickly available. Moreover, from our balcony we have identified twenty-seven species of birds, including glossy ibis, Egyptian geese, a variety of herons, and a fishing osprey which, judging from his bungling, could be this year's nestling from Scotland.

Aswan is the door to Africa. You see it in the chocolate skin of the Nubians, taste it in their Sudanese drinks, see it in their geometric designs and southern Nilotic handicrafts. Life is exuberant here in the narrow strip of green between the Libyan and Arabian deserts.

"We are not like the Egyptians, praise God," says our driver the next morning as we rocket towards Kalabshah. "There are no religious extremists in Aswan and no incidents between Muslims and Christians." Illustrating his city's liberating lack of orthodoxy, he relates a tale of bootleg local booze, which unfortunately resulted in "forty dead and fifteen blind." Silently, we resolve to be thankful for Omar Khayyam.

Amelia Edwards found that the Nubians are "inferior people,"[1] which I translate to mean she found them gentle folk whose nature and relative economic backwardness had made them prey to the more forceful Egyptians. Nor has the position of the Nubians with regard to their Arab conquerors improved much since that time. Although modern mass tourism means more jobs for them, it is the people from Cairo who own the hotels and monopolize tourism.

The Temple of Kalabshah near the Aswan High Dam is a Ptolemaic beauty dismantled and reconstructed by a German team between 1961 and 1963 in a race against the rising waters of Lake Nasser. It is also a monument to Nubian civilization. Here the ancient gods continued to be worshipped under new pharaonic, Roman, and later Christian names. Here, too, the area's tie to the south is also seen in rough pilgrim carvings of elephants and giraffes.

We reach the site by motor launch from a shore littered with decaying boats long stranded above the dam. Our boatman has the leonine features of a leper, several missing fingers and an open sore on the hand he extends to steady his passengers' descent. We ask about tourism; he laments and asks for good baksheesh.

At Philae we find several small groups of tourists, mainly Italians. They follow their guides closely through the Temple of Isis, allowing us peace in which to examine the Kiosk of Trajan. Though it is December, the sun is brilliant, reaching into the shadows of the great buildings where it caresses friezes and massive columns. And here, too, is the story of religion and culture in transition as hieroglyphs give way to demotic and Greek inscriptions. The additions by earlier tourists, Coptic crosses and nineteenth-century European names and dates, deface several sections. But recent graffiti are mainly in Arabic for the Egyptians downstream have also discovered the allure of Nubia.

Like so many people, Egyptians can be uncouth tourists. On Kitchener Island we are swarmed by several score young male students from a Cairo college who want to have their pictures taken with us, demand to know our names and address, ask the time to show they can speak a little English, and altogether destroy the peace of the lovely botanical garden with loud music and constant shouting. Surely, it is they, or brutes like them, who have written their names in paint over the great rocks in the river!

The scene is the same at the tomb of the Aga Khan, where aggressive young men who do not seem to understand our desire to be left alone block the steps. No, they will have conversation, names, addresses, the time. They block our way shouting into our faces "What's you name?" and "Germany? Germany?"

To escape we climb over the new wall and find again the old road that leads after half a mile to the ruins of St. Simeon's Monastery. Here in the ruins we find the peace we need. But not for long. Next door, the Coptic Christians, preparing for their own influx of tourists, are constructing a new monastery, and the noise of hammering, shouting, and radios floats over the plateau. What, we ask ourselves, will the Islamists say when they find out what is going on here?

"You could as easily keep a monkey from chattering as an

Arab," Edwards wrote in her smug nineteenth-century British way.[2] Cruel words, indeed, and wounding. Travelers need to learn to adjust to different cultures. Every morning at seven we are awakened by workmen shouting beneath our window and hotel staff loudly greeting one another in the hallway. And though Aswan is not a city of cacophonous mosques as are many other Egyptian cities, at the airport we are nearly blasted from our seats by the amplified call to prayer. It is perhaps indicative that despite the strident call, we saw no one answering the command.

"Amplified Islam," we say to one another—whether expressed by a muezzin with a loud speaker or by the Party of the Beards—can easily become, not a call to worship, but an order to obey authority. Is it not as well a travesty of faith, an expression of aggression that arises from deep feelings of powerlessness and frustration? Meanwhile, the beard itself has become a mark of the desire to push back, to take power from those who have it, not in order to share it with those who are downtrodden, but so as to wield it oneself. Amplified religion, we tell ourselves, is the epitome of "I'm okay, but you're not okay," shouted by those who in their hearts are not certain this is true. For are not the heretics and unbelievers rich and God's people poor and powerless?

Upper Egypt has entered into this tunnel of noise. Aswan, although it is Nubia, cannot remain apart and has already felt the impact. Having tasted the economic opportunities provided by tourism, the Nubians will become more vulnerable to the noise of the Party of the Beards. For the moment, however, one can at least hope that no more hotels will be built on the most beautiful stretch of the Nile.

24

Monkey Business in Wadi Natrun

31 December 1992

Wadi Natrun, the "Valley of Salts," is where the ancients found natron, an essential ingredient for mummification. But preservation, even of the desert itself, seems far from modern minds. Along the main Cairo to Alexandria road the desert is filling up with "farms," meaning that the wealthy are staking out their claims in an era of rapid development. Behind each magnificent gate there is usually only desert. Even the monks of Wadi Natrun have had to put up sand walls and buy from the government land considered theirs for hundreds of years.

To reach this once-remote wadi, sixty kilometers long and six wide, we drove halfway from Cairo to Alexandria and then turned into the desert at an amenities area where shops sell sun cream and trendy, over-priced casual clothing. In the playground children of rich parents slide down the elephant's trunk or careen about on rented tricycles as the latest music from Cairo blasts out of the cassette kiosk. In the parking lot a ragged attendant will wash your car for fifty piasters while you use the rest area's unusually clean facilities.

However, if you are an Egyptian fighter pilot, you can skip the Desert Highway and reach Wadi Natrun off road. Simply fix your sights on St. Bishoi's monastery and make a few strafing runs, seeing how close you can get to the highest tower. No harm in cocking a snook for Allah over the official residence of the Coptic pope, Shenudah III.

"How long has this been going on?" I shout at Father Sidrac.

We have finished our salty tea, and the tour of the monastery has begun. The monk's long, sad face collapses further. Twenty-five years, he says, but thank God, not every day. Father Sidrac finds us, too, a nuisance but dutifully leads our ragtag group of Italians, Egyptians, British, and one American through the disused refectory, around the ninth-century walls and into the twelfth- century qasr, the keep of the Monastery of St. Bishoi.

Christian presence in Wadi Natrun grew out of persecution. In the reign of Emperor Diocletian, thousands fled for safety to the desert, and by the fourth century there were said to be over a hundred monasteries in Wadi Natrun. Most returned to sand over the centuries, and by the early 1970s, the remaining monasteries of St. Macarios and St. Bishoi contained only five and eight aging monks respectively. However, a miracle was about to occur.

By the early 1990s, some one hundred monks were living in St. Macarios monastery and 160 at St. Bishoi—and there were long waiting lists of applicants to both monasteries as well as to several others. This increase apparently had as much to do with politics and identity as religion although no one likes to talk about it.

At the gate into St. Marcarios monastery, a teenage boy with a Fayoum portrait face and large fly-encircled eyes waved us through and up the road. Later, our guide to the St. Bishoi monastery admonished us that "People come for the blessing. Miracles occur here. We are always open, twenty-four hours a day."

While at St. Bishoi we passed a monk in green plastic slippers going about his daily chores amidst a crowd of playing children. Adults kissed the hand he extended and then pulled back before the kiss could be planted. In the main church we examined the red-covered casket that contains the uncorrupted body of St. Bishoi. Pilgrims jostled for a look.

Just over a year earlier, before my last visit to Wadi Natrun, there had been "an incident" in the Cairo suburb of Imbaba, an attack by Muslims on Christians, perhaps provoked, perhaps not. Our visit this time came in context of severe police action against Imbaba's Muslim extremists, who had advanced from bashing Christians to shooting policemen and occasionally even tourists. Most Egyptians, Muslims as well as Christians, support the crackdown on violent behavior but vigorously debate whether the government's rather arbitrary iron fist policy is the right tactic for handling unrest based on socio-economic malcontent—with religion only a minor irritant. Meanwhile, the "Emir of Imbaba" is said to have been arrested along with some six hundred of his followers, and there is recent news of the arrest of sixty "religious extremists" in Cairo's Ain Shams district.

"What if all the Copts leave Egypt?" I recently asked a monk at St. Mina Monastery near Alexandria. The monk, a medical doctor who ten years earlier had left a successful secular life to take divine orders, laughed at the obviously absurd question.

"Whatever happens, there will always be Copts in Egypt," the monk said. "We monks will always be here. We Copts are the true Egyptians."

This statement, frequently heard, is based in part on a Coptic claim of descent from Christians converted by St. Mark who introduced Christianity to Egypt in the first century. Most Copts see Islam as an unacceptable break with Egypt's glorious Christian past while Muslim Egyptians often speak scornfully and suspiciously of the "arrogant Copts who boast of their identity by tattooing blue crosses on their inside wrists"—an act frequently interpreted by Muslims as a semi-secret sign of less than true allegiance to the modern state.

On this visit, Father Sidrac, our guide, carefully avoids modern controversy. Instead, he describes attacks by "barbarians," meaning Berbers from the Libyan Desert, during the early Christian era. His large, muscular hands clinch, and his dark eyes glare from beneath his cowl as he recites the historical litany of excess. It is easy to image Father Sidrac as a warrior for his faith.

"Our music, literature, language, art, and architecture are all inherited from the period of the pharaohs," Father Sidrac says. In Bishoi's main church he pauses, reaches into a cupboard and extracts a triangle and then cymbals he uses to demonstrate. Chanting, his face lights up, and his eyes flash. I remember the sword, said to have been found in an ancient well and now on display in the monastery's refectory, and whisper to myself: "The sword of the Lord and Gideon."

The nearby monastery of Deir El Sourian is the site of St. Bishoi's hermitage and a reminder of controversy among the monks themselves. Why else build two large monasteries cheek by jowl? Indeed "El Sourian" was founded in the sixth century during the heyday of the "Gaianite Heresy," a debate over whether the body of Jesus was corruptible. To accept this notion was felt by some to question the Incarnation and thus to lower the status of the Virgin Mary. In wrath, therefore, orthodox monks removed themselves from Bishoi and founded their own monastery hard by, defiantly dedicating it to the "Mother of God." Later, when theological feathers had been smoothed and the two groups reunited, Syrian monks took over the second monastery, giving it the name, Monastery of the Syrian, by which it is still known.

At Deir El Sourian we examine St. Bishoi's cave and the chain to which he tied his hair to prevent nodding off at prayers. Although visitors have carried off many ancient manuscripts since the eighteenth century, there are rich, albeit damaged frescos in several of the Wadi Natrun churches, and El Sourian contains at least one particularly interesting treasure. While cleaning frescoes in the monastery's Church of the Virgin in 1991, French experts found a delightful Byzantine fresco behind the more primitive Coptic painting. The now exposed older fresco gives the final word on Mary's continued virginity. Standing near her, the Prophet Ezekiel holds a placard on which is written Ezekiel 44:2: "And the Lord said to me, 'This door shall be shut. It shall not be opened and no man shall enter by it; because the Lord God of Israel has entered by it.'" The ancients who built this place must be mightily pleased with the French.

Sadly, modern artistic abilities have declined. Directly opposite the splendid Byzantine painting is hung an enormous work by self-styled "talented artist Alfonse Ratib." Mr. Ratib has selected Mary's Son as his subject, depicting him surrounded by real iron pinchers, spikes, a wooden mallet and bright globs of thick red paint. Artistic standards have also declined elsewhere in the monastery. Moreover, the strain on modern monks is enormous.

In outbuildings, modern monks seek privacy and seclusion from both the eyes of the curious day-trippers from Cairo and their own persistent fellow religionists. But unlike the "hermit holes" in nearby hills and wadis, there is an air of prosperity here, and the new buildings look rather like seaside bungalows. We suspect there are no chains in use to prevent nodding off at prayers. But we are about to be surprised.

We are leaving the monastery after our lengthy visit when we notice several black-robed figures sitting together in the doorway of their bungalow some distance away from the central part of the monastery. We start to walk across the sand towards them but are waved away. We hesitate for, in a small area in front of a bungalow, a black-robed figure wearing a monk's cap, stands with his arms affixed to a cross. But this is no scarecrow and I am close enough to see the face of the unmoving figure.

Perhaps we have erred greatly in deciding standards have slipped. Are we looking at punishment for infringement of the rules? Or is this perhaps the usual method of preparing another "incorruptible" corpse? We retreat quickly as the monks shout at us again to move back.

Are punishments from the Middle Ages being applied? Have the tourists and the noise driven the monks into deeper, more serious self-mortification? But it will soon be dark, and we have tarried here for so long that the Deir El Baramus monastery is beyond our reach today. As another fighter plane screams over the monastery, we walk, mystified, towards our parked car. Let us, then, leave quickly allowing the monks of Baramus to pray and to repent in holy solitude. And may we repent for having disturbed them.

Monastery in Wadi Natrun, December 1992

25

From Cairo to Kharga

3 January 1993

We left Cairo at 6:30, passing through Helwan in time to catch the sun coming up behind cement plants belching filth into the cold morning air. The Range Rover purred south, roof rack singing, along the East Bank's new desert road. Farmland alternated with desert and by noon we were crossing the Nile at Assyut. A sign on the rattling bridge announced "Ipswich, England, 1935."

The first thing I noticed about Assyut was the cropped ears of many of the donkeys, sometimes one ear, sometimes both. Later we saw a few of the same lopsided little beasts in Kharga but when we asked why, the phenomenon was denied. Just like that. Dogs, yes, to keep their ears from being torn during fights. But no one cuts donkey ears. Still, I have seen it, and it adds to the mystery of the fellaheen.

There is a petrol station just after the taftish, the checkpoint that guards the entrance to the desert. Soon after that a large sign announces "Interior Ministry: Central Security." But we have seen no evidence of the "Party of the Beards," only the university, a sign for the Badr Hotel, advertised as "beyond the train station," and cheerful soldiers at the check point. Darb El Arba'in, The Road of the Forty, on which slaves and camels took at least that many days to struggle through the sand to Assyut from Western Sudan, stretches out for 223 kilometers between us and Kharga.

Rocky hills increased as the road neared the oasis. The passable, but in stretches fairly miserable, road disappeared for a while into liquid tar, which splashed high on the Range Rover's sides and windows. Finally, we came over the escarpment—all oases are depressions—and down seven kilometers of winding road still guarded by ruined Roman fortifications. There are no villages, just the Valley of Melons, curiously rounded stones that litter the desert floor, and then a field of enormous yardangs, wind-eroded rock outcroppings shaped like crouching lions.

Qasr Kharga, capital of both the oasis and of the New Valley, still lay several kilometers ahead, and it was only mid-afternoon. Time, then, to visit El Deir at the foot of Jebel Umm el Ghanayin. Though its name means monastery, which the site may have been in some past century, El Deir is actually an immense mud brick fortress. Its twelve towers make it one of the most imposing Roman fortifications in Egypt.

After several incorrect directions given by farmers winding up their day's toil in nearby date groves and cane fields, we found the correct track behind the village of Munira and set out on a three-kilometer drive over the drifted remnants of road alternating track which ended at the base of a great sand dune. El Deir hid itself somewhere behind this moving yellow mountain over which it was impossible, and around which perilous, to drive. The day, moreover, moved in drifting shadow towards sunset, and we were weary after a ten-hour journey.

The impulse to go forward was, nonetheless, very strong. At the base of the dune, stuck upright in a pile of gray ash carefully heaped on the sand, stood a Stone Age flint spearhead. Without thinking, I took it up and felt at once that I had connected myself to this place. "It" wasn't the Deir, wasn't the dune, wasn't the desert itself. Something else was here, something much older. Something not frightening, just present and very powerful.

At the Hamad Alla, Qasr Kharga's "three-star" hotel, we found ourselves in the midst of a party of Assyut University students. The only other guests were two more-than-middle-aged Italians and two youthful Scandinavian backpackers, all like us confounded by the extraordinarily loud music with which the students filled the hotel lounge. Among the students were several women, all wearing headscarves. Amplified instruments including tambourine, drums, and Egyptian versions of the flute and violin were accompanied by enthusiastic singing and licentious, vigorous dancing by men only.

At length a large and heavily made up woman arose to recite. The poetess swayed eyes and hips and the audience groaned enthusiastically. Repeatedly she mentioned the Muslims and Mohammed and, at least once, jihad.

But though we could not converse above the noise, the dinner of grilled chicken was not bad. The waiter apologized for the students, and we told him "Malesh. These people, too, are tourists, and what could you do anyway?" I caught the eye of one of the elderly Italians, and we both grinned and shrugged. A bottle of Beaujolais Village, brought from Cairo and entirely out of place, helped a great deal. Then we wandered off to bed.

Before sleeping I reread Bagnold's chapter about the inaccessibility of Kharga Oasis[1] Bagnold had nothing to say about Roman ruins or the even more ancient history of Kharga. Perhaps he knew nothing of these. However, his description of the desert and the hardships of the Darb El Arba'in is almost unbearable. The carcasses of camels may still be seen where the worn out, thirst-tortured beasts fell on the march north. But where are the bodies of the hundreds, surely even thousands, of men, women, and children who perished en route to the slave markets of Cairo? Kharga is an island of ghosts. But when the music finally stopped, we slept.

26

Around Kharga

4 January 1993

Breakfast at the Hamad Alla is quite indifferent: frozen butter, sandy bread with jam, and a tiny, cold hard-boiled egg. The coffee is like muck, and we do not tarry over a second cup. Emerging from the hotel, we half expect to find Major Ramadan of the Tourist Police who had accosted us in the street the night before. Anything I can do, the Major said, just ask. He had just been promoted and, charmingly, kept forgetting and calling himself captain. But Major Ramadan is nowhere around and so we head for the Tourist Office.

The three or four people seated behind desks in the Tourist Office barely return our greeting, and though we wait a while, no one offers information, so we leave and have the tar cleaned off the Range Rover. Possibly because they are unused to seeing foreign women close up, the men at the petrol station stare and stand so close that I feel uncomfortable and move away. Kharga, it seems, is an aggressive place, though perhaps this is mostly unintended.

At the Ptolomaic era Temple of Nadura, just outside Qasr Kharga, the guard asks a multitude of nosy questions which center on our relationship, my age, whether we have children. He insists we stay for tea, and we refuse as politely as possible and as much for the press of time as to be done with his persistence. Nearby is Hibis, a large Roman temple that every year requires further buttressing to keep its walls from falling outward. The temple will not be allowed to perish, another guard reassures us. It will be moved to safety. Most of Hibis is covered by cultivated fields and ground water is rising. Inexplicably, the trees around the temple are dead or dying. Salt perhaps? On then to Bagawat, which may also be seen from Nadura.

If Egypt were today a Christian country, a UNESCO grant would have been sought to save Bagawat. The site is an archive of church history in an almost totally unpreserved fourth to seventh century cemetery. Crumbling white plastered walls and mud brick domes, some with still brilliant frescos, reach up the hillside and remind of the brooches produced by a trendy artist in Mohandiseen, items which are currently all the rage in Cairo.

Bagawat is the first place in Kharga where we have had to pay admission, an indication that the local authorities have some inkling of its historical importance—or at least of its touristic appeal. Our obligatory guide turns out to be extraordinarily arrogant and uninformed, insisting that a fresco of a Roman soldier with a Greek inscription is pharaonic and identifying a mosque in a fresco painted long before Islam. He is, however, proficient in the practice common to illiterate people (and some who are not) of interrupting conversations in a language they do not understand.

To this guide we are not people but freaks from another world. Still, he tries to make the most of it and, as I step into one tomb ahead of him, runs his hand along my backside. Really I am getting extremely unhappy about all this touching, and my response does not increase his understanding or appreciation of foreigners. Obviously I am supposed to like being fondled by a man I have just met. Isn't that what he sees on television or perhaps hears from his fellow guards?

Infuriatingly, Alan again chuckles over my wrath and then turns the situation to advantage. Our guide declares that the nearby monastery of Mustafa Kachef and the monastery/church complex of Ain Za'f are "mamnoo'," forbidden, out of bounds. We can see them through our binoculars but may not go there.

"But Madam wishes to pray there and is very unhappy at not being allowed to do so," Alan says. His tone implies that if Madam does not get her way there will be hell to pay, including perhaps a report about feeling up the tourists. I look as piously fierce as I can and, while the guard is deliberating with his fellow at the gatehouse, feed leftover mince pies to his starving dog. When the young men remove rocks from the entrance to the track, conceding that we may head out towards Mustafa Kachef, I repent of my anger and give them some mince pies, although I don't tell them about the alcohol in the pies.

The region has been extensively farmed in years past, and there is evidence of an underground irrigation system. But today all is desert. Despite new vitality in parts of the oasis as the result of the newly paved road from the Nile, the oasis is dying. There are crumbling frescos in the broken walls of both Mustafa Kachef and the nearby monastery, and we picnic at Ain Za'f among the mounds of potsherds and largely unexcavated ruins. Archaeologists, not now in residence, have recently been at work, probably the reason access to the site has been limited. A fitful wind sweeps sand in and out of the tiny cells where monks once lived and died.

It is time to return to Munira and make another attempt on El Deir. Parking at the base of the great dune, we leave the car and walk for some forty minutes, sometimes on an old road, sometimes through heavy sand, to the foot of the great fortress. The approach is eerie, and the guidebook speaks of a well within the fortress. We cross the buildup bed of ancient fields long abandoned. Nothing has grown here for several hundred years. But the garden near the fort looks like it has suffered a nuclear attack, trees bent over and only recently dead. There is no living well here, only history, destruction, and the names of the dead.

The plastered internal walls of the ruined fortress appear to contain the signature of every British soldier who ever served in the Western Desert and some of their addresses as well. The towers of the fortress have been undermined by brick hungry locals—and perhaps by British soldiers as well—and several seem in danger of collapse. Hard by are the remains of what must have been a British military camp. A lone white-crowned black wheatear flits among the ruins, the rusting tins, the dead trees. There is nothing but sorrow to keep us here.

We hurry back along the way we came navigating by the great dune. The afternoon deepens, the wind picks up and a few drops of rain quicken our pace. It will be a relief to put the dune between us and El Deir.

Back at the hotel, we devour another chicken—there is nothing else on the menu–and retire early. Something about Kharga promotes sleep, and I dream of shadows moving amidst the ruins. But what or who they are, it is impossible to know.

27

South to Dush

5 January 1993

The weather is considerably warmer today, though overcast and very windy. At 9 a.m. we set off for Dush, 116 kilometers south along the Darb el Arba'in. Once the southwest frontier of the Roman Empire, Dush is some 300 kilometers from the Sudanese border and as close as we can get without permission from military security.

The picturesque village of Ginah is the first stop and because the secondary road is unmarked and our map inadequate, we soon encounter difficulty.

"Is this the road to Ginah?" we ask a man in a donkey cart as we pull up beside him.

"No."

"Then where, please, does this road go?"

"To Ginah, of course."

"Oh, thank you. And are there Roman houses in Ginah?"

"No, there is nothing there!" The donkey driver looks amazed that we should think anything old worth visiting and prods his small gray beast into action.

Undeterred, we press on, conjuring with our scant knowledge of Egyptian fellaheen beliefs and responses. Ask a fellah about dates and the response is likely to be that the event or structure in question is "min zamaan," meaning "from a time," a category which appears to cover everything older than one's grandfather. A conversation might go something like this:

"When?"

"Before."
"How long ago?"
"From a time."
"How many?"
"A lot."
"What size?"
"Big."
"What sort of bird?"
"A bird."

Lack of exactness seems childish to most Westerners and leaves us frustrated, ill tempered, and feeling superior. But could it be that measurements and precise specification are alien because they don't matter here? Sleep until you awake. Eat if you are hungry and have food. Work so you and your family may eat. Rejoice when you feel happy. Shout when you are angry. Weep when you are sad. Go with the flow of life. God is good.

Unlike the people of the desert for whom the margin between subsistence and disaster is much thinner, oasis dwellers can afford to be more extravagant. If your house falls down, build another. If you are thirsty, drink. If the taxman comes after you, give him just enough to make him go away. The nomad, who has no excess at all for the taxman, does not waste water, protects and names his few trees, knows a bustard from a sand grouse, and keeps on the move whenever that is necessary.

We leave the ancient well at Ginah, now gushing its waters into sprawling date plantations, and head for Qasr El Ghueita, a hilltop fortress built around a temple attributed to the Persian invader Darius I. The ruined fortress looks down on a desert plain, and the temple which it embraces has been defaced by passing tribesmen whose fires have blackened its ceilings and whose knives have gouged out the loins and faces of its pharaonic friezes. The vineyards of the Fortress of the Beautiful Gardens once supplied wine to the royal court at Thebes. But these, like the people who planted them, have long vanished.

Nonetheless, the small yellow sandstone temple retains a note of majesty, reinforced by contrast to the mud brick fortress. A guard asks for 8 LE each, high even by Cairo standards, but the government is out to get its pound of tourist flesh. A jolly group of young men engaged in repairs to the temple's delicate wall carvings tell us they are moonlighting employees from the local date factory. One says he has studied agriculture, and another claims a degree in commerce as the others scurry off for a tea break, leaving behind their buckets of cement and the trowels with which they have been daubing the friezes.

When asked, the guard claims that "an engineer" from the Ministry of Antiquities is in charge of the restorations. But he seems to find our question frivolous. After all, an educated man is an educated man, agriculture or commerce, and an effendi is an effendi. Alan takes a photo of me seated cross-legged on the high altar, and then remarks that "The foreigners are mad." This is a phrase the guard has heard enough and, embarrassed, he giggles.

Qasr El Zayyan comes next, likewise a small Roman temple encased in a Roman fortress. Again both are in ruinous condition, especially the fortress where we climb around the walls and almost fall into the deep but dry well. Of major interest are the concrete-like cylinders left by bees on the external walls, similar to those at the Monastery of Hammam in the Fayoum oasis where bees are credited with building the monastery during years in which it was abandoned.

Hassan, a leather-handed old guard, asks us for 8 LE each and then grins that I, as a woman, can go in on the Egyptian price of 50 piasters. He does not produce a ticket, however, and simply pockets the 2 LE change from the note Alan gives him. After exploring Qasr El Zayyan, we decline Hassan's enthusiastic offer of tea and continue south where desertification is again everywhere apparent.

But although most large trees stand dead, the area is not uniformly dry, and the desert is interspersed with groves and small fields in watered wadis and, surprisingly, often on hill tops where springs sometimes emerge. Beautiful marching dunes cross the area, and at one place we squeeze through an opening where the highway is being swallowed by pure, golden sand forty feet high. The road south traverses several villages built in the last decade or so and named after Arab states and cities: Aden, Algeria, Sanaa, Baghdad, Port Said, Palestine. All these seem dreary, poverty-stricken outposts where incomers from the Nile Valley live in low, blockhouses. Although there is electricity in these villages, they seem to be without television antennas and even minarets. Many of the small houses are empty, and Damascus, marked by a road sign, does not even exist. Clearly, the people of the real Valley do not transplant well to the New Valley.

A lovely town of domed buildings, New Baris, is a monument to the famed architect Hassan Fathi. But New Baris is likewise defeated, though for very different reasons. Never occupied, it was supposedly the victim of peasant reluctance to continue living in native architectural style. Comparing this beautiful place to the boxes we have just passed, I am incredulous and sniff a controversy between officialdom and the recently deceased and now nearly deified Fathi.

Bureaucracy is certainly at work. The road to Luxor, connecting the New Valley with the Nile, flashes by. But though this road has been paved over its entire length in the New Valley governorate, some forty kilometers in the Qena governorate remain nearly impassable. The word is that Luxor fears a drain-off of tourist resources to the New Valley, which, although it seems unreasonable, is just as well. The poor seem seldom to benefit much from tourism but are frequently doomed to become venal and aggressive in proportion to their contact with rich foreigners in coaches or, come to think of it, Range Rovers.

At the military roadblock twenty-two kilometers from Dush, we are told to turn back as we have no permit to visit Dush. Permits, the soldiers assure us, are obtainable only in Qasr Kharga. Recent renewal of controversy between Egypt and the Sudan over the Hala'ib enclave on the Red Sea has apparently increased Egyptian vigilance on this border as well, and the taftish has been moved north a few kilometers.

Dilemma and palaver. Alan keeps the engine running. Finally a young man in a tracksuit, who seems to be in charge, says we may go on if we return in an hour. The barrels are rolled aside, and as we accelerate we shout out a request for an hour and a half.

At the base of the hill on which the fortress of Dush stands, French archaeologists have built a dig house worthy of Hassan Fathi. A steep climb through sand to the hilltop reveals two noteworthy structures, a small rectangular temple which looks rather like a church and an enormous warren of a fortress, probably Ptolemaic, which abuts a Temple of Osiris built around the turn of the millennium. There we discover our two old Italians busily deciphering the hieroglyphs. They claim to have a permit.

The French have blocked off the fortress entrance, but the guard leads us up a goat path in the broken walls and onto the treacherous internal domes and stairways. Dush commands the surrounding plains and many miles of the Darb El Arba'in. But there is no time to tarry. Mindful of the waiting soldiers, we turn back for Qasr Kharga. At the checkpoint a soldier accuses us of overstaying and suggests that he ought to check the contents of our car. But Alan tells him we are in a hurry, and our offer of a couple of packs of cigarettes temporarily overcomes his curiosity about what foreigners carry around in Range Rovers.

It is well past lunchtime when we find the track to Shams el Din, the Sun of Religion, site of a fourth century church and its necropolis. Sand fills the church, and we picnic in the sanctuary gazing out over three-foot mud brick pillars covered with patches of white plaster. The desert is empty save for the distant road and a few passing donkey riders. In remembrance of those who came before, perhaps even Athenasius and Nestorious, both once exiled to Kharga Oasis, I pray the Lord's Prayer while Alan is rummaging in the Range Rover. Then we sit reading in the weak sunlight until the wind drives us forth.

Back in Qasr Kharga we find the Darb el Sindadıyya, a tiny alley leading into the tenth- century medina which is ruined, uninhabited, and encroached on by modern slums. The Darb el Sindadiyya is blocked by fallen masonry, but a young man offers to lead us into the city, dark even at midday and composed of tiny rooms and tortuous alleys, proof against attackers on horse or camel. Together we scramble over walls, along dark passageways, and up collapsing staircases. Within minutes we are thoroughly lost.

Inexplicably several areas are littered with animal skins, mainly of dogs. We examine a bread oven topped by a beautiful but discarded clay pot. Though I long to do so, I dare not take the pot least it suddenly assume value and importance to someone else. Alan almost breaks his ankle when he puts his foot through a very old skin container that the guide had urged him to jump down upon. The medina protects itself against intruders.

Back outside the medina, our guide refuses a tip but accepts the cigarettes we press upon him and his waiting friends. The Hamad Alla and a bottle of ouzo await us as night falls and we head back towards our hotel.

"Is this the road to Ginah?" In the desert between Kharga and Dush, January 1993

28

In Dakhla Oasis

6 January 1993

The day is splendidly bright, much warmer and less windy. The Italian professor of Egyptology—for thus it proves—says he will be going to Dakhla today. This he says at breakfast when I ask him if his friend, too, is a professor. No, a policeman and a dear traveling companion of many years. They seem a sweet old couple, but our mutual languages are limited.

From Kharga to Dakhla, 120 kilometers almost due west, the road wanders through golden dunes. Broken segments of road end in the bellies of marching dunes until finally a way through is found. The hills are conical like miniature pyramids, and there are yardangs in fantastic shapes. Soon we enter a broad plain, which extends right and left to the distant escarpment. We are driving at the bottom of a bowl.

At the phosphate plant, I stop for a hitchhiker in an iridescent blue tracksuit who says he is a farmer going back to his 200-feddan farm. Ten kilometers, he says, and settles comfortably into the front seat while Alan, having taken over the wheel, rides the ridge for forty kilometers until we reach a large government-sponsored farm and the farmer gets out. Soil here is rich when watered and fossil water, pumped from underground aquifers, had brought this part of the desert to life. Beyond the sown, we pass the Professor, the Policeman and their driver.

There are few checkpoints on the road today, but—as everywhere beginning at Assyut—people ask if we are Germans. Alan's response—a 'outhu billah, (I take refuge in God)"—is an Islamic saying denoting abhorrence of the very idea. The miles are eaten up by discussions of the tracksuit as the national uniform of the developing world, in further rumination on imprecision and the Egyptian fellah, and in speculation about who is manipulating whom in the tourist/fellah competition.

Just before the village of Tineida, we search for prehistoric graffiti on great sandstone outcroppings at the roadside. This area has been a crossroads for millennia, and travelers, from Neolithic man to a certain Jarvis, British governor of the oases, have left their names. But though we find a few primitive looking sketches of men and animals, the majority of the inscriptions are modern. Ahmads, Mohammeds, and Ramadans have scrawled their names, sometimes over ancient inscriptions. Happily, most of the ancient drawings seem to have been removed, salvaged, we hope, for the new museum in Kharga whose opening has been indefinitely delayed by bureaucratic befuzzlement. Ironically, at this place of inscriptions, I lose my fountain pen and drive on feeling bereaved.

A short drive offroad brings us to the thriving village of Bashinda—Pasha Hinda—where a local school teacher offers to take us to the tomb of Kitines, which is a second-century mastaba with several underground rooms and pharaonic wall carvings. But although we pay 8 LE each for a ticket "to the village," we are told that all else, save the kilm factory is closed. Strange how people from Scotland to China think they are the only ones who ever worked a loom or a mill and wish to involve visitors in the most detailed demonstrations of these useful but essentially quite boring contraptions.

Our preference is for something with a less vital, more funereal, bent, but we are denied entry to the tomb of Sheikh Bashindi, a domed structure rising over the original Roman tomb. What sort of conversation can they be carrying on down there, the sheikh and the mummy, or perhaps their ba and their ka? Are they eternally debating the design of kilms and whether or not underground irrigation systems should be revived?

As we wander back through the town of small, neat, whitewashed houses, our teacher/guide stops a six-year-old girl whom he describes as his best student. On order the child traces neat Arabic numerals in the dust, recites the first sura of the Koran, and demands a pen. I, alas, have none, but take her picture, kiss her forehead, and give her 25 piasters, all of which she finds highly acceptable. The women selling bits of broken jewelry and palm mats are, however, disappointed.

In the desert behind Bashindi is Ain Asil, which we locate with some difficulty, explore, and then lunch in the shade of an abandoned one-room mud house with a beautiful conical bread oven in the side yard. Ain Asil was probably capital of the Dakhla oasis during the Old Kingdom and the First Intermediate periods, but archaeologists from the French Institute seem to have taken the day off. Stillness hangs over the site like a blessing, a guard dozes in a white tent, and jackal tracks lead off through the sand towards a line of trees.

Nearby Oila el Dabba, the necropolis of Ain Asil, contains five enormous mastabas, one of which has been stripped down and opened to reveal the deep interior. This site, too, is officially closed, and the French archaeologists, either at work or asleep in their domed dig house, miss out on the wine and chocolate with which I was prepared to part. But an engaging young Egyptian archaeologist, native of Dakhla and a graduate of Cairo University, kindly shows us around.

It is mid-afternoon when we leave to search for the Roman city of Kellis, Asmant el Korab, Asmant the Ruined. Failing, we drive around the ancient walled medina at Balat. Then, behind the village of Sheikh Muftah, which is filled with raucous children of the "Helloo, Mister" ilk, Alan heads the Range Rover into the desert. But we can find neither the Roman cemetery of 250 rock-hewn tombs near the city nor the further distant cemetery of 100 more Roman tombs. The desert track peters out into sand, and we are in a vast, near-empty world less than an hour before sunset. It is time to retreat.

Backtracking past wells with their isolated trees and small fields, we return to Sheikh Muftah and continue the few kilometers towards Mut, capital of Dakhla Oasis. The off-track Qasr el Kassaaba, one of Dakhla's few Roman fortresses, looms in the distance as we near town. Mut, when we drive through, appears to be a modern, carefully laid out town, similar in its broad roads and few cars to Qasr Kharga.

In the hot spring pool at the Tourist Resthouse (8.50 LE per room per night), we find the Professor and the Policeman. They beckon to us, but I am put off by the russet water and the gaggle of male onlookers. Back into town then, to the Mebarex Hotel, opened sixteen months ago, according to a helpful manager who then tells us, before turning on the water and electricity, that he has worked abroad for twelve years. The wind has come up as the sun has gone down, and we are glad to be under shelter.

Our host promises a delicious supper of kebab hala, an oasis specialty he says, and when the meal turns out to be mainly chicken, compensates with a recital of his life story and personal philosophy. Though he is an oasis man and loves Dakhla, he is looking for a job in Kuwait as a stepping-stone to Europe. He does not covet money or power, he tells us, then goes on to boast of his father, a local sheikh and landed official. "I am a person of loyalty and faithfulness," he claims, adding that he never sees his children as they live in Syria but, anyway, he had hoped to visit a woman in America until the American Embassy in Cairo turned down his visa application.

"Give your hand to many, but your heart to only one," he intones. "This is my philosophy," repeating the cliché so we can savor its originality. "There is no one like me in Dakhla," he continues reassuringly. "I am the only one like me."

A "famous Egyptian movie star," whom the manager had pointed out at the only other occupied table, rises to go, and the manager rushes after him. We are not sorry to see him off for the Professor and the Policeman have just come in, looking pink from the wind and their hot springs bath. We uncork a bottle of Chianti for them.

29

On Tour from Liberation Square

7 January 1993

The day began with a visit to a tourist office where Omar shows us his name in Cassandra Vivian's controversial guidebook[1] before providing helpful directions to Kellis. We note these down for later and set off via "Lipration" Square, as one helpful citizen charmingly called it. Today we shall tackle the oasis's western loop. But first we drive to Rasha where we find great views of the escarpment but no Roman ruins. Nearby is Deir Abu Matta, an absolute ruin of an early church behind which are Roman tombs. Earthenware coffins found there are reportedly awaiting display in the Kharga Museum when it opens. A very cold wind forces us down from the mud brick walls, and we leave the tombs and their scattered bones unexamined.

At Budkhula, an agricultural village with a splendid penile minaret, we decide not to explore on foot due to time and abundant children. The main difference between traveler and tourist must surely be that the former takes more time. But the press of time and the persistence of importuning people make us edgy so that we lock the car doors and snap at one another.

The Bir el Gebel affords what is surely the oasis's most spectacular view of the multicolored escarpment. Here, there is a hot spring and, in a secluded spot, a pool for bathing. But when we alight to test the water, gabbling men appear and ask if we are Germans, tell us there is no hotel here (we didn't ask), and want to know all about us. Today there is something maddening about this sometimes-endearing Egyptian inquisitiveness. To be always considered an oddity, constantly under interrogation when it is we who have come to see the sights, is wearing. Not unreasonably, the people of Dakhla regard us as a diversion and hope to make us tarry. But today their queries hasten our departure.

At Qasr Dakhla we find a small boy to lead us into the fascinating and now almost abandoned medina, a warren of tiny rooms and alleys with beautifully carved lintels, treacherous stairways and broken roofs. Soon an older man drives the boy away despite our protest and takes us to the madrasa where a young plasterer interrupts his work to lead us around for a good forty minutes. The plasterer is justifiably proud of his city and its history and finally, as a professional, hurries off to avoid a gratuity.

After asking directions several times, we reach the pottery factory where I buy a couple odd-shaped Dakhla pots, including an oblong water jug for comfortable under arm carriage. On a pond at the town's edge we see black-winged stilts, little grebes, and many moorhens.

At lonely Mozawaka, off track in the desert, there are three hundred second-century Roman tombs. But all are locked to protect their frescos, just as Omar at the tourist office warned. The friendly guard has no key but takes us to see a jumble of broken mummies, including one sad figure with red hair. Rather than stay for tea as he implores, we apologize by giving him baksheesh and a handful of dates. This is only a reconnaissance trip, we console ourselves as we drive away. We will return some day, we hope.

Deir el Hagar, the Monastery of the Stone, also closed due to Canadian archaeological work, is not so friendly. The Egyptian archaeologist we met at Qila el Dabba yesterday advised us to give the guard a few pounds and he would let us in. But this does not work. Obviously, the guard has been warned of dire Canadian retribution. We point out that we have driven across the desert to reach this jungle of broken Roman temple walls but the guard warns us off, and we compromise by parking nearby for lunch. The guard watches us sourly from a windswept hilltop.

The next objective is Amheida which Omar has advised us to skip as "you need an expert to understand it." But Amheida is a major, if incomprehensible, site on five kilometers of desert, and there are no guards there to drive us away. Ptolemaic, ruined, unexcavated for the most part, Amheida is indeed a mystery. Still, we enjoy shuffling through the mounds of potsherds and gawping at the great walls. How large is it? "Big." How long ago was it abandoned? "From a time." This is all we understand. But it is enough for now and, despite the fierce wind, for the first time today we feel peace in the bright sunlight.

Driving through Mushiya and Gedida villages, we do not stop. Life there is fascinating for its distance from our experience, and the oases interest us for both ancient remains and modern culture, although the contrast between the sophisticated past, at least for some, and the primitive present is perplexing. There are few tourists in the far oases, but yesterday we saw an enormous German "rolling hotel" at Kharga and today found that it has followed us to Dakhla. Behind the tourist coach is a bunkhouse of three tiers, each bunk with a tiny window. No wonder local people often think "the foreigners are mad."

But strangers are still rare enough for even adults to wave and shout a greeting. However, the salutations today are aggressive, and we sense they could turn ugly if we run over any of the myriad chickens and ducks—to say nothing of children—that fill the narrow alleys.

The loop ends at the "Fish Pond," a man-made lake some three or four kilometers from Mut. Here we discover some of the best birding we have had in Egypt, including white tailed plovers, rare in the Middle East outside Iraq, and red necked phalaropes in great flocks. Alan, however, is still determined to find Kellis.

Eventually we do, driving on a cross-desert track on which we miss the sign that says in English, "This site is closed." An irate guard with a shotgun rushes up to ask how we can have done so. "The Canadians are working" he says fiercely, but we have come thus far and are not to be put off. We pass the guard and his dogs and drive up to the dig house just as the archaeologists are leaving to go into Mut for their nightly bath in the hot springs. A young Norwegian we last saw in Cairo two years ago greets us, but the dig leader is not pleased. He does not introduce himself, just repeats angrily that the site is closed.

The desert, it seems, has been rented out to foreign scholars whose professional futures depend on fending off the tourists during the all too brief winter digging season. This we understand. I give the Norwegian his promised chocolates, and we leave by the "proper" route. No Egyptian would be so rude, we decide, and self-righteously restrain from hurrying on to the rest house, renting the entire place, and declaring the hot springs closed when the archaeologists arrive.

Back in Mut we visit the Ethnographic Museum by torchlight as the electricity is off. The museum is only of modest interest to anyone at all familiar with primitive farming and rural Egyptian life, though I suppose a dress enthusiast would find something to please. Modern women of Dakhla no longer adorn themselves in traditional dress, though all wear ankle length skirts and head covering. Searching for film, we tour the nighttime streets where many shops are open but most empty of customers.

After chicken dinner at the Mebarex, the Professor and the Policeman, whose name is Aldo, waved us over to their table and opened a bottle of fortified Verona wine they had originally planned to drink on St. Aldo's feast day. An hour and a half later we have finished two bottles of wine, the Diplomat is speaking fairly fluent Italian, and the Professor and Policeman are telling us about their troublesome wives.

We part with invitations for them to see us in Cairo next trip and for us to visit them in Verona, where the Policeman promises us tickets to the opera—he sings a few notes—even if all are sold out. A lovely old couple, grown round from pasta, wine, and travel, we say to ourselves as we stagger off to bed.

30

On to Baharia

8 January 1993

Today is Friday and trucks, quiet all night, do not awaken us before dawn as they did yesterday. Breakfasting at eight, we greet a lone Japanese traveler, a woman we have been watching for several days as her touring overlapped with ours. Only with great difficulty can I make her understand my question concerning when she plans to go on to Farafra. We cannot understand how she manages to travel alone with elementary English and no Arabic.

"He speak little English," comments the waiter with a superior air. His condescending manner illustrates the common Egyptian error that knowledge of English places the speaker closer to civilization and sophistication. There is no room here for interest in the cultures or histories of the East or even perhaps of those of Spain and Italy. "Good Golly, Queen Victoria, what *have* you done?"

We leave the hotel at 9 a.m. and, before heading north, visit the ruins of Mut Khorab. A young woman, an Egyptian, stops to observe us, and I ask her if she is "okay," kwayisa. She does not understand so I try asking if she is "content," mabsouta.

"Yes," she says, then asks what that means.

Well, is she "happy," saida?

Oh, yes, and I may take her picture. Alan wonders if in Dakhla mabsouta means "beaten," as it does in Iraq. But the woman looks rather tough to me and well able to stand up to any normal-sized husband. She and I grin at one another.

On then to the desert road towards Farafra Oasis with our day's target Baharia Oasis. We avert our gaze from the tempting "Fish

Pond" with its wonderful birds where we would willingly spend the morning if time would allow. The frequent qubbas, tombs of sheikhs, indicate that this is Sufi country. Yesterday at Qasr Dakhla we found a niche full of freshly burned paper in a sheikh's tomb, and those we questioned would say only that this "belongs to the sheikh." Today at a taftish we see a terracotta stele depicting a demon in the guise of a Turkish officer with fez, another indication of traditional, unorthodox religious practice. I long to know what Sufis believe here and if the Sanusiyya, and its ties to Libya, still survives in the desert oases.

Beyond the town of Dakhla, herds of goats and a few "kine of the lean years" are being driven across the desert to some place of sparse grazing. Local women appear as hitchhikers, certainly a lifting of taboo brought on by necessity. But as we no longer have room for people in the back of the car, we do not offer a lift to a middle-aged woman who importunes us as we flash by. Was she desperate to reach a sick daughter, and would she have gotten out at the next village, I ask myself. Have I no compassion for people in need? We find the next village only five kilometers later and then enter 200 kilometers of flat, empty desert.

The checkpoints today are less friendly, more inquisitive, and slower—as well as simply more. Once, very unusually, there were three checkpoints in the space of two kilometers. At the checkpoint in Abu Minqar, we are 100 kilometers from Libya, the closest our road gets to that country. A slack-jawed soldier asks if we are Germans, takes our residence permits and car registration papers, ask again about our nationalities, and then has no pen to write down the details. His colleague suggests we may have one. No, we say sourly, recognizing a ploy. After more delay, the soldiers produce a pen while I am offering a tangerine to a staring child. The boy accepts without a word, peels the fruit, and eats, never taking his eyes off us.

Past the taftish, we soon cross the escarpment into Farafra oasis and immediately are in a region of mining and efforts to promote farming. The desert is a mess here, filled with ruffled mounds and new ditches, but people are few and the settlements far between. The area was clearly better watered naturally than Dakhla even before the present use of fossil water. In this area small oases with interesting names are encroached on by stark new shantytowns, which do not seem to have put their roots deeply into the desert.

Farafra city appears sooner than expected and holds little of interest. Hajjis have stenciled camels, cars and airplanes on their house walls as in Dakhla, a neater mode of expression, though perhaps less artistic, than the usual flamboyant paintings in the rest of Egypt. At the new and only petrol station in Farafra, where gas must be pumped manually, the attendants attempt to overcharge us. We are rich, of course, compared to these people. But they are well versed in the ways of manipulation and exploitation. Did they learn this from the desert, from contact with careless foreigners, or simply from human nature? I feed week-old quiche to two kittens while Alan settles the disagreement and, winning, tips the attendants generously for their work at the pump. Fair is fair and everyone is happy.

We lunch in the White Desert, a fairy tale area of white calciferous stones, sculpted into fantastic shapes by wind, time and sand. The road is good from Qasr Dakhla to the Farafra Oasis and on into Baharia. But Baharia, being in the Giza governorate, is starved of funds in favor of more impressive business nearer Cairo. We recall that last month a road was built overnight near the Giza pyramids, thrown together to accommodate a single visit by President Mubarak to a new archaeological excavation. Then for almost two hours we jolt forward on the worst road thus far encountered during this trip.

Twice more we reject would be passengers, the first a soldier and the second a schoolboy who wants a lift on the last fifty kilometers into Baharia. But we are in bad humor caused by the very rough road, little better than a track, which runs the last 100 kilometers or so into Bawiti, the oasis capital. Besides, we tell ourselves self-righteously, the boy and an older man had used an improvised taftish to stop us. Surely that is against the law! And, anyway, we ask ourselves even more unreasonably, why don't people organize their lives to use the bus?

When eventually we check into the Hotel Alpenblick in Baharia, the manager tells us the road to Farafra is ziffer, a rude play on words greeted with much laughter by his friends. We agreed, of course. But first we had to alert the manager to our presence by asking him to turn down his extremely loud music and interrupting his conversation with two German girls seated with him around an open fire in the courtyard. We have arrived back in touristville where the Hotel Alpenblick offers "parties and fetes with local flair."

The joint owners of the hotel turn out to be a young man from Cairo who has built the hotel in partnership with an oasis sheikh. Gazelle are no longer plentiful in Baharia, the younger partner tells us, blaming this on hunting parties of Saudis whose exploits were forbidden by the Egyptian government three years ago. On his desk sits a forlorn gazelle skull.

At supper, which features chicken, the cook who doubles as a bellhop, comes out of the kitchen three times to feel Alan's biceps. It is not clear if this is intended to remind us of the virtues of his cooking or of the effort he expended carrying our bag of books. A most irritating Egyptian mannerism, we mutter to one another, is the propensity to make a production of everything. We complain to ourselves as well about intrusive hotel staff that, for example, linger overlong in flourishes of table laying that interrupt conversations, prevent eating, and are intended to underscore the solicitude of the waiter. This frequently occurs amidst loud talking, nose blowing, and other efforts to help the customer remember that the server is present, and inshallah available and worthy of a grand tip.

A German couple and a Dutch couple eat supper with us in an icy room beneath a loud buzzing fluorescent light. We share with them a roll of toilet paper placed on the table as a bit of local flair in lieu of table napkins. We are a dour company until later, around the campfire, we break out the sherry, warm everyone up, and turn the discussion to terrorism against tourists.

The next morning we discover that all archaeological sites in Baharia are "closed." So we drive off-track to Bir Matar, site of a small reservoir and a former British airfield and then go on to Bir Ghaba, a well-known site for tourists in quest of hot springs. Irritating swarms of children shout as we pass and rush into the road so that we find it impossible to get out at the springs. Before noon we are back on the main highway heading towards Cairo.

As with the road into Farafra, the road out of Baharia is carried over the escarpment on a sand bridge. Lifeless and flat, this road to

Gaza is, nonetheless, well paved. We pass the "rolling" hotel whose passengers, after peeing on the sand, are collecting desert rocks.

Back in Cairo, we learn there have been two more attacks on tourists: Japanese in Dairut and Germans at Giza where a small explosive device was thrown between two buses. Egyptian authorities claim that the Dairut incident was the result of tourists caught in crossfire between police and extremists. But, alhamdulillah, we are told, no one was injured in either incident.

31

A Gift at Dimeh

10 February 1993

You can reach Dimeh of the Wolves by driving over the escarpment from the Baharia road, by boat across the Birket Qarun, or by four-wheel drive over the dry lakebed. The lake, now much shrunk from its size during the classical age, abuts a desert of ruts and sand traps and, amateurishly, we chose this approach without an accompanying vehicle. Later, trapped in deep sand, it seemed we would have to pay for our foolishness by spending the night in the desert unprepared and with no means of calling in rescue.

Remembering how cold the desert becomes after nightfall, we put rag rugs meant to cushion sleeping bags under the car wheels and managed to extricate the Range Rover. We pushed on, then, until Dimeh stood stark on the skyline like a row of bad teeth. Dimeh es Siba, known to the ancients as Soknopaiou Nesos, may once have been an island. Occupied in Neolithic times, the site was later a major port and starting point for caravans to the coast carrying goods bound for Rome. Then, sometime in the third century A.D., after six hundred years of life, Dimeh was abandoned to the wolves.

Long before we arrived, the magic in those crooked mud brick walls pulled us forward so that our stop at Qasr el Sagha, a Middle Kingdom temple, was brief. The warm yellows and browns of the Fayoum's internal desert nearly conceals Qasr el Sagha until the traveler is almost upon it, snuggled on a low hill behind which are broken rock walls filled with the caves of long-dead hermits. Qasr el Sagha's walls are made of rock strangely cut in irregular angles, which fit together like a jigsaw puzzle. We clambered to the top for a splendid panoramic view of the surrounding desert. No people, no animals, no trees, no other vehicles, only desert.

Then on again towards Dimeh. Splashes of blue paint on rocks, placed there for modern drivers in the Pharaoh's Desert Rally, guided our approach between areas of impossibly soft sand. Finally the road climbed an incline and ended beneath the ten-meter high walls of the temple area.

Silence grips Dimeh and reverberates within us as we walk, hushed, among the sand saturated ruins. Centuries of pillage by passing Bedouin had left little for the archaeologists who arrived in the 1930s. But chunks of blue faience, millions of scattered potsherds, and occasional coins and fishhooks may still be discovered in the drifting sand. We ate our sparse lunch quickly in a sheltered alcove watched over by the great leaning walls.

Outside the temple area is a spacious house whose intact underground chambers are half filled with sand. The intruder stoops to enter, humbling himself before the abode of the ancients. The inevitable question arises: Where are the people? Here are their works, their storage vaults and sleeping quarters, their places of worship, fragments of the vessels in which they kept the oil and wine that gladdened their hearts. But where are they? On a nearby hill we found one straggler.

I knelt to examine the grave wrappings and scattered bones. Someone else had recently done the same, yielding first to the impulse to dig and then recoiling, as I did, when a lock of black hair fluttered between my fingers. Apologetically, I covered the hair as that other explorer had done and added a few more protective potsherds on top. Likely, as this was a Roman cemetery, the bodies were heat-dried, not mummified according to the ancient religion. And certainly, they had long since been stripped of all items that might be considered valuable.

But the site had assumed a new significance, and I stepped carefully, alert to the presence of dead people beneath my feet. Human bones, scattered by man and jackal, protruded from the sand. On the next mound of sand the sense of human presence grew stronger. I shut my eyes but opened them immediately as giddiness overcame me. Something, someone, was there still, and I would gladly have known who.

Searching, hoping, waiting, I wandered in circles until an unusual object stopped me. Nudged by my foot, a small wooden bowl popped out of the sand. The bowl was beautifully shaped, incised with a circular band and, curiously, had a small wooden plug in the bottom. I received this gift with gratitude and passed on, stopping to examine potshards and bones, one of them the heavy jawbone of a tusked mammal, which could only, I thought, have been a pig.

It was mid-afternoon when we left Dimeh and set out to return to the world of the living. The towel-wrapped bowl, key to a past that could never be fully known, rode securely under a car seat. After Dimeh, the Auberge du Lac seemed a shocking place of confusion and sensory overload. A five-man band announced our arrival with drums and rasping fiddles. Photographs of Omar Sharif lined the entrance hall. The sense of isolation and of adventure had departed.

Although the solidly constructed Auberge, once King Farouk's hunting lodge, is still beautiful and now bills itself as a five-star hotel, its water-stained carpets were filthy, and in our room we were greeted with wilted flowers and a foul odor from the small refrigerator. Later in the bar, forty fans cheered as Zamalek scored a goal against Ahli. And in the dining room a sign announced that here Winston Churchill had hosted a banquet for King Farouk.

Dimeh, too, must once have been an odorous place, its lakeshore, as here, filled with floating debris. Once the rich and powerful loitered in the temple courtyards and along the Avenue of the Lions, as they do now in the sumptuous lounge of the Auberge. But, with the retreat of man, builder and destroyer, the desert has reclaimed and cleansed Dimeh. Although this Ptolemaic city is perhaps less than ten kilometers across the lake from the Auberge, most of the visitors to the modern hotel have never heard of Dimeh and would probably have no desire to go there even if they had. What has brought so many of us to a state of disinterest in the history of humanity?

The Auberge is where the action is today. Nonetheless, across the road, as night falls, men load eight weary and still saddled horses haphazardly into an open truck. So I could be wrong, I tell myself. Perhaps some modern Egyptians still do seek solitude on the road to Dimeh.

Back in Cairo, I show the wooden vessel to an American archaeologist. "Coptic," he says definitively. "Yes, absolutely. I'd say tenth or eleventh century. And monastic. They served up small portions of meat to the monks, you know, and this hole was for letting out the gravy."

The archaeologist swigged his G and T and looked serious. I retrieved my gift from the dead monk with the black hair and changed the subject. It's hard to argue with an expert, but whoever heard of a hungry monk letting his precious gravy run out a hole in the bottom of his eating bowl? Moreover, last year at a Buddhist temple in Gansu, interior China, I had purchased a similar vessel with a hole in the bottom, a monk's begging bowl. But Dimeh itself, once on the caravan route to everywhere, remains an enigma.

Relaxing at Dimeh of the Wolves, north of Fayoum, February 1993

32

Port Call with the Honorary Consul

11–13 February 1993

There is an element of violence about Port Said that is not quite possible to quantify. An aspect of terror even, which sits quietly and with folded wings but clearly waiting, waiting. What this terror awaits is difficult to say unless it be opportunity. When that comes, much now hidden will be revealed.

On the road into Port Said, after the customs barrier that serves as a frontier to the duty-free zone, came our first impression of Port Said. A man stood in the road savagely beating his harnessed donkey with a heavy pole. The little animal's legs quivered, and his eyes rolled in mute agony as the pole lashed down again and again on his head and neck. Alan braked the Range Rover as I shouted from the window, "Oh stop! Oh stop! This is not permitted. Are you mad?"

The farmer held back his arm and we drove on, not daring to look back. But it was a scene of violence repeated later in the day when we came upon eight young men in a heavy cart racing an old horse down a main street, lashing its skinny frame as it ran, ears flat back in terror, through the traffic.

Our host, the Honorary Consul, awaited us in the lobby of the Helnan Port Said when we arrived at noon after a three-hour drive from Cairo. He plied us with cups of sticky coffee during a briefing on what he had arranged and what he thought should be discussed: more fiscal aid, a gift of books, commercial concessions, and the possibility of a visit by the Ambassador. Is there nothing the British should ask for, I queried naively, for it was apparent that in all these ventures the Honorary Consul had business interests.

"You are in my area," the Honorary Consul replied aggressively. "I have been in this position for ten years." Then we set off to call on the Governor who, by contrast, appeared a moderate man, reserved, exuding the confidence of one who feels the responsibility of power.

"No," he said mildly in answer to our questions about security. "There is no danger to foreigners here. The recent shooting of a Russian tourist was merely the result of a price dispute. These things happen, of course." Nonetheless, he had provided an armed escort for us during our visit.

"Just to be on the safe side," said the Honorary Consul. We smiled and nodded as a television crew captured presentation of the obligatory plaque. The Honorary Consul made certain that the reporter interviewed him alone, smiling and reciting fine words about British-Egyptian friendship and his own valuable role therein.

The rest of the afternoon was devoted to meetings with a bank manager and the director of the Port Said industrial zone. Smiling broadly and with thick smudges of coffee in the corners of his heavy lips, the Honorary Consul escorted us grandly, taking us at length to "the finest restaurant in town."

The enormous meal pleased the Honorary Consul and, relaxing, he confided in us that his teenage daughter, light of his eyes, had demanded a car of her own even though she was not yet old enough to drive. As he could deny her nothing, he had paid 50,000 LE for a new Mercedes and was counting on his contacts in the local police to get her out of trouble should it arise.

"You will meet me at 7:00 for another interview I have arranged," he said, leaving us at the hotel. "Then there is a speech on heart surgery and a following dinner at 8:00 with the Rotary Club."

By the next morning we had decided to push back. We'd had enough of the Honorary Consul's city, or at least that portion he chose to reveal, and when day came, left a note and gave the Governor's guards the slip. For a few hours we tasted freedom, driving through wasteland to Damietta and, off-road, searching for birds. But although the area is coastal marshland, there were few birds except migrating starlings, spur-wing plovers, one or two redshanks, and a few overlying cormorants. The complete absence of ducks and even waders was explained by the many shooting hides, some within gunshot of the next. The area had been overhunted and apparently few birds come here now. Seeing our binoculars, a man stopped his truck to ask suspiciously what we wanted and where we were going.

Back at the hotel lobby at 12:30 as ordered by the Honorary Consul, we discovered that the lunch cruise he had arranged did not leave until 2:30. Time then to do a bit of shopping, but only after a few wounded questions as to how, on the Honorary Consul's turf, we could possibly have considered it appropriate to arrange our own program and even to spurn the escort?

When the overloaded boat finally sailed at 3:30 we knew there would be no time that day to visit Port Fuad, visible across the Canal. Nor was the Governor on board as the Honorary Consul had promised. However, we had not expected him because the Governor had told us the day before that he spends every weekend in Cairo with his family.

On board, our host introduced us to our fellow guests, a retired Canal pilot and his wife, and then lapsed into unusual silence while feeding himself on grilled lamb before ordering for us another impossibly large quantity of shrimp, curried rice, fish and calamari such as we had eaten the day before.

"I cannot eat too much fish," the Honorary Consul proclaimed, digging in.

The pilot gave us a detailed description of how local companies defraud passing ships with counterfeit invoices for services rendered. His wife said little except to lament that "there is nothing to do in Port Said" because there are "only two good restaurants" and, besides, her family lives in Cairo. However, conversation in the lower-deck dining room was soon ruled out by a keyboard synthesizer connected to several loudspeakers. Somehow amidst the noise the Honorary Consul, who seemed to know everyone, managed to chat up the waitresses as the shoreline moved by replete with new buildings and the hulks of scrapped ships. Over our protests, he ordered desert for everyone and then told us to meet him at 8:00 for dinner in "the Italian restaurant."

He was angry when we declined, politely at first, but then more firmly as his persistence grew. But we had seen little of his troubled city, evacuated in the late 1960s during "the war of attrition" and revived when the Canal reopened in 1975. The evening would need to be spent wandering in search of the real Port Said. Although we did not spell this out to him, certainly the Honorary Consul suspected what we were up to and was greatly opposed.

The pre-Ramadan night markets of Port Said reminded me of China with every imaginable commodity on sale and food stalls around every corner. Once grand and now crumbling French colonial buildings with wooden balconies fill the downtown area, and the milling multitudes jostled us along. More men were bearded than in Cairo, and most of the Egyptian women were in Islamic dress although few wore veils. We remembered the Honorary Consul's cryptic remark that an unfinished school and an unfinished mosque we noticed had been left that way "for government reasons."

Down by the resplendent Suez Canal Authority building blue-eyed Egyptians in fedoras mingled with Asians and Eastern Europeans drawn by duty free bargains and goods not available elsewhere in Egypt. While I was examining dry goods on a street stall, a man offered to sell us a pistol, cupping an illustrated card carefully and looking over his shoulder lest the police take notice.

Ataf, a young devotee at the Italian Catholic Church of St. Eugenia offered to help us find the Anglican church, consecrated in 1889 and now closed as much for lack of congregation as for lack of clergy. He extinguished the candles in St. Eugenia, locked up, and led us forth. Before 1952, Port Said's population was at least 60 percent European, and among the buildings they left, the churches are surely the most interesting.

Two black-clad young soldiers asked our business at the small Anglican church. But though they allowed us into the tiny compound, the church itself was locked, and Atef could not find the man who holds the key. We wandered on past Greek Catholic, Greek Orthodox, Coptic, and French Catholic places of worship, all under guard.

Most, save for the Coptic properties, were in advanced disrepair judging from outside appearances, but kept alive by small congregations. If this were Israel, we mused, these buildings would probably long since have been converted into museums, art galleries, or civic halls, as has happened to the mosques in northern Israel. But this was Egypt, land of forbearance, waste, and waiting.

We retired at length to the Helnan Port Said, where the barman served us no-beer he claimed was Stella Export at 9 LE the bottle. But the bottles were old, uncapped before arrival at our table, and undrinkable. So we ate the peanuts and asked the barman to give us some warm Stella from behind the bar. Afterwards, feeling a bit repentant, we looked up the Honorary Consul who was, as every evening, drinking coffee with his friends in the lobby. Again we apologized that we could not face one more meal that day.

"No one has ever won over me like this," he said, eyes glittering. And then, addressing himself to me: "Madam has won." We shook hands and told him we looked forward to seeing him in Cairo. It was a lie, of course, and we all knew it. Nonetheless, except for our unexpected resistance to manipulation, the visit had gone well from his viewpoint. Yet he remained displeased, as were the security escorts when we told them the next morning that we would visit the museums before leaving town.

The Museum of History was empty of visitors, and we anticipated a leisurely hour browsing through the museum's excellent overview of Egyptian history, poorly labeled but carefully divided into periods. Instead, a young woman attendant was summoned by the police to "explain" the exhibits to us. This she did in loud rapid fire Arabic, which even Alan found difficult to follow. Eight of us marched around together with the police escort eager to move us on and determined to avoid being given the slip once again.

The Museum of Military History is a sad place and took even less time, although here at last we came face-to-face with Port Said's violent past. However, as the museum has only one entrance, we were allowed to wander at will past artillery pieces and war debris in the gardens and inside among vainglorious paintings with misspelled English captions. In these, Nasser and Sadat emerged as heroes, and Mubarak, their chief adviser, despite having been a virtual unknown for most of the period under consideration. Major displays centered on the personal effects of captured British "spies," including a can of denture stain remover. A large oil painting depicted the kidnapping by patriots of a young British intelligence officer in 1956, followed by a display of the dangerous contents of his pockets such as his pipe.

Finally we left the museum, thanked our escort, and headed back towards Cairo, a police car behind and a truckload of soldiers before. Sirens wailed as we crossed the customs barrier, passing the marshlands where we'd hoped to do some gentle birding and flashing by the turnoff where we had intended to search for an ancient site. Not until we were nearly 100 kilometers from Fort Said did the last escort peel off at a military base. We were left feeling that we had been run out of town on a rail.

The rest of the journey back to Cairo was used to plan how someday we would sneak back into Port Said and explore the markets, churches, French colonial hotels, and crowded streets. Then, we told ourselves, we'll be able to talk to "real people."

The Honorary Consul was so peeved that he failed to show up as promised at a Cairo reception given by the British Consul two days later. Still, perhaps, it was he who won for who knows whether or not we saw what he and the Governor did not want us to see? Or if seeing, we failed to recognize? One discovery does stand out: Nowhere in Egypt, save the Fayoum, have I seen so many shotguns as in Port Said governorate, the smallest governorate in Egypt.

33

Consultation in Zagazig

18 February 1993

At the right turn towards Ismailia by the airport, I considered asking Adel to stop the car so I could take a taxi home, feigning sudden illness. Only seriously stretched loyalty to the Diplomat prevented my escape. He, after all, was stuck in the back seat next to the Consultant, whose metallic voice filled the car. Today the sweepstakes for "Greatest Bullshitter of All Time" had ended. The winner was in a class of his own—and in our car.

The Consultant did not speak, he shouted. He interrupted. He boasted. He never stopped talking. Conversation was impossible for no one else was allowed more than half a sentence before interruption. A formidable clattering laugh like flat stones striking together ricocheted through the car and even Adel appeared stunned, hunching his shoulders and resolutely gripping the steering wheel.

"Actually," the Consultant shouted, "We know, in fact, that at the end of the day it's performance that counts. As I say, this is our way." He then launched into a detailed recital of all the organizations on whose boards he sits or to which he serves as consultant from his twin bases at the Zagazig University Centre for Environmental Development and his own company, Environmental Quality International.

The Diplomat pointed out a brick factory spewing filth into the countryside, but the Consultant brushed aside the observation. What is one factory when there should be many? That reminded him of a favorite theme: one day the entire desert between Cairo and Zagazig would be developed and "filled with industry and apartment buildings." Adel swerved to miss a truck whose driver had parked in the middle of the highway and the Consultant warmed to his idyllic vision.

"Zagazig will be part of Cairo," he thundered. "The way to keep people at home and out of Cairo is to improve their sociosphere." I suggested they might want help to do that for themselves, but he wasn't listening. "For every problem there is a solution," he cried. "As I say, at the end of the day it is performance that counts." Three trucks entered the highway simultaneously from our right, and Adel stood on the brake, swerved, and then accelerated hard, determined to reach our destination before we all went mad.

At last, crossing a branch of the Ismailia Canal, we entered Zagazig, a backwater until a few years ago and now one of Egypt's fastest growing urban villages. Zagazig University, started in 1974 by the Consultant's father, "with permission from President Sadat, who was his great friend," dominates the city.

"A city in a university, not a university in a city," bellowed our host. "We have 100,000 students, including those at the branch in Benha. But I will be honest with you. The government is not allowing new universities these days. There must be some control." What percentage of the graduates find employment, we wondered.

"That's what we at the Institute of Productive Efficiency want to find out," the Consultant shouted cheerfully and then took the opportunity to describe for us the numerous financial grants from which he benefits. Recently he'd become part of a project to retrain unemployed university graduates, but first there had to be research. There was, it seemed, nothing we could ask about for which he was not a consultant or for which he didn't have a student researching.

Guards waved us through the university gate onto a campus thronged with strolling students, among whom almost all the women were veiled. We got out at the administration building and followed the Consultant into the Vice-President's office.

"Acting President now!" the Consultant shouted as we were introduced. A large man in a suit several sizes too small motioned us to sit with him in overstuffed chairs. A man with grimy hands served tea in dirty cups, and we were examined from afar by several unsmiling men who sat or walked about the large office. Unemployment seemed rampant here. The Consultant took over the conversation, including answering the questions the Diplomat addressed to the Vice-President.

No, there is no religious extremism problem at the university. Most students come from villages and are "not aggressive like in Cairo." In fact, they know how to obey "the Big Man." Also, "Because they are used to the ways of the village, in the university there isn't much political involvement."

"We make a good control," the Vice-President managed to interject. Then the Consultant allowed as how the administration rigs student elections "for their own good," adding proudly that "the Islamic groups are stronger in the villages than in the university."

An hour later, in the downtown office of the Governor of Sharqia Province, we learned that all problems of religious extremism in Egypt are due to outside influences, and all problems in the governorate are caused by troublemakers from outside Sharqia, especially riffraff from Cairo.

"There are bombs every day in London," the Governor told us sternly and changed the subject. Still, his concerns were many: 100,000 unemployed, massive pollution down to seventy meters in the subsoil as a result of waste water from Cairo, the recent arrival of the Asiatic palm weevil. He showed us a letter from the Institute of Entomology in London confirming the identity of this villainous immigrant and hoped the Diplomat might find means to help. But the Consultant could no longer tolerate not being the center of attention.

"I want to announce to your Excellency today," he told the Governor, "that we have selected Sharqia as a pilot project. We have decided to build for you a model environmental affairs office financed by the World Bank. We will do the research on environmental pollution, and at the end of the day we will know what will be done. We will begin in April." Then he settled back to receive applause from the Governor, his secretary, and the group of eight or ten petitioners waiting to lobby the Governor when our turn was up.

But the Governor was not so easily deflected. "Will you begin on April 1?" he asked smoothly.

"By God, we put our trust in Your Excellency," cried the Consultant, unmoved. "I want to say to you that this is one of the main reasons that we put our confidence in you, Excellency. At the end of the day we rely on you as we, in fact, manage the biosphere and the sociosphere." He signaled to the Secretary, who brought the Governor's engagement book and set up an appointment for the coming week. The Governor arose, and it was time to go.

"We shall speak another time," he said quietly to the Diplomat, "when there is opportunity to talk." The Consultant, who was grandly greeting the supplicants, did not seem to hear.

Leaving Zagazig, Adel drove for an hour through desert and then fields of alfalfa and orange groves to reach the Consultant's farm, "deep in the desert" as promised. Before arrival we caught glimpses of Ten October City, the abode of poor desert dwellers. By contrast, the Consultant's country house was lovely and its surroundings verdant and well watered. We were shown into a villa of modest size where four or five small servant girls, one no more than seven, hurried to supply us with fresh orange juice.

"We take them from their families and bring them up here," the Consultant declared. "Thus they raise their social condition, and when they are twenty-two, we find husbands for them. This is our duty. As I say, it is performance which counts, and you will hear this from my father, holder of the family's parliamentary seat, who will meet us for lunch." With this thought, his face darkened.

"But let me be honest. With all due respect, my father is seventy-two, and I believe he will soon decide to let me have my turn. This is our duty. The eldest son must take the office, or our family position will suffer." This was his cue to embark on a recital of the family's political views, charitable involvements, and monetary successes, a monologue that continued as we strolled down a sandy road between fields and orange groves. The day was lovely and, other than noise pollution, so was the walk.

"This was all desert in 1974. We paid five Egyptian pounds a feddan. Now it is all profit." We passed two women seated beside the path with a large duck in a basket. They lowered their eyes respectfully, and the Consultant did not greet them until after I did.

The Consultant's mother, who had cooked the excellent meal, did not eat with us in the ornate living room where we sat in gold-laminated chairs and ate off our knees. Not until we had finished did the Member of Parliament arrive with his daughter, second son, and various other family members and retainers. As the great man ate inside, we sat on the patio in fading sunlight and listened to the Consultant describe the relationship between his family and "our villagers."

"People don't want to participate in political parties," he said. "If we meet the needs of the people, they will leave politics to us. That is our philosophy for, as I say, it is performance that counts at the end of the day."

Later, when the Member of Parliament, joined us, he confirmed this viewpoint, though it was immediately clear that he had no intention of yielding his parliamentary seat any time soon. A sensible man, he had spent many years teaching in the Sudan before founding his university in Egypt. But it was impossible to explore his views as the Consultant dominated the conversation, feeding his father phrases and changing the subject when the whim took him.

The Consultant's small daughter played in the garden with the servant girls, and our conversation turned to modern life and the changes it brought. I was intrigued by the way the family referred to other Egyptians as "they."

"I am on the committee for Miss Africa," the Consultant told us, still searching for approval. The Diplomat asked how this fitted in with economic and environmental issues. But I was wondering what would happen if the servant girls quarreled with the youngest member of The Family.

34

Alifa Rifaat's Vision

14 March 1993

Is Egypt being destroyed by those who claim to know the will of God for the affairs of mankind? The Pasha fears it is so. Before the iftar, he paced nervously, continuing the denunciation of the Islamists that he'd begun as soon as he opened the door of his Zamalek flat. Outside, the fading light of late afternoon enhanced a panoramic view of the Nile. All this—and so much more—he has to lose.

"The newly rich," he said in American English, "if I may say so without sounding like a snob, don't know how to live. The gap has widened between social classes, and the poor now rebel against the conspicuous consumption and power abuse of the new class of entrepreneurs. For them it's a world in which the elder brother slaps the younger, the father slaps the son, the employer slaps the father. They don't know how to live, and they share a big part of the responsibility for what is happening to us all."

Over the past ten years, Egyptian society has witnessed a steady increase in all types of violence, a prominent Egyptian sociologist wrote recently. "The result of the erosion of moral, social, and political authority is that young people have sought solutions in religious extremism, confrontation, and crime."[1]

Recent acts of violence have shaken Egypt's soul: the attacks on law enforcement officers, the police raids on a mosque in Aswan and homes in Imbaba, the day earlier this week when sixteen "terrorists," three soldiers, and a mother and child died in security operations in four governorates. But, said the Pasha, the February 26 bombing of a crowded cafe in Cairo's Tahrir Square, in which four of the six dead were tourists, was the most terrifying development of all.

"You remember the Ayatollah?" the Pasha asked. "Khomeini was nobody, an unknown living in exile in France until the press made him into Superman. Naturally, seeing how the Westerners feared him, the Iranians welcomed him as their leader. Now the same is happening in America with Omar Abdul Rahman. It doesn't matter whether or not he actually had anything to do with the bombing of New York's World Trade Center. The people of Shubra, Imbaba, and upper Egypt see him as a hero who fights in the name of God against those who oppress the poor."

Darkness fell and nine of us gathered around the iftar table, breaking the fast with bowls of thick chicken soup and kerkadeh juice followed by meats, rice, and vegetables cooked with cheese. It was a joyful feast, a celebration of faith as well as physical and spiritual endurance, to be shared with family and friends. The Pasha and his teenage son bantered about the rebelliousness of youth while passing pasta to one another.

Conversations were intermittent as those deprived since dawn of food and drink tucked into the heavy meal. People ate quickly, getting up to help themselves to seconds and returning to their seats to consume with gusto. At length we handed the plates over our neighbors' heads and started on the mounds of fruit and sticky sweets carried in by the suffragi. Conversation turned from one guest's recent minor pilgrimage to the subject on all our minds.

"It isn't just the Western media," someone said. "It's Iran, and Sudan, and even the Saudis who fund Egyptian extremists. They're all to blame. And, of course, Americans and Europeans now seize the opportunity to claim an international Islamic conspiracy."

"Maybe that guy the Americans arrested for bombing the World Trade Center was really hired by Mossad," someone suggested. "But that hardly matters now. The Zionists will benefit, and we Egyptians are seen throughout the world as Islamic terrorists."

We sighed collectively and retired to the sitting room for cups of thick Turkish coffee, mint tea, and the traditional Ramadan mixture of dried fruits and nuts. The room was beautifully furnished in a style the Pasha described as "conservative Arabesque." A table displayed the decorations awarded by King Farouk to the Pasha's Turkish grandfather. I chose a chair from which I could watch the lights along the river.

Terror did not begin with last year's attacks on tourists, but those attacks laid bare the fragility of an economy dependent on some three billion dollars a year in tourist revenues. This week, forty-nine of the so called Islamic extremists were brought before a Cairo military tribunal on charges ranging from attacks on tourist buses and a Nile cruiser to conspiracy to overthrow the government. Proclaiming the fugitive Sheikh Omar as their leader, the accused carried banners which declared, "Our objective is to hit tourism and not tourists."

Foreigners do not understand this. Nor do they understand official Egyptian anger when press coverage of violence in Egypt harms tourism. What about bombs on the London underground, Egyptians ask, gang warfare in New York and mob violence in India? The response that such attacks do not specifically target tourists is pushed aside. And although the suggestion that the Islamic preachers call us all to address the plight of the disinherited elicits sympathy, most affluent Egyptians then turn aside into empty words of apathy and self-pity. "We are not our brothers' keepers," they seem to say. "This is the responsibility of God and of government and, besides, we don't know how."

At another recent dinner, I reflected, a senior government official had praised the "iron fist" which would smash the rebellious, those who seek change through violence. In vain a leading political analyst argued that violence only breeds greater resistance and more violence. I remembered the sad smile and shrugged shoulders of Nour, our aging suffragi, when I asked if he had voted in last year's elections—and also the vehemence with which an Egyptian student of political science recently told me, "I am twenty-five and have never voted. It's all rigged. Why bother?"

At the Gezira Club some days later, I laid these conversations before an Egyptian millionaire while his Labrador romped with my street dog.

"But I understand this perfectly," he said. "Power corrupts and there is no way to remove or change those in authority over us. The end, of course, will be in blood. It has happened before; it will happen again. We may have to leave." Thinking of the coming plight of wealthy Egyptians he, too, smiled sadly, although he has at least one non-Egyptian passport and sufficient funds abroad against the evil day.

Is Cairo burning? Not yet. Not yet. But by coincidence this week, I read two books which troubled me further about Egypt's future and one other which gave hope. The first, Brian Keenan's poignant telling of his four and a half years as a captive of Islamic Jihad, described the impotent fury, fear, and failure of young men driven to violence as an answer to political inequality and economic deprivation.[2] The second book, by a Lebanese woman novelist, described the hopeless despair and horror of those whose families, homes, and society were torn apart by such young men. However, for the novelist, pre-1975 Lebanon was "the Golden Age," a time of "unprecedented social and intellectual affluence."[3] I wondered that she had not seen the plight of the Palestinian refugees, the poverty of the Shia villagers, the unresolved hatreds which in 1970 caused a young Druze woman to tell me, when I asked of the Maronites, that "Someday we will have to kill them."

For the most part Egyptians remain unwilling to acknowledge the truth, to accept their responsibility for what is happening here. Someday, when the stench of death has filled our senses, we may describe the Egyptians, too, as victims. But I am held back from absolute pessimism by the stories of Alifa Rifaat, Egyptian author of a third book, *Distant View of a Minaret*.[4] This is a comforting book about women struggling to take charge of their lives. The author has no university education, speaks no foreign languages, and, as a committed and conservative Muslim, would not, her translator assures us, question the right of men to rule over women. But her characters live in a world of immense inner strength, of contempt and rebellion when the behavior of man, the leader, falls short of his mandate. And here, too, is the clear-sighted humor Brian Keenan found so vital to survival and to the overcoming of violence.

Despite the monster that stalks Egypt, I cannot grieve. Not so long as Egyptian women carry such strength and resolve within themselves. When Alifa Rifaat's fictional character Badriyya understood at last, after years of passive faithfulness, that her man had betrayed her, she walked home asking herself "how it would be

possible for her to find the strength not to open the door to him."
Egypt is Badriyya. If there is salvation for her, it lies in swift social action and the sharing of political power to close the doors to violence.

35

Restoring Icons at Abu Seifein in Old Cairo

19 March 1993

The Restorer tosses her short blond hair impatiently. "Use the microscope for working on the face," she says sharply and, one imagines, for the hundredth time. A chastised assistant bows humbly to this task and dares not answer back. The enormous cult icon of St. Mercurius Abu Seifein lies supine on the workshop table, its holiness now masked, the icon itself protected by five centuries of prayer. Two of the Restorer's acolytes daub gently at the icon's grave wounds: the grime of centuries of candle smoke, holes caused by corroding nails, the miscalculations of earlier restorers.

Weeks have passed since St. Mercurius was laid here, and so far work proceeds only on the scenes around the edges of the icon. The saint himself awaits the attention of the master. Wearily she lifts a silk rag and wipes carefully at a corner of the holy picture. The assistants maintain a silence redolent of respect, affection, and fear. God has given them a difficult task and, it must seem to many, an impossible taskmaster.

Deir Abu Seifein, the monastery of the Father of the Two Swords, is surprisingly off the tourist track. Yet, with the exception of St. Catherine's monastery itself, Deir Abu Seifein is said to contain Egypt's most important collection of medieval icons not examined in modern times. Here are pictures whose mysteries are as much secular as religious. Armenian, Russian, Byzantine, Greek, Serbian, even Mongolian influences inspired the artists whose holy pictures are venerated by Egyptian Copts. The skein of history is more puzzling than the difficulties involved in restoration.

Tourist buses bypass Deir Abu Seifein for nearby Mar Girgis, the heart of Coptic Cairo. In this small area are the Coptic Museum, several notable ancient churches, a synagogue that was once a church, and the walls of Babylon, as the ancient city was known before it became Fustat, and later Cairo. The area is ringed with Christian cemeteries and contains the oldest mosque in Africa, that of Ibn Al As, where the first Islamic conqueror stopped to pray and which I often visit for its beauty and prayerful atmosphere. Coming from the Nile, the pilgrim turns right in front of Ibn Al As, avoiding the donkey carts, pot sellers, and children playing football in the street, and proceeds a short distance to Deir Abu Seifein. The street is potholed and obscure, like the monastery it contains.

But the Restorer herself is a hybrid. A polyglot Czech with a Dutch passport, she has stumbled by chance—some say divine intervention—upon one of the last great uncatalogued ancient Christian art collections in the world. Her work is dogged by bureaucratic obstructionism, professional jealousies, indifference, xenophobia, and ignorance, to name a few of the impediments. Against the onslaughts of others, who sometimes destroy under the guise of protection, she battles to save the records of a little-known segment of church history. And she chafes under the scrutiny of priests and other officials who demand quick results. Moreover, as a foreign expert, she is forbidden to publish. Therefore, her work with people must be as careful as that on the holy pictures themselves. Needing a sympathetic listener, she has chosen me—despite my ignorance—and I am both delighted and apprehensive.

"I never touch the icons which other restorers have just ruined. Not if I had a chance to warn them beforehand. Quite simply, I refuse. And I never touch those icons that weep blood or exude holy oils for healing. Never." Is this art or is this faith? The Restorer does not reveal, and the listener finds it difficult to ask.

An enormous icon of St. George in the guise of a Mongolian prince dominates the far end of the makeshift workshop above the Church of St Mercurius. Fully restored, the Prince shines in an array of gold, red, green, and blue. Who was the artist who composed this mythical man, his shoulders full forward in the pharaonic style, his left hand twisted in the manner of Bodhisattvas depicted in the cave murals along the Silk Road? Was the artist familiar with these? Surely at least he was a copier of older pictures, the heritage of Christians, who in the thirteenth century traveled from Central Asian exile back to the Middle East with the Mongol hordes.

"The Nestorians," the Restorer muses. "What became of them?" Though no church historian, this mother of icons is a woman of vast energy and knowledge, and her questions lead in a thousand directions. Should I mention to her the Chinese general who ruled Baghdad in the fourteenth century and the Nestorian general who rode into Damascus at the head of the conquering Mongols? The Restorer's eyes catch the reflection of a thousand icons awaiting resurrection. She does not yet fully understand, but already she knows.

We tour the tenth-century Church of St. Mercurius with its myriad chapels and icons. Here Philip meets the Ethiopian eunuch in a Byzantine painting that portrays the Ethiopian in a pharaonic-style oxcart drawn by two droll, doglike oxen.

"Naïve," the Restorer pronounces. "Naïve, in keeping with the people." But far from pejorative, the word assumes new relevance for the faith and reality that bring these pictorial sermons to life. We pause briefly before the hermit cave of St. Barsuma and his serpent. An icon gives the serpent lustrous feminine eyes of great intelligence. And does the Restorer wonder whatever went on here? Once more, I forbear to ask as she seems unwilling to discuss.

We stop longer before an early eighteenth-century icon of the Virgin. Again the features are oriental, with large, slanting eyes, and small pursed lips. Mary's feet are bare, and she wears trousers in the Eastern mode. The picture is simple and primitive, and the effect is extraordinarily powerful. The infant, moreover, is minor to the painting. This Virgin, I tell myself, is Kuanyin, Goddess of Mercy, the Queen of Heaven. Serenity and beneficence flow from her, and she cries out for the Restorer to worship by ministering to her.

From the gallery we look down at an iconostasis containing the twelve apostles. Though recently restored, the Apostles' faces appear washed out, less clear than in a photograph taken before the applications of acetone and careless scrubbing.

"I begged them," the Restorer begins. She chokes off and collects herself. "A lot of iconoclasm is carried out by eager, overconfident, and arrogant amateurs, who do whatever they please." It is a metaphor for Egypt's modern society, and the results are deeply shocking. The Restorer cannot bear to look any longer, and we move on into an upper chapel. Here, onlookers in a passion play, we cringe before more faded wall murals. Large empty bottles of acetone are thrown together in a corner. The Restorer's response is biblical: "It is finished."

But, like Christ at Golgotha, the Restorer is not finished. There are at least 175 icons in this church alone. And as we continue to walk, she lectures on about the work of Yuhannas the Armenian, the influences from Jerusalem, the lack of an available translator of classical Turkish, and the need to determine the materials in an icon before starting to clean. Her enthusiasm and hope slowly ease our gloom.

The morning ends in Mar Girgis at the Church of St. Barbara, where we stand in awe before a large thirteenth-century icon of Mary and Child.

"I restored it without permission, upstairs in the gallery," the Restorer says gleefully. "Anyway, they were renovating the church and all the icons had been moved, so for a while no one even noticed what we were doing." An adoring assistant nods behind her.

Severely damaged in a 1984 cleaning, the Virgin now gazes serenely down upon us. Sunlight filters into the church and reflects off the glass shield necessary to prevent the prayers of the faithful being written directly upon the holy icon. We move about to examine the Virgin more carefully, and her eyes follow us.

In a back chapel is another restored Mongolian picture. Across the iconostasis stretch other bright icons, recently cleaned but replaced incorrectly. The Restorer's amazement and fury overflow at lasts.

"Blasphemy," she cries. "Wrong order! Six months ago I told them! Saints look *away* from the Christ! Blasphemy! Doesn't anyone listen?" Here surely, I tell myself, is a saint in the making. Then, as suddenly as she had cried out, she changed the subject.

"Look," she said. "Do you have an old silk nightgown? I need one for the cleaning."

Icon of the Crucifixion at Abu Seifein church, Old Cairo, March 1993

Icon at Abu Seifein church, Old Cairo, March 1993

36

For the Love of Camels

March 1993

The drive from Cairo through the dripping Ahmad Hamdi tunnel, under the Suez Canal, and across central Sinai to the Red Sea takes about six hours. Recent rains had coaxed strange plants from the desert sand, including a spiky flower that looks like a bright yellow corncob, or perhaps an old-style hand grenade. We press on up the Mitla Pass, through landscape littered with the military debris of 1967 and 1973. Relief stops require care: tread only where there are animal droppings or, better still, tire tracks. A Bedouin boy appears at roadside waving an empty water container.

"Don't stop," says the Egyptian Engineer. "Never stop when flagged unless it's a police post. People have been robbed or even killed." We, who often amuse ourselves by portage of interesting human cargo from one part of the desert to another, scoff silently, if a bit uneasily. Later we do stop—on the Engineer's instruction—to examine calligraphy in a limestone pass. Here, two hundred years ago, a Mamluk ruler "opened the way" east for pilgrims "to the glory of God." We five modern travelers—Egyptian, British, American, and two Finns—gape at the inscription.

Then down the thirty-kilometer decline that snakes between colored cliffs to the sea. The Taba Enclave is just to our left, but we turn right, south along the edge of the Sinai Peninsula. The campground of Basata, a few kilometers on, spreads itself on the Red Sea shore like a nomad's dream of paradise. Having checked in, we are soon floating lazily above the coral reef among brilliant fish and rejoicing silently. But this, too, is prelude. Night falls suddenly over the coast of Saudi Arabia across the narrow sea, and we nest in our sleeping bags as a salty wind hums through the thatch. Tomorrow. Tomorrow.

It is 9 a.m. the next morning, and we five are already several miles south of Basata. Our food, water, and sleeping bags have been strapped to five bull camels, and it is time for us, too, to mount. Our guides, three boys and a man, motion each of us towards the beast they deem appropriate. The White Camel and I look one another in the eye for the first time before I swing my leg across his back and settle into the awkward wooden cradle. The camel rumbles loudly, lurches forward and then back, lifting himself on spindles that seem too fragile for his own weight, let alone mine as well. Tentatively, I hook a leg around the pommel as the train sets out.

The White Camel's great two-toed feet, smaller in back than in front, pad silently across the rock-strewn sand. Great tufts of white hair spout from his constantly twitching ears. His eyes are to die for, and even his long, symmetrical eyelashes are white. I think I am falling in love.

"Ya walad," I address the teenager who leads this white marvel. "What is your name?"

"Mubarak," he replies. "Hosni Mubarak"

"Oh, yeah?" I reply. "And what then is the name of this camel?"

"Him? That's Mohamed Hosni Mubarak. Same family."

Having lost round one, I settle into the camel's rhythmic gait as we swing down the wadi. Satisfied, Hosni Mubarak feeds an orange to Mohamed Hosni Mubarak. The White Camel takes the offering in his great soft lips and munches thoughtfully. I notice then the leather thong through the tender tissue of his right nostril and realize that among those things I need to learn about camels there is much I would rather not know.

Time for a truce. When I begin to sing, Mubarak joins in. Though his tune and words are different, we have each chosen a marching song that matches the White Camel's stride. Eventually the boy gives me a shy smile. Mubarak, as it turns out, is indeed his name. But the White Camel is Shilan, the Carrier. He is four years old, hates bananas, likes to sleep close to campfires, and is doted on by Mubarak—among others.

Trouble is not long delayed. A dirty brown beast named

Al Azraq, upon which the Diplomat is uneasily perched, manages to sidle up to the Carrier. Shilan lurches sideways as Al-Azraq lunges, bellowing his desire. Only an instant passes before Muzallaq, the eldest Bedouin, regains control, jerking the string fastened to the brown camel's nostril. When the roars of pain and frustration have subsided, we plod on. Mubarak seeks out tasty patches of vegetation through which he leads the White Camel. Self-confidence restored, Shilan resumes his stately smorgasbord. They ignore me, a hindrance to full enjoyment of their morning walk, until my shrill vexation over the fate of a young acanthus tree being chewed to a nub by Shilan provokes Mubarak to respond.

"There will always be trees," he says, amazed at my ignorance. The Carrier belches and drops a few neat round turds to punctuate the remark. Al Azraq attempts to eat the turds of his beloved and is beaten back. We move on.

In midmorning we leave the camels and hike further up the wadi, along a twisting path littered with enormous boulders and impenetrable except on foot. The mountains close and open, their walls black, orange, yellow, red, and violet. An Israeli family joins us, and we send their teenage son to swim across the first pool, swing up the rope at the far end, and explore whatever is beyond. The lad returns with news of a second, bigger pool enclosed in a rock canyon with unscalable walls.

"I know," his father says quietly. "I came here once before, many years ago."

We leave the Israelis eating tinned peas and straining water through a hat and slip into the dark water. When we return, mud splattered, from the higher pool, they have gone, replaced by two American backpackers, who regard our awkward, slippery descent with silent mirth.

The sun grows hotter, drying our clothes and hair as we trek down the wadi and around a second jebel to rejoin the camels. Our hobbled herd browses, seeking spring shoots among the rocks. The bedu have baked a large flat loaf in the ashes and heated up the contents of several tins: peas, lentils, tomato sauce, and tuna fish. Squatting, we scoop up this mixture with pieces of scorched and sandy bread.

"There were Jews at the pool," says Musallam. He is ten, has a chronic cough, and like the others, has never been to school.

"Sons of dogs," the adult Bedouin replies, but it is clear that his response would have been the same to any foreign presence. Our attempts to engage the desert men in conversation embarrass them, and because their vocabulary and accent are of the east, even the Engineer has difficulty understanding them. One thing they do get through to us: they do not consider themselves Egyptians, for they have nothing to do with the Nile. When asked, they call themselves Tarabin, a proud and ancient tribal title. Shilan, hopping nearby with front legs hobbled, begs like a puppy before being driven off with sticks and stones.

"Harry! Harry!" The bedu order the camels away.

"As in 'God for Harry, England, and St. George,'" the Diplomat suggests. Chagrined, I follow the White Camel with fistfuls of bread, which he accepts eagerly, gazing into my face. Yes, I decide, this must be true love.

Before night falls, we make camp in the Wadi Mulha Riyyan, the Wadi of Salt and Water. Tomorrow's mountain looms behind, and stale water seeps from cracks in the wadi floor. We taste the white stains and wish we had not.

A biting wind blows up the wadi, lifting sparks from the small fire beside which we huddle. When the bread, wine, and cheese are finished, all five of us khawagas crawl into sleeping bags. But the bedu are already asleep among the camels, which, couchant like sphinx, chew cud, rumble, and blow. They are hungry, though each has been given a small bag of grain. There will be no water for two more days.

Twice in the night I awake, as sand-muffled feet creep warily through the camp. The wind reaches into my sleeping bag and tugs at the scarf knotted around my throat. Once, I am certain I feel a nose on my hair but, awakening, can see nothing but brilliant stars. Jackals, I decide.

"No," says the Engineer when dawn comes. "fasit afreet, (demon's fart). That's all." I inspect the pad prints in the sand next to my sleeping bag and say no more. Shilan, who kept vigil and knows all, purses his silky lips in my direction.

Today is the day of the Colored Canyon, reached after a steady two-hour walk, first following the camels and then leaving them, as we head alone into the narrow wadi. There is no access other than on foot; and, through binoculars, we watch two vehicles on the canyon rim. More Israelis.

The canyon walls move in until we are surrounded by multicolored layers of stone, which at times come so close they almost tunnel before opening out again. A small white snake, a scarab beetle, and a few desert larks amidst the sparse desert plants seem to be the only life other than our own. We crawl beneath a wedged boulder through an opening the size of a small window and up onto another plateau. Today, I think, if the hills followed the Psalmist's injunction to clap their hands and skip for joy, we'd be crushed like beetles.

Camp that night is in the Wadi Milha Atshan, the Wadi of Salt and Thirst. It has not rained here for three years, the bedu say. Still, they hack branches from the few remaining trees and build a fire for the tea and bread. Do not sleep there, they warn, indicating the sheltering rocks behind which we have placed our sleeping bags. Though a search produces no scorpions, we move away. Stars and a quarter-moon light up the wadi. Shilan chews with great concentration on a small tree that no longer has any branches.

"There are men among the Tarabin who know about the stars," Muzallaq admits, rolling some of my pipe tobacco into a cigarette. He pokes at the small fire and refuses our offer of wine. As spokesman for the bedu, he answers our questions patiently. Khawagas, it seems, always want to know so much but learn so little.

"There was a group of Germans who tried to run away into the desert rather than go home. Their leader shouted at them and was very angry." Muzallaq puffs on the cigarette. The boys, faces hidden by darkness, say nothing.

"Perhaps tomorrow we, too, shall run into the desert and not return to Cairo," one of the Finns suggests.

"What would you do then?" Muzallaq does not hesitate. "*You would die,*" he says. And then, reading my thoughts, the man of the desert adds, "Even if this woman were to run off riding the Carrier, she, too, would die. The desert does not welcome strangers." It was a final pronouncement.

The next morning Muzallaq is particularly brutal with Al Azraq, tugging fiercely at the nose thong while the camel is still kneeling, bending the animal's head back until the brown camel screams. Why, we ask, why?

"Unless I do this, next year when he is fully grown, he will be very mean and dangerous," the desert man says. The boy Salamah, whose dark eyes are rimmed with kohl, nods agreement.

Later that morning, when the camels have knelt for us to dismount before a sharp ascent, Al Azraq suddenly lurches upward and leaps upon the fully loaded Carrier. The brown camel's eyes blaze, and he lashes out with teeth and feet. When the screams and shouting have subsided, Muzallaq forces the big camel back to its knees and beats him savagely with a stick. Blood runs from Al Azraq's mutilated nostril.

"Would it not be more merciful simply to castrate this camel, or at least to keep him far enough from the others to avoid stimulating his natural behavior?" I ask in anguish.

The drivers are amazed as much by my outburst as by the question and refuse to discuss the matter. Angrily, I slam down a camel jawbone picked up nearby. "Not ours," the bedu say. "Not ours."

I turn away pondering over whether something quite complicated may be involved here. No man, I suppose, wants to be master of a castrated camel. The culture is ancient, macho, and endangered. It is a culture in which women are often held accountable for provoking aggressive sexual behavior, no matter what had occurred. Yet Muzallaq has beaten the aggressive animal, not the seductive object of Al Azraq's desire. I ask myself if the Bedouin has, by so doing, admitted to the lie. Is he, knowing the price of sexual trespass in his society, warning himself—and the boys who work with him—of the consequences that come from breaking unwritten laws?

We ride down the wadi towards the sea and then briefly along the highway. Someone in a passing car has tossed out a notebook, which Mubarak picks up. He shuffles along at Shilan's head, examining the curious scrawl and then turns to me.

"Do you read Arabic?" he ventures hopefully. But I cannot help. Disgusted, Mubarak flings away the hateful yet seductive object of his humiliation.

When the journey ends, I feed Shilan an entire package of biscuits. The White Camel gobbles them all, ears twitching. But when I turn to thank Mubarak, the boy has vanished. He, too, loves the White Camel and knows what is in store.

Travels into the Heart of Egypt 193

On camelback in Sinai. March 1993

37

Watching on Sham-e-Nessim

27 April 1993

Traffic clogged the road from Cairo to the Bitter Lake before eight in the morning, as citizens of Cairo fled their city in every known variety of motorized vehicle. Mercedes jostled with dilapidated trucks, tractors, overcrowded buses, and motorcycles along the road to Ismailia. Sham-e-Nessim, spring holiday with pharaonic origins, requires that Egyptians return to the countryside to "sniff the breezes," a reaffirmation of rural roots and a celebration of the unity of mankind and environment. Carefully we wedged the Range Rover into the slow moving parade.

The mood was exuberant, punctuated by car horns and celebrated by busloads of young men packed several to a seat and still able to shout, sing, and hammer on tambourines. Speed increased as we moved into the desert. Sedans passed us packed with rejoicing families, flapping inner tubes tied to car roofs. In one vehicle, four children were stuffed into the front seat, while Papa and Granny and several more leaned out back windows through which we could see Mama and Aunt Leila resolutely clutching baskets of lunch. The flailing legs of at least two toddlers filled the back windscreen. The entire rejoicing Egyptian population seemed to have crammed itself into small steel containers in order not to miss the great occasion.

Before we reached the halfway point to the Canal, breakdowns had become common. Dejected families squatted beside their jacked-up cars, as cousins and uncles changed tires and tried to prevent children running into the road. Appropriate to a day of license and leisure, many men wore shorts, and a few had even taken off their shirts. It was a rejection of winter, a celebration of the heat to come. Later, making up time, many drivers crossed the dual carriageway and rocketed ahead on the wrong side of the road. But what did it matter, after all? No one seemed to be heading *into* Cairo on such a delicious and important spring morning.

The noisy caravan represented all segments of society. "St. Luke's Travel" proclaimed the sign on a busload of singing Copts. The male group advertising itself as Gehad Travel was also suggestive. But who were all those people bumping along in buses owned by Glob Travel? Ordinary folk, we decided, out for a sniff of sea breeze and a chance to boil up a pot of tea by the lake and wade into its cool water. From the back of a pickup truck a teenage mother and her two children dressed in the tattered galabiyahs of the poor waved cheerfully in our direction. Sham-e-Nessim levels social and economic distinctions, and perhaps even religious divisions. On this day once a year Egypt becomes one and goes to the beach for lunch.

The approach to Ismailia threads through a number of military camps. Here the travelers wave to young soldiers tending their tanks while bravely trying not to appear heartbroken, as they surely must be, at being on duty while the rest of the country is on holiday. The long barrels of field artillery, carefully kept far from Cairo, point skyward in neat rows. The soldiers wave back, hoping for a breakdown by a rich family, who will surely give them a few sandwiches and yusif effendis in exchange for helping them repair the car.

Eventually we turned right off the main highway and drove slowly through several lakeside villages where revelers outnumbered residents. It was easy to tell the difference: the Cairenes wore about half as much clothing as the locals. Then, just before turning into the driveway of our friend's villa at Feyad, we saw three enormous Smyrna kingfishers sitting on a wire over the irrigation canal. This, the Diplomat and I decided, clearly foretold a red-letter day.

Our host was out of the country, but we were greeted by his wife and the Doctor, their dear friend, and fed a late breakfast of fried cheese, colored eggs, smoked salmon, and flaky bread smothered in honey. Aunts, uncles, and children were everywhere.

"No faseekh this year," the Doctor said firmly. "Not after over twenty deaths from bad fish last year. Never again." Thinking of death, he grew contemplative. "Besides, I hate the stuff. Some day the fundamentalists are going to poison the whole nation with faseekh." So we all drank several glasses of champagne in celebration over the absence this year of faseekh, the pickled fish that for centuries has been the staple of Sham-e-Nessim.

Two or three hours later I swam out into the salty, milk-colored water of the Bitter Lake, with Malika following close behind me. Her ten-year-old body cut the water like a small golden-brown porpoise.

"You swim fast," Malika said reprovingly, and I altered my stroke to hers. We poked along for a while, watching the far-out line of tankers heading for the Canal. Could I teach anything to a child already fluent in three languages? A child whose ancestors were documented much further back than mine? A child growing up in a country far more troubled, far more divided than mine along political and religious lines? A child whose identity and future, no matter what politicians say, was possibly in peril?

"Keep your head down for the crawl," I said. "Turn your face like this for breathing. Now keep your arms and legs straight and your hands cupped. Reach. Reach. See how you pick up speed?"

Meanwhile, the wind was picking up, and far out in the lake the Doctor had fallen off his sailboard and could not right it alone. Five teenagers in a paddleboat pulled the boat back in and left the Doctor to swim back. When he finally reached the beach gray with exhaustion, they were still laughing. How could a man so strong, so loved, so important to their lives have been in danger of drowning? But I, too, had been wrong. Although I had almost gone out to encourage him, I decided that he seemed to be swimming strongly, if slowly, and anyway, I had no training for lifesaving. Meanwhile, almost everyone else had gone inside to check on lunch.

When the Doctor finally landed, I helped him to a chair on the grass above the sand and gave him a towel. "No water," he whispered in French. "I think I might vomit." The sun beat relentlessly down as we sat quietly together, grateful that what almost happened had not.

For the rest of my life, I told myself, I shall remember that day when Egypt seemed united, I tasted the salty Bitter Lake, and swam with a beautiful little girl innocent of choices to come. But on that day, as well, the Doctor had escaped death, and I had not gone to help him.

As we started our return to Cairo in early evening, the three enormous red-billed kingfishers sat together on a wire, watching, watching. It seemed an omen I could not understand.

38

Tourist Trash in Sinai

17 May 1993

Southern Sinai is a region of contrasts: Flat sea and mountainous desert. Carefree Italian tourists on the beach and US warships stopping Panamanian-registered freighters in the Straits of Tiran. Topless sun-worshippers across the narrow strait from Saudi Arabia. Giant dun-colored lizards sunning in an uncleared mine field, and Green Sea Turtles swimming among the snorkelers off Ras Mohamed. Here eons of history, both geological and biblical, filter into Egypt's modern economy.

The six-hour drive from Cairo took us to Sharm El Sheikh, a town as artificial as a plastic bucket, on the Sinai Peninsula's southern extreme. Once the headquarters of pirate kings, South Sinai is today a dreamland of tourism. Washed and brushed up in the Presidential Suite at Namah Bay's Aquamare Hotel (could the corpulent Mubarak really have wedged himself into such a small bathtub?), we visit one of the many restaurants that cater to international clients.

Two young Frenchmen at the next table watch as the waiter uncorks their wine. An expression of astonishment crosses the taster's face, and he sends the bottle back with a flourish. "Corked," he tells his companion. It takes two visits by the restaurant manager, three by the waiter, and finally an intervention by us to convince the Frenchman that Omar Khayyam wine always tastes like…well, to be kind, the product of a government monopoly.

After dinner, we amuse ourselves by strolling along the beachside pavement. Fanciful signs invite:

"Rent biscle!"

"We rent bicycle. Come have some fund with Khalid."

"Glass bottom boat: 20 LE Ride the Banana! 10 LE Caned: 5 LE"

"Qafyland Camp" (Qadhafi? Not in evidence, but there *is* a very large tent pitched nearby....

"Desalination pipe for sea water." This sign seems intended to forestall unpleasant queries from fastidious foreigners. We step over the pipe, which disappears into the surf, and move on down the pavement.

Jet skis and motorcycles. Beach buggies and a miniature golf course. Shops for developing underwater photographs, learning scuba diving, renting flippers, purchasing sun cream. There are many gawping Egyptian men wearing tiny bathing suits, and almost no Egyptian women.

An exhausted young camel kneels awkwardly beside the boardwalk, upset by the prodding of the after dinner crowd. His head jerks nervously, blood seeping through the white bandana tied around his neck. Has some crazed tourist tried to slit the camel's throat? More likely he has just been brought in from the desert, and his outgrown halter has been removed by the Bedouin owner, who now offers rides.

Snorkeling the next day below the Hilton Residence outside Namah Bay, we enter a world of fantastically colored angel, clown and zebra fish, purple sea anemones, and schools of fry. Moray eels hide among the rocks, and manta rays fly along the bottom, occasionally leaping into the sunlight.

Rapt, we float beyond the reef examining its wells and inlets. The sun hammers down, but in this cool blue world of endlessly varied life, the heat and din of Cairo are filtered out. The words of an old hymn comes back to me:

> O Love that will not let me go,
> I rest my weary soul in Thee.
> I give Thee back the life I owe,
> That in Thine ocean depths its flow
> May richer, fuller be.

When we turn at last towards shore, the tide is out, and we must float carefully over the emerged reef. Enormous sea urchins, waving poisonous spines, appear beneath our faces, and giant clams snap shut their jagged purple lips. "There are things still coming ashore," the anthropologist Loren Eisely wrote. "It pays to know that."

Southern Sinai arouses admiration for those Egyptians determined to preserve the region's endangered ecological balance—and fear that they will not be able to do so. The Ras Mohamed National Park, established with funding from the European Community, covers the tip of the peninsula. Here fishing and hunting are prohibited, and access to some areas of the coral reef restricted.

Namah Bay and its hotels are in fearsome contrast. Most of the hotels are new, some still going up. But building rubble pollutes the water, and plastic sacks and motorboats destroy the age-old silence. Postcards for sale on the walkway show divers feeding hard-boiled eggs to the giant groupers, and in the water tropical fish follow swimmers looking for handouts. And were it not for the tourist hotels, would there be a sewage farm? Described in the birding book as "the best migratory bird trap in southern Sinai," the sewage farm provides a rest stop for a variety of birds on yearly migration between Europe and Africa. Braving the stench, we circle the ponds identifying sandpipers, stilts, ruffs, and collared pratincoles.

"Whose lands are these?" we ask about the newly cultivated land that abuts the sewage works and are told, "These belong to the Lord of Sanafir. Come drink tea with us." Workers welcome us to eucalyptus-lined lanes, between orchards of young citrus trees replete with spotted flycatchers, yellow wagtails, and herons. Feral dogs wait while another group of men finish butchering a bullock, whose carcass they then hang from a tree. The dogs fawn, grovel, move closer, and are driven back.

The next day, after a second visit to the sewage farm, we decide to explore further. The desert drive from Sharm to the town of Dahab, also on the Red Sea, passes through canyons and between sharp peaks that replicate the offshore underwater world. But although the one hundred–kilometer journey takes only an hour and a half, Dahab seems a more primitive place, tawdry, even freakish. The town styles itself an oasis, but appears to be the most rubbish-strewn site on the peninsula.

Barbed wire enclosures on Dahab's outskirts are decorated with thousands of wind-blown plastic bags. Side wadis, which serve as rubbish tips, are littered with broken glass and rusty tins. Ancient rock-hewn hermit cells, that honeycomb the entrance to one wadi, have been turned into modern storage bins by the bedu. But storage for what? A Chivas Regal carton blows in the wind.

Dahab is divided into two. In one area, luxury villas and hotels, a new mosque, social club, and civic buildings are being constructed. In the other part of town, signs in English reveal the source of this new prosperity: "Black Prince Disco," "Crazy House Camp," "Naughty Boy Club" and, more ominously, and perhaps as a result, "Lawyer."

On the waterfront, backpackers spread themselves and their belongings among fortunetellers, camel touts, and providers of water pipes. Beyond is a concrete Bedouin settlement, where new pickup trucks are parked next to tethered camels. Just outside the settlement, a group of young girls suddenly jump screaming into the road. When I stop, they jeer loudly and, as we drive on, one slaps me through the open window. Foreigners, it needs no reminder, are contemptible, and Dahab makes it clear why.

Ten kilometers of dirt track lead to the Blue Hole. Among those who know such things, this is one of the world's most renowned dive sites. Jagged sandstone hills reach down to a rocky beach, and there are no signs of animals, birds, or fresh water. At the Blue Hole, a group of European scuba divers check gauges before descent.

Back at Namah Bay, two hours later, we sip araq on the terrace of the Presidential suite, ignoring several shouting Italians in the bar below. The Red Sea washes in, political and religious extremists seem far away, and most of the foreign tourists have been left behind at Sharm El Sheikh. As a full moon comes up over the water, I think of the girl who slapped me, and wonder what her life will hold.

39

Following Jehovah through Sinai

Late May 1993

It is easy to understand why man has always sought God in the Sinai. Alone, with extremes of heat and cold, punished by thirst, threatened by sudden natural violence, man hears the Still Small Voice. And so is purified and led forth.

"The Lord knows the way through the wilderness. All I have to do is follow." Hymns of my childhood about being led and safeguarded, psalms that germinated in Sinai, come back to me as we churn north from Sharm El Sheikh through the center of the peninsula. "Guide me, O Thou Great Jehovah, pilgrim through this barren land."

Rugged mountains of pink, gray, and green alternate with sandy plains. The land is indeed barren, but patches of vegetation and frequent acacia trees whisper of hidden springs, and a more verdant past. Wadis open outward, inviting the unwary traveler further into Sinai's stony heart. There is little sign of human life, save for an occasional semipermanent Bedouin encampment, and traditional tents replaced by tin shacks around a small spring. "Open Thou the crystal fountain whence the healing stream doth flow. Let the fire and cloudy pillar lead me all my journey through. Bread of heaven, feed me 'til I want no more!" Hymns of my childhood accompany us.

Abandoned hermit holes checker the walls of a wadi. Who sought God here, and did or did not allow God to find him? The anchorites have always known that evil as well as good achieves incarnation in the desert. The voice of the Tempter wails through the wadis, and visions bedazzle the unfortified heart. Yet it remains possible that "He hideth my soul in the cleft of the rock that shadows a dry, thirsty land. He hideth my life in the depths of His love and covers me there with His hand."

Up, up, to the Sharirah Pass, where stands a blind Israeli memorial, all identification removed when the weary land was transferred back to Egyptian sovereignty, following the Camp David Agreement. We stop to taste the silence of a place of memories, a place where for untold centuries, man and God have danced together. "I will lift up mine eyes unto the hills. For whence shall my help come? My help cometh from Jehovah who made heaven and earth" (*Psalm 121: 1-2. The Holy Bible.* standard version 1901).

The asphalted road cuts like a scar through the landscape, and we follow it down the pass. "Follow, I will follow Thee, my Lord, follow every passing day. My tomorrows are all known to Thee. Thou wilt lead me all the way." Two soldiers rest in the scant shade of a smashed and overturned red van. "We are Thine! Do Thou befriend us; be the Guardian of our way!"

Eventually, the road forks: right towards Nuweibah and left to St. Catherine's Monastery and the Mountain of Moses, spiritual heart of Sinai. We rise through a spectacular pass, where waiting bedu leap suddenly from behind a rock wall screaming like brigands, imploring us to halt and buy their trinkets. "The storm may roar without me, my heart may low be laid. But God is round about me and shall I be dismayed?"

It is noon when we reach El Tafa. Low stone and cinder block houses line the road. Tamarisk and manna trees fill the extensive gardens. "Bread of Heaven! Bread of Heaven! Feed me 'till I want no more!" On then, down to Firan, Sinai's largest oasis and the seat of a fourth century bishopric. Palm trees nestle at the foot of Mt. Horeb, where Joshua upheld Abraham's arms against the Amalekites.

Tombs cut long ago in the living rock pepper the hillsides. A ruined citadel with the remains of a basilica rises on a hill to the left. Lower down, new buildings are replacing the homes swept away by the spring 1991 flood. And everywhere, tiny kids follow their small black mothers. "Saviour, like a Shepherd lead us. Much we need thy tender care! In Thy pleasant pastures feed us. For our use Thy folds prepare. Blessed Jesus! Blessed Jesus! Through hast brought us, Thine we are!"

About three o'clock, and fifty kilometers from the west coast highway, we pick up a travelling salesman. No, he is not a Bedouin, but a Saidi from Upper Egypt, and he has come here to sell cloth. He places a large bundle in the roof rack, and climbs into the backseat of the Range Rover.

Although the Saidi seems near collapse when we stop, still he drinks only sparingly from our water bottle. This is not his land, and we are not his people. But he will come with us, for we are heading towards the Ahmad Hamdi tunnel that connects Sinai to the Land of the Nile.

Or, to put it another way: "When I cross the verge of Jordan, Bid my anxious fears subside. Bare me through the swelling current, Land me safe on Canaan's side. Songs of praises I will ever give to Thee! Song of praises I will ever give to Thee!"

40

Befriending Cairo

6 June 1993

In Imbaba, on the Nile's west bank, is an ornate villa where King Farouk kept his mistresses. Known today as "The Swiss Club," what remains of the villa's grounds is the last vestige of green, in an area which fifteen years ago was still farmland. Stately royal palms, last holdout of majesty, rise above the villa, but are themselves dwarfed by surrounding tenement blocks. The dwellings of the poor do not simply crowd the Swiss Club, they embrace it.

To reach the club, you must drive through some of the most chaotic and unrepaired streets in Cairo. More accurately, Imbaba is an urban village, home to several million rural incomers, who crowd together in population density greater than most cities in India. They have come hoping to find work in what is literally "the Big Smoke." But theirs is a deafening world of heavy trucks and donkey carts, lurching through throngs of street hawkers, roadside tea drinkers, and women carrying heavy loads on their heads and children on their shoulders.

Seeing these women as we enter the Swiss Club grounds, I am reminded of an Egyptian doctor who recently told me that, according to her research, over 90 percent of rural Egyptian women—and 75 percent of those in Cairo—have been subjected to female genital mutilation, known as "female circumcision." How, she asked me, do I help a woman, who by a brutal childhood operation has been rendered frigid, sterile, and sometimes hopeless due to infection?

At the Swiss Club gate, a ragged porter waves back the gaggle of even more ragged children, and allows the privileged to enter.

The Diplomat buys a beer at the cash bar, and disappears into the crowd of Voluntary Service Organization (VSO) representatives and their guests. He is working but, of course, I am as well. I go in search of a telephone, and finally locate one inside a small room on the villa's ground floor. Waiters hurry by, carrying trays of canapés, as I dial and redial, but continue to receive a busy signal. That's a good sign, but I must get through.

The people of Imbaba, barred from this green haven, are nonetheless connected to me, although few of them know this yet. Befrienders Cairo[1] has been operational for only six months and, with official registration delayed by bureaucracy, we may not advertise broadly. But some day, I hope, there will be a branch center in Imbaba—perhaps here in the Swiss Club—where the despairing will find emotional support through "listening therapy," even those who have no telephone.

When I manage to tell the befriending center where to find me in case of emergency, I wander back out beneath the palms. At the bar, I slip several cards with the Befrienders phone number under an ashtray and, turning away, hear nearby a well-known silver laugh. From behind, I recognize a young Egyptian woman, last seen two hours earlier holding a telephone, shoulders hunched, her scarf concealing her marvelously sympathetic eyes. At the other end of the line, a young father who gave no name poured out his anger, his sorrow, and his fear.

"There is no way," he told Number 31. "It's all my fault. I deserve to die. There is no other way." Number 31 bent further forward in concentration.

"Can you tell me more?" she said gently. "Please trust me. Please believe that we care." The shift leader placed a reassuring hand on Number 31's shoulder, and then scribbled a note on the telephone pad. Two other volunteers sat tensely in the quiet room as the phone line held a man back from possible suicide.

Recently an ambassador's wife questioned me sharply at lunch, lifting her eyebrows, and finally asking triumphantly, "But what can you 'befrienders' *do* for people? How can just listening help? The Egyptians need housing, jobs, financial security. What can just listening to their problems do for them?"

"That's it," I told her. "We're nonprofessionals. We aren't

qualified to help people solve their problems. But what we can do is listen, and that very often helps a despairing person hold on to life until he or she can figure out what to do." But the lady was not impressed.

"Well!" she said. "If *I* ever have a problem, it wouldn't work for me. I'd want an answer!"

What solution, I wondered silently, would anyone dare offer a woman who, circumcised as a child, is now frigid, sterile, and hopeless. And I thought about Number 11, listening to a woman whose husband had taken a second wife; Number 2 (the ambassador of Singapore, but this is unknown to anyone outside the Befrienders), hearing out a refugee who had lost his job, his family, his country; Number 20, listening to a troubled teenager; and Number 15, befriending a young man who had been beaten because he is gay.

"No one ever before let me tell this," the young man wept when he came on line. "But I want to say how I feel. Oh, please listen to me. There is no one else I can tell."

Today I took our consultant psychiatrist to the center for the first time. Several months ago, when befriending was explained to him, the Psychiatrist was among those who asked me, "Where have you been? Where have you been?" From the beginning he has referred to the Befrienders as "us." But the Psychiatrist is a very important Egyptian, and I was nervous and apologetic as we climbed the dirty stairs to the third floor.

"It isn't grand," I said. "And we still have only one telephone line, although technicians at the British Embassy are ready to put in another two." I showed him the waiting room, with its secondhand chairs, the interview rooms, and the stuffy phone room, where we have to turn off the air conditioner whenever the phone rings.

The Psychiatrist read through the Standing Orders, suggesting here that we encourage a family befriending, and there that an offer of medical consultation might be an option. He accepted a cup of coffee and listened as a volunteer sat, mainly silent, while a torrent of pain poured from the telephone.

"It's working," the Psychiatrist whispered. His eyes glistened. "It's working!"

Under the royal palms a short while later, I sipped my beer and talked to the VSO volunteers, one a splendid old carpenter from

Scotland, who probably deserves the Order of the British Empire for the work he has done. On the other hand, Number 31 will never be publicly honored: her identity is confidential. But the Befrienders* know they get far more out of their voluntary work than they can ever put into it. I do it, I know, in celebration of life.

Across the crowd, Number 31 catches my eye and grins. I edge over to the bar, and find that the stack of telephone cards had disappeared.

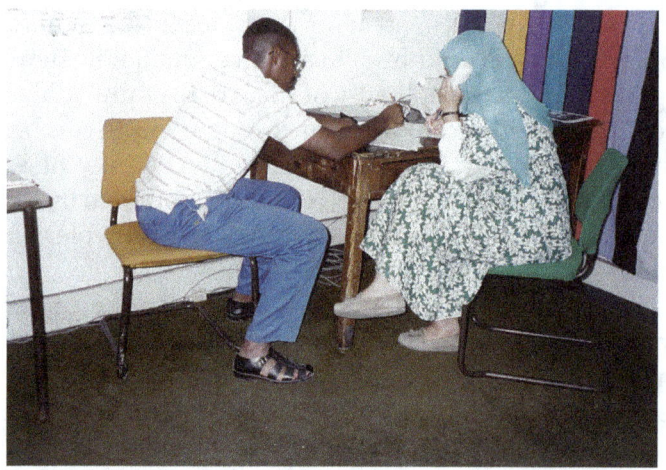

Befrienders in action, Mohandiseen, Cairo, May 1993

Befrienders at rest, in the Befrienders' center,
Mohandiseen, Cairo, May 1993

41

Birding at the Barrages

7 June 1993

Never go to the Barrages on Friday. Thirty years ago, when there were only about six million people in Cairo, a Friday outing to the Barrages would have been a good idea. But these days, Saturday morning makes a lot more sense. Take the water taxi from in front of the Nile Hilton. Or drive out through Imbaba. But go early, before heat drives the birds into hiding. Take drinking water and binoculars, of course, but leave your Labrador retriever behind, no matter how persuasively she insists on accompanying you. Labs usually bark just when you've focused on a black-shouldered kite or, preferably, something smaller and more exotic. Labs also attract unceasing insults from their country cousins, the Baladi Boys, and tend to fake heatstroke if not allowed to lumber into the canal every few minutes.

The Barrages is one of those "built by the British" places that seems not to have been cared for since the British finally and reluctantly relinquished control over Egypt. Constructed to control the Nile flood, the Barrages have long been a favorite destination for families and courting couples. Only a forty-minute riverside drive from Zamalek, the area remains one of greater Cairo's most accessible green areas. At the Barrages, moreover, though few people know this and fewer still care, colonialism has again reared its head—but in the form of birds rather than humans.

After crossing to the east bank over the top of the main barrage, you turn left along a lane that parallels the river. The small teahouse is always empty on Saturday. Park here and greet the waiter who rushes out to interest you in refreshment.

"Later," you tell him and he grins and nips off to hang a few more Pepsis in the canal to cool.

Now stroll along the elevated eucalyptus-lined lane. Little green bee-eaters hunt from the branches, uttering their liquid cry. But you are looking for the bright red Avadavats, native to India and recent settlers here thanks to catching a boat from South India. If the Avadavats are "in," you'll see a small flock of these colonials feeding among the reeds.

A flash of black and white, and a pied kingfisher descends at speed from a dead branch above the reed bed, hitting the water with a great show of bravado. Missed! She returns, unembarrassed, to the branch and continues to wait patiently. Now you are surrounded by small boys determined to interest you in a motor launch trip to the small islands. Resist this. Birds do not like noise and have a particular disregard for small boys. But be patient, and the boys will accept that a boat trip is not in God's plan for you today, though it could be tomorrow if the apricots bloom.

Try to ignore the heaps of burning rubbish attended by starving dogs along the riverbank. What else are people to do if the authorities won't haul the trash away? But stop to thank a picnicking family who, in the kind Egyptian way, invite you to join them. You may accept a sandwich, if you wish, after exchanging pleasantries with them, and perhaps give their son a ballpoint pen. What you don't eat of the sandwich will gladden the heart of a baladi dog—unless the Labrador (who insisted on coming) hoovers it up first.

The morning has begun to stoke up, and you are glad to have remembered a sun hat. You exchange macho salutations with the bored young soldiers, guarding a geriatric piece of field artillery inside their barbed wire enclosure.

"Don't take pictures," they cry, hoping for business.

"But, look," you say, pretending to be deeply wounded by their accusation. "These are binoculars, and I've just seen a fine Senegal coucal in the bushes behind you." The soldiers laugh indulgently and flex their muscles. You wave goodbye, imagining that, as usual, they are reassuring themselves that "the foreigners are mad."

Several more flashes of black and white, and three little bitterns fly low across the water. The space widens between the river and canal, and you walk through plantations of citrus, mango, and banana. Here rufous bushchats, busy nest building, signal frantically to one another with their long, spotted tails.

Laborers hoe between rows of trees, or at least some of them do. It's a lovely morning, and most of the cultivators seem more interested in gossip and the music blasting from a transistor radio. A man on a bicycle pedals up behind you, and shouts down at the lolling workmen the Arabic version of "Ahmed, don't mess around." Meanwhile, the Labrador is creating a sensation among a pack of nearly identical Baladi boys, who bark and lunge in a frenzy of exaggerated bravado. You hurry off, towing the object of their disdain. Insults, clearly referring to the "fat blonde in the fur coat," see you off the premises.

At the first bridge right, you pause to rest in welcome shade, then stare in shocked recognition at the large blue and brown bird fishing from a wire across the canal. Smyrna kingfisher! The heavy red bill makes identification unmistakable. And the Naturalist had just published an article claiming Smyrnas are found in only two places in Egypt, neither anywhere near the Barrages. A triumphant phone call will set him right. But that must wait, because a flash of yellow on a small brown bird among the canal reeds lets you know you are on to something equally as exciting.

"Don't mess around," you tell yourself, desperately adjusting the binoculars. Steady as she goes. This is serious business, and when you're hot you're hot.

You cross the bridge and squat on the canal's opposite bank, eyes straining. Yes! There are several of these yellow-headed birds, weaving oblong nests with filaments plucked nearby. Streaked weavers! More immigrants from India, though to be fair, they became colonists only after escaping from the Alexandria zoo. One weaver diverts to drive off a persistent intruder who, to judge from his insufficiently yellow head, is an immature member of the tribe. You scribble a few notes, which you hope will impress the Naturalist.

Turn back then along the canal's far bank, trudging past fields of roses and dahlias meant for the drawing rooms of Zamalek. Water pumps throb, and women in black robes, and men in ragged trousers beckon you to stop and drink tea. Through fly-infested eyes, tethered donkeys, and mud-caked water buffalo watch you pass. Graceful Warblers thrill the joy of living, and moorhens parade their young down the center of the canal. You think you spot a water rail, and then you don't. Too soon, on the opposite bank, not far from the teahouse, you see a rowboat tied to a large tree.

"O Boatman, Sir," you cry and a lad of fourteen emerges from his hut, unties the boat, and crosses to fetch you. The Labrador prefers to swim across, her broad head cutting a crocodilian wedge through the green water, her eyes alert for moorhens.

"My name is Ahmed," your captain says.

"In that case, Captain Ahmed," you reply, "here is fifty 'ursh. And I happen to know there is beps cooling at the teahouse. So please don't mess around if you want one."

42

Mena House and Minor Pyramids

8 July 1993

The Diplomat had a birthday and, lo, he was gloomy. A weekend in the Churchill suite at the Mena House Hotel[1] on the edge of Cairo would—at LE 915 a night, even with the 20 percent discount—surely have further darkened the mood that oppressed his spirit. Still, the Mena House seemed a convenient bolthole, and a room with a view over the pyramids of Giza had been booked.

We arrived late Thursday afternoon, the beginning of Cairo's weekend, after a jolting drive along Pyramids Road. The crush and cacophony of cars leaving Cairo suited the Diplomat's current belief that life is a slippery slope on which he was hurrying towards his grave. A burnt out tourist bus, parked just outside the main Mena House gate, did little to alter this conviction.

His packing had been rushed and, as we dressed for dinner, the Diplomat realized that he had forgotten to bring a tie. This lapse, so alien to his career and training, seemed to confirm creeping senility. The silence into which he lapsed demonstrated the resolve with which he steeled his heavy heart against the morrow. Forty-six and counting.

That night the proprietor of the Mena House's famed Indian restaurant tried, so the Diplomat told me, to poison him. Rumbling and malaised, he returned to our room, planted his aching body on a balcony chair, and tried to enjoy the moonlight on the pyramids of Giza. But it was hopeless. Mosquitoes, which always choose his flesh over mine, drove him inside.

So he went to bed, and didn't see the explosions of light from the summits of the tombs of Cheops and Chephren, or the barn owls that glided on swift white wings between the royal palms in the empty gardens below. Something, I decided, would have to be done. Perhaps a trek across the Giza plateau on the morrow.

Had he not already been awake, pondering morosely that over 60 percent of visitors to Egypt suffer intestinal disorders, the 4:30 eruption of the call to prayer from the apparently switched off radio would have jolted the Diplomat far more severely. Exhausted, he questioned whether fundamentalists were after him, but managed eventually to fall asleep again— until hammering on the door at 7:30, accompanied by cheerful cries of "Wake up call," drew from him some very undiplomatic language.

"But I didn't *ask* to be awakened" he cried, and wondered aloud if the world conspired against him, or whether it was only that advancing age had bred a persecution complex. But the day had dawned, and sleep came no more. From the balcony, he surveyed with binoculars the hordes of camel touts and horse punters on the Giza plateau. They awaited, he knew, the tourists who would not come and acknowledged himself too weakened by age to face their importuning. Being the proud son of a Scottish mother, he refused to admit that he was ill. And so, with a bottle of water and a bird book, we set out to find our way by car, along the canal road south that leads to the village of Abu Sir and its Old Kingdom pyramids.

Three ruined pyramids rise behind the village, beckoning, but seemingly inaccessible as the Diplomat tried one blocked lane after another. There seemed no way out of the maze and into the desert. Small boys shouted aggressive greetings and hitched rides on the back of the Range Rover, and small girls in bright dresses shrilled demands for baksheesh as they charged by us, whipping their donkeys. A group of old men gathered outside the mosque before prayers sent us off down yet another blind alley.

"Turn back, and go left after the canal and then cross the second bridge," a young man told us finally, leaning through the open window companionably. Thus, we arrived at last at the final line of trees before sand sweeps upward to the Fifth Dynasty (c. 2494–2345 B.C.) pyramids of Abu Sir.

Emad, age thirteen, stepped forward from the trees as we parked. Yes, he would watch the car well, he said with a smirk. Not reassured, we set forth up the shard-strewn slope crowned by the pyramid complex of Sahure and a guardhouse.

The sun beat down on the Diplomat's aching head. Continuing to deny that he was ill, he wore the present which I had given him for his birthday, a t-shirt with a picture of a nineteenth century explorer reeling beside a pyramid, and supported by a dragoman who said, "That is nothing, Effendi. It is but a sunstroke." The legend in Arabic, which I had hoped would be much ruder, said only, "O poor thing, Ya Doctor!" But at least the Diplomat had remembered to bring his hat.

The desert view at Abu Sir sweeps north to the pyramids of Giza, and south to those at Saqqara. We stood at the end of the causeway and began to feel time receding. Indeed, the Diplomat's luck seemed to have turned. There followed a delightful hour of uninterrupted wandering before the day stoked up in earnest.

Attracted by rhythmic snoring, the Diplomat peered cautiously into the open window of the guardhouse, and saw its three occupants in deep slumber, which he could only envy. Carefully, we backed away, and continued our ramble among limestone fragments, across black basalt floors in the temple complexes, and around the crumbling sides of the pyramids.

An Egyptian Red Fox, with black-tipped ears and white-tipped tail, started up at our approach. The dirty brown vixen trotted rapidly up the side of a crumbling pyramid, squatted, and then vanished. Not a bushy tail, but still not the hairless-tailed specimen for which the Naturalist had told us to remain alert.[2] With harsh buzzing cries, two Little Owls warned their offspring to retreat further into a niche in the side of a pyramid.

Reaching the Valley Temple of Nyuserre, we found that Czech archaeologists had blocked the entry with stones. Their signs warned us off. But this being Egypt, we soon located the rickety ladder, placed by the guard for use of paying customers, once the archaeologists had returned to Prague. More Little Owls fluttered away as we descended into the temple, and then climbed a wall to exit on the far side.

The sun had moved toward its zenith, and we were turning back towards the Range Rover, when we looked up at the guardhouse and saw a horrified face gazing down upon us.

"Allah!" cried the guard and his two companions took up the lament. Two tourists and they had been napping! Three forms emerged from the guardhouse, adjusting their galabiyahs on the trot. Shouts of "Hey, Mister" ricocheted off the pyramids.

But we have seen the pyramids and are just leaving, we tell them politely, shaking the leader's hand and wondering how anyone but a mummy could have such brown teeth.

"Ya salaam!" the guard exclaimed in remorse, the equivalent of "Lord, have mercy." There followed a lengthy explanation of the lack of tourists for the plucking, and then an exchange of funds, which, though generous, was, of course, not enough. No, we would not give more for the benefit of the children of the man still lounging at the guardhouse, scratching his groin.

"Those who are too old to work and can only sleep should not be paid," said the Diplomat, and the head guard, stunned by this logic, shook our hands again. Go in peace, he said as we ambled off towards the tree line, with everyone pleased by the morning's business. Back at the car, Emad had been joined by Yahya, a somewhat older boy, who limped towards us with the aid of a crutch, his crippled right leg dangling.

"Ya Professor," exclaimed Yahya jovially. This the Diplomat declined. "Doctor, then," exclaimed the youth. We replied in the negative. "Surely then Engineer," cried the enterprising Yahya. But this, too, the Diplomat was forced to deny. The young man then showed himself equal to any diplomat but decided not to pursue his advantage.

"Well," he said, "at least you are a gentleman, and there is hope for baksheesh." This we duly delivered to both car watchers, before climbing into the Range Rover and heading back along the rutted path towards the canal road.

That night, the Diplomat and I celebrated his birthday in splendor in the magnificent oriental dining room of the Mena House, once a royal hunting lodge. A bearded musician, who resembled a lugubrious religious fundamentalist, played muzak on a synthesizer. The bevy of waiters fluttered about, reaching across us many times to pour the wine, whisking away plates before we could finish, and showing their attentiveness by frequently interrupting our conversation to ask if we were enjoying ourselves. There wasn't much else for them to do. Almost all the tourists had fled and we were the only diners in the grand hall.

Next morning, beside the swimming pool, we were startled to hear sharp cries of alarm from one of our few fellow guests. Near the pool, a middle-aged British couple hunkered in panic, gesturing at something in the grass. A snake perhaps? Or a bomb? We joined the pool attendants who charged to the rescue, and found that a large damselfly had alighted next to the bikini-clad woman.

"Is it a mosquito?" she cried terrified. "Get the bug spray!" Her husband, who cowered behind her, demanded that the attendants "Take it away!" adding "We have never seen such mosquitoes before!"

"The khawagas are mad," said the Diplomat mildly and I was pleased to see that the pyramids were working their magic on him. He was almost back in form. Moreover, it was noon, and time to leave the Mena House and collect another pyramid, that of Djedefre who reigned between Cheops and Chephren.

This fourth dynasty tomb, the most northern of the ninety or so pyramids of Egypt, lies near the Delta village of Abu Roash, about five miles north of the Giza plateau. Why Djedefre turned his back on Giza, and chose to build on this other splendid vantage point, is not known. But by so doing, he ensured the destruction of his monument.

In the 1880s, according to Sir Flinders Petrie, stone from the Abu Roash pyramid was carried away at the rate of three hundred camel-loads per day.[3] No one knows how large the pyramid was, only that it contained several unusual features, and was probably never finished. It may even have been a step pyramid, not a true pyramid at all. Today, only a core remains, surrounded by immense heaps of granite chips, the remnants of the original casing. Few tourists go there in the best of times.

We took the Desert Road towards Alexandria, and then cut back towards the Nile, on a road rutted by heavy trucks through newly built up industrial areas, sprawling and ugly. Several times, we stopped to ask about the pyramid, and were told firmly by peasants and a policeman that, if pyramids were of interest, we had best head back to Giza.

Finally, at the village of Abu Roash, we found a twisting lane that led towards the high plateau on which we knew the remains of Djedefre's pyramid would be found. But how to get there remained a problem. The road passed out of the village and skirted a modern rock quarry. More villagers emphatically denied the existence of a local pyramid or, scratching their heads, thought they could remember something about one, but whose or where remained known only to God.

Our lane finally ended at a machinery repair shop on the outskirts of wilderness. But here we found our guide. Bedawi, who proclaimed himself a skilled mechanic earning 300 LE per month, put on a clean shirt and jumped into the backseat. Under his instruction, we snaked along a dirt track between cultivated areas and desert, and at last, up a long incline to the top of the plateau.

The pyramid, when finally Bedawi called a halt, was hardly recognizable. Massive rubble encrusted blocks, melded to one another and to the hilltop, which formed a low mound. Wind from hell embraced us as we picked our way over the rubble, and descended carefully into the open and unusually large tomb chamber. The core was like a blast furnace. But though there was plenty of fox scat, all traces of the pharaoh had vanished.

Back on top, we were joined by a guard, who clapped his hands rudely to attract our attention, ordered us to show a tasrih, and demanded to know how much we were prepared to pay him. He shadowed us as we examined the adjacent boat pit and temple complex, and circled among sand-filled excavations that looked like pit tombs.

Rejecting our story of the camel trains carrying Djedefre's building blocks off to the lime kilns, Bedawi insisted that "foreigners" had destroyed the pyramid—true, of course, given that the British took over Egypt in 1881. Moreover, Bedawi said, the wall paintings once here had been "destroyed by a great rain." Smaller excavations in the surrounding rock faces were reminiscent of monk cells, and I asked Bedawi if there had ever been a monastery on the site.

"God forbid," our guide intoned fervently, perhaps fearful that Christians might be encouraged to stake a claim.

From Djedefre's vantage point we could see, despite heavy smog, the still largely intact pyramids at Giza. The Diplomat looked at his watch–we might still be able to get back to Zamalek before the evening traffic jam. We paid the guard, packed Badawi into the back seat with promises of excellent baksheesh, and headed back towards the cool waters of the Nile. It was time to leave–the Diplomat had obviously been fighting a bout of flu all weekend, and needed to go to bed. This, being a man, he denied.

The Diplomat is feeling better, at Giza, July 1993

43

Spiritual Journey on the River

27 September 1993

The Nile is an electric current that flows through Egypt, energizing earth and living creatures. Wastelands crowd against the great river's green border, a fringe that narrows as the traveler moves south from Luxor until at last the cruise ship stops before the barrier of the first cataract at Aswan.

The American Cousin and I left Cairo at dawn, our one-hour flight over the eastern desert a reminder of the penalty for being cut off from the river's energy. She carried a pamphlet, linking select spots on the river to the chakras of the human body, points of accumulated energy, sources of seeing and knowing the divine. We read the pamphlet together, not altogether believing, but at least hopeful.

Ugly with new buildings, Luxor sprawled below, engulfing the great temple complex of Karnak. The pink brown hills of the West Bank, still hiding many treasures, are beautiful by comparison. Along both sides of the river, a thick line of dark green palm trees and cane fields hold back the desert.

A minibus dropped us near the moored *Nile Commodore* that would carry us two hundred kilometers upriver to Aswan. Two Egyptian sisters, one visiting from abroad, accompanied us as we staggered, carrying our cases, through two other tourist ships before finally fetching up before an obsequious steward on the correct boat. *Death on the Nile*, I thought, delighted by the white gloves. Death and rebirth are intertwined here in both imagination and reality and we were eager to begin.

Our fellow travelers, most of them British, were in prior occupation of the Commodore, spread over chairs and sun beds. Several of them, having boarded the ship in Cairo, were already deep pink, bordering on serious sunburn. When, after lunch, we were loaded into three coaches for a visit to the East Bank temples, our detachment grew. Ignorant cattle, we were herded by a young Egyptian woman, whose contempt for tourists could not be concealed. She chided our fellow travelers for not remembering what she had told them the day before, finally exclaiming in consternation, "Do you understand anything?" As a sometime university lecturer, I rather sympathized with her.

Afternoon sun bore down as the guide knelt to draw diagrams in the dust of a temple floor. Here is how the hypostyle hall was roofed, how the obelisks were raised, she told us. I recalled a lament by Florence Nightingale written over 140 years earlier that "The contrast could not be more terrible than the savages of the Present in the temples of the Past at Luxor,"[1] only this time it was tourists, not residents. I left the group to wander among columns that suggested energy, rejoining the others beside the Sacred Lake near the Great Scarab enthroned on his pedestal.

"Local women still come here to receive power," said the Guide. "Five times around the scarab for marriage and seven for pregnancy."

"How many times for divorce?" one of the Egyptian sisters asked, and we all laughed. Then, wondering if only barefoot peasants feel the surges of power that come from the great river, the Cousin and I left the sisters contemplating their chances at the scarab's pedestal.

Behind the dam, Lake Nasser swells like an embolism, with waters that for centuries inundated the riverine low lands, washing, renewing. The energy generated by the dam supplies but a tiny portion of Egypt's needs. Stretching towards the Delta, the lands reclaimed from the annual flood are turned into tenements and industrial areas. Those which remain under cultivation are loaded with debris once removed by the Nile and with chemicals now necessary for continued fertility.

But below the great dam the Nile continues its course, smooth, deep, and sometimes swift. Though it is a captive river, its power remains enormous. Peasant women washing clothes along its bank still offer prayers.

As the ship descended the river, we passed rows of rock cut tombs, hieroglyphic inscriptions, mud brick villages, and abandoned lime kilns, which in their time had devoured the stones of countless ancient temples. We floated by a sheikh's domed tomb, high on a barren hilltop, then flocks of black goats followed by brown, black, and red cattle feeding belly deep in the lush grass. Water buffalo reclined in the shallows. On the sundeck, Londoners spread their fleshy, tattooed, and half-naked bodies across the deck chairs.

Waiting to pass through the locks at Esna, we were accosted by boys and men in boats and knee deep in the river shallows. Shouting, they flung their merchandise onto the deck, gesturing, bargaining frantically over tablecloths and galabiyahs offered at high prices. The tourists purchased willingly, for fancy dress night was coming when we must all "go native." A teenager twirled a tiny crocodile and shrieked his price. Where, below the dam, had he obtained this unfortunate creature? Stray dogs lolled in the slight surf, among village rubbish and plastic waste from cruise ships.

Night fell before we reached mooring at Edfu. But darkness does not halt the river traffic, and despite the constant lament that tourism is "down," at daybreak, we discovered ourselves in company of eight other tourist vessels, all waiting to disgorge. Lines of coaches and carriages drawn by miserable horses jostled to carry us to the Ptolemaic temple. The entire town is a market where the soul of Egypt, personified in statues of Horus, is on sale.

The Cousin was suffering severe stomach cramps, but joined me on the coach that deposited us minutes later at the entrance of the temple dedicated to the trinity of Horus, Hathor, and Horus the Younger. But first, we must push our way through lines of makeshift stalls, manned by voracious hawkers of statues, tablecloths, galabiyahs, and scarabs. The merchants pursue, drape us with dresses and necklaces, shouting cheerfully into our faces as though we are hard of hearing: "Come into this shop, O My Queen. Only to look. Very cheap prices today, My Dear One!"

"But we have come to see Horus," I say.

"And to search for a pharmacy," mutters the Cousin who looks blanched, but determined. Our Guide waves us forward and down a passage beside enormous temple walls.

Around a corner, and we are face to face with immense basalt statues of Horus guarding the temple entrance. The gaggle of tourists treads carelessly on the sacred way. Time is short, for we must visit and reboard within an hour. Cameras flash in an effort to capture the unknowable.

I wander morosely, for I have been here before—alone. The guide, who yesterday threw her arm companionably around me, today looks away with a shrug. But the Cousin's pamphlet tells of "an Initiate" at Edfu, doubtless the guard who spots us now, two lambs separated from the flock. Silently, carefully, he sidles up and signals.

"Om. OOOMMM," he says and the walls respond "OOOM-MM." The passage is stuffy, musty with stale urine and bat droppings, and its walls are covered with fine carving.

"Stop here," orders the Initiate. He places me in a corner, where the stairway bends and pushes the Cousin against the opposite wall, our hands upon the carvings. "OOOMMM" we all intone. From the walls, energy flows into our hands.

"You are water," the Initiate tells me and to the Cousin, "You are light." Then, in a louder voice, "Horus! Horus! HOR-US!" Energy buckles and surges in the walls, as the Initiate makes obscure movements above our heads. We press our faces to the walls, transfixed. Three voices chant in unison, and the walls respond. Then the Cousin coughs and I remember the waiting ship—and the pharmacy.

"Are you a Muslim?" I ask the Initiate.

"Of course," he says. But I cannot follow his further explanation, although he speaks of his wife, Gamila, and of certain women who gather to pray.

"Light," he says. "Light and water. HOR-US." Scarcely breathing, we fix him with our half-believing eyes.

When the tourists have moved on, the Initiate leads us down the stairway, and behind the stone alter that houses the inner sanctuary. Again, we press ourselves against the stone and intone "OM." But although this time, there is no responding surge, we tip the Initiate handsomely, before moving out into the courtyards bright sunlight. Our fellow travelers gather for a group photograph around the best-preserved Horus statue, while the Cousin and I escape down another side passage, from which we eventually exit and find a pharmacy.

Too soon, we are back on board the *Commodore*, and Edfu is far behind. The Nile carries us quickly, so that by late afternoon, the walls of Kom Ombo rise before us. This time, we are within walking distance of the temple, though once again the way is hindered by scores of vendors selling Nubian caps, scarves, and still more galabiyahs.

Inside the temple complex, the group stops to admire a pile of crocodile mummies. The Cousin and I amble away once again and explore the temple, one section of which is propped up and off limits due to earthquake damage. Twice we feel energy points, though not so strongly as at Edfu. The Guide catches up, and points out stone friezes of surgical instruments, and an agricultural calendar.

That night, back on the *Commodore*, we all dress in our galabiyahs for dinner, after which we gather in the lounge. There, the British tour leader narrates, while the chosen members of the group act out the story of Osiris and Seth. Egyptian waiters, who have seen this countless times, watch silently as Seth slays Osiris and cuts him into pieces, which he flings to the hysterical crowd.

The vital bit, a cucumber in aluminum foil, is retrieved, and re-attached when Amun allows Osiris to be resurrected for a brief dalliance with Isis. A scrawny Englishman in a short gold shift, who represents Isis, climbs on board the alive but slumbering Osiris, now reunited with his cucumber. Soon, thereafter, Horus is born, emerging as an enormous fat Englishman in a nappy from under the skirts of the enthroned Isis. To universal delight, Horus slays the evil Seth, and a round of drinks is called for by all.

The Egyptian waiters hop to. Had the Diplomat been with us, he would definitely have intoned "Most unsuitable." What Florence Nightingale wrote was "And will England turn into Picts again, after a certain number of harvest years, as Egypt has turned into Arabs?"[2] Feeling self-righteous, the Cousin and I looked at one another and said "OM," after which we laughed for a long time.

It was very late, and I sat on the empty sundeck and watched the dark water sliding by. There is power here, energy and hope, and we have encountered it, I told myself. "One wonders that people come back from Egypt and live lives as they did before," the heroine of the Crimea wrote.[3] But, of course, she did not, and nor would I. The Cousin and I had talked through most of the night, and she and ancient Egypt had helped focus me on the Lord of Life. There is only one God who calls us.

When at 6 a.m., dawn splashed the Nile with color, we were on possibly the loveliest stretch of water in the world. Rock walls reach down to the river at several points, and the vegetation in secluded coves is exotic and deep green. Villages are few, birds legion. We journey through a pristine world of light and water, crying birds, and grand silence. Glossy ibis feed at water's edge, and a great mystery unfolds us as silently, majestically, as the enchained but northward flowing river carries us south towards Aswan.

The river runs briskly between great rocks, and then opens to a brown expanse bordered by banana and date palm plantations that alternate pink, yellow, white, and brown hills, closing down to the river before opening again and again. At Aswan, floating reed beds are sprinkled with purple water hyacinth blossoms, fishing herons, and pied kingfishers.

When the others, including the Cousin, have all crowded into buses for Philae, the morning is mine, and I ask the barman to turn off the music on the sundeck. The boat is moored third in a file of three, so that I have full view of the reed beds where fishermen in feluccas work with nets and beating sticks. A squacco heron, inexplicably unable to fly, is carried by the current towards a moving cruise ship. Desperately, I will energy into the struggling bird. But although it squabbles frantically at the side of the ship, the bird is quickly sucked under. I ask myself if this is a sign, but find no answer. All I know is that the Voice wishes to speak to me, and that I am resisting because of fear.

That afternoon, the Cousin and I take a felucca across the river and hire camels to carry us up to the ruined sixth century monastery of St. Simeon. Mohamed, the caretaker, knows all the secret places where monks sought refuge before the monastery finally closed in the fourteenth century. He crawls into a drainage pipe and leads us through a hidden passage and mimes how the monks slept in their short clay cots. But he treats the altars with respect, giving names to faces in the vanishing frescoes.

"Then you were once a monk yourself," I challenge him. Mohamed looks at me closely.

"Yes," he says shortly, and we move on to another part of the monastery.

The next morning, we take the people's ferry across the River to the Tombs of the Nobles. Irregular rock steps lead up the cliff, where we are intercepted by the guardian of the tombs. He leads us along the rock face and, before entering the first of several sixth-to-twelfth dynasty tombs, evokes God's mercy. Then, because the late afternoon flight will take us back to Cairo, we climb the hill behind the tombs to pay our respects to the river.

The ruined qubba of Ali Ibn al Howa, Son of the Wind, commands the highest point at Aswan. A pale crag martin, evidently guardian spirit of the tomb, for he has been there every time I visited over the years, keeps close watch as we mount the hill, past open tombs and crumbing bones, to the enormous rock on which the *qubba* stands. The crag martin soars and swoops for he, too, is son of the wind, a creature of light and water. The Nile spreads magnificently around her islands and rocks. The moored tourist boats and ugly hotels are a temporary blight.

When we descend the hill towards the people's ferry, an elderly sheikh instructs the young men to make room for us on the bench. As the boatman pushes off, the sheikh asks God's mercy on our crossing. But I realize already that this most recent time on the Nile has been a breakthrough for me. God wants me to listen and I have decided to follow the invitation to which Love is inviting me. "Though you slay me, Lord, yet will I trust you."

"Michael, row the boat ashore! Hallelujah! The water is deep, the river is wide. Promised land on the other side. Hallelujah!" I sing softly as the small ferry crosses the Nile.

Fun in a canal near the Nile, 1993

44

Looking for Michael in Middle Egypt

1 October 1993

Few tourists visit Sohag, Assyut, and Minya. Minya, to be sure, contains the nearest hotels to Tell Amarna, Tuna el-Gebel, and Ashmuneim. But Assyut is full of terrorists, so the newspapers say, and Sohag is remote and of little interest. Even the university in Sohag is really only a branch of Assyut University, hotbed of the Party of the Beards. Best, we are advised, allow such places to squat in isolation on the great river. No one, meaning no one with any brains, comes from there—or goes there.

Except the Diplomat. A local gossip columnist heard of his plans for an official tour and wrote of the "holiday destination" sought by "an adventurous political spirit," expressing hope that the Diplomat would survive, if only to give another of his garden soirées. However, it had been four years since an official British visit to the governorates, and some people in London were grumbling about the dearth of supervision of funded development projects, abandoned VSOs[1], and general lack of an ear to the ground by the British Embassy in Cairo.

We left Cairo on a Friday morning. At the wheel was Ahmad, a kindly and stolid man who exists from shisha stop to shisha stop, and who was eager to show off skills recently acquired on an evasive driving course in London. El Saff, the first major town south of Cairo, was a jungle of Friday markets. Newly slaughtered animals hung from hooks or lay at roadside. "Avoid contact with freshly slaughtered animals," warned a recent bulletin from London, intended to quell our fears about an outbreak of Rift Valley fever.

Ahmed threaded the Discovery through the warren of carcasses, mud brick, and concrete buildings. On the outskirts of town, we stopped for tea, and for Ahmad, a shisha, before striking out on the Desert Road that winds through a stark depression, surrounded by a wind-molded escarpment. Periodically, women and children lurched to their feet at roadside, waving cucumbers. Where in this wasteland had they grown them?

The Diplomat and I hunkered in the backseat, as Ahmad accelerated to 140 kilometers on the smooth, new road. Our minds idled, as miles of desert enveloped us. Sitting doing absolutely nothing was bliss. Sometimes we just held hands, especially on the curves. And occasionally I sang "On the road again. Makin' music with my friends. I just wanna be on the road again" and, after that, "Michael, row the boat ashore. Hallelujah!"

Ahmad, preoccupied by need for nicotine, said little. I'd brought along a large hat, suitable for audience with three governors, and kept checking that it had not fallen under the suitcases behind us. The Diplomat mused about the Governor of Assyut's refusal to receive him. Security? Rank too low? Actually, as we were soon to discover, a parallel visit of the Egyptian Prime Minister.

Some thirty kilometers from Minya, we spotted a sign to the Church of the Virgin and turned off the road. Here the Holy Family, plus Sallouma, their midwife, are said to have spent three days during the flight into Egypt. In 328 AD the Empress Helena, mother of Constantine the Great, erected a church over the cave where the foursome stayed. Our approach was through a village that is home to 3,500 Copts and no Muslims, although Muslims as well as Christians consider the church a place of pilgrimage. We drove up past rock quarries, where most of the villagers work, and then through an extensive cemetery of above ground tombs. A large rest house, built in 1985, faces the church. And British money had built a school here.

Abu Kyros, or Gebel El Teir, the Monastery of the Birds, the site is called, although neither monks nor birds are in evidence anymore. The birds, perhaps migrating storks, ceased their annual pilgrimage in the seventh century, according to Magar, our guide. Thus other names have been supplied: the Monastery of the Cave and the Monastery of Bakara (who may possibly, we are told, have been a water witch).

The once-glorious church is today small and poorly furnished, but contains at least one fine icon of the Virgin and Child, said to date from 1554. Rock-hewn pillars, a lovely baptistery carved into one, and a door lintel with fine stone carvings of birds, fish, animals, and saints are said to remain from Helena's era. The cave is simple, and there is little decoration. But the church's pillars are covered with red hand prints and crosses, smeared henna offerings placed by brides and grooms, Muslims and Christians, who seek the Virgin's blessing.

On the second story, up a stone staircase, are chapels to St. George and the Archangel Michael, both built by the Bishop of Minya in the nineteenth century. These are shabby and poorly kept, and there are no chairs here or in the main church itself. But the proximity of the chapels suggests affinity between the two spiritual warriors, guardians against the Evil One.

At Minya, we stopped in spacious riverine gardens for our picnic. Below, a fine Nile steamer rots at quayside. Ahmed dined on bread, cheese, cucumbers, and, in the absence of shisha, several cigarettes. Then, on towards Sohag, along the agricultural road past high cliffs honeycombed with Greco-Roman tombs. By four p.m. we had reached Sohag, and were sitting on a balcony of the university guesthouse watching the Nile flow past.

But not for long. Soon the guesthouse sitting room had filled with university, government, and police dignitaries and officials, including the small round Inspector of English Instruction. The Inspector overflowed with flowery phrases and attempted to have us transferred to the government guesthouse. But the Dean held firm.

Then the Voluntary Service Overseas representative arrived and we were whisked off to the nearby town of Akhmim for a moonlight look at the gigantic statue of Meryt Amun, favorite daughter of Ramses II. Sirens wailed, and pickup trucks filled with uniformed police and plain clothes men in galabiyahs with long rifles, drove before and after. Ahmed tailgated as we careened through the village. This was what he had been trained to do in London, and his smile was beatific.

Meryt Amun, found face forward under the rubble three years earlier, now stands enormous in the floodlight, traces of paint still apparent on her full lips and finely carved granite clothing. A great entourage of officials followed us through the site and told of plans to move the town's entire population into the desert, so that layers of hidden history could be revealed and tourism could spring forth. An owl alighted on Meryt Amun's shoulder.

Next, a visit to the weaving plant, where workers had been ordered to put in an appearance on Friday night for our benefit. The looms clattered, driven by hand and foot, as boy workers pulled cords that ensured correct design in bed covers and dress materials. Then, soft drinks, soft words, and gifts, followed by the drive back to Sohag for a tour of the "cultural stadium."

"What's your name?" demanded the first English lesson tape, just as we had heard it hundreds of times earlier from young and old Egyptians. After the language lab, we saw the children's library, the computer lab, sports fields and tennis courts, all credited to the farsighted Governor. It was 11:30 before we sat for dinner of cold fried pigeon and several other cold fried meats, served beside the Olympic size outdoor swimming pool. Over dinner, the Inspector of English assured me of his abhorrence of American English.

"Impure," he said. "Confusing. I can always tell the difference." When he asked where I was born, I gritted my teeth and replied, truthfully, that my ancestors came from Scotland.

By 8 a.m. next morning, the guesthouse had already begun to fill with assorted officials. We were taken first to the university, where the Dean described his concerns over Nile pollution. A tour of the medical school laboratories revealed a dearth of cadavers for the students ("People are very conservative"), as well as several recently purchased and very expensive Japanese microscopes and computers, some with coffee stains already in place.

I browsed in the Social Sciences library: *Dictionary of Physics* (1922) and *Dictionary of Statistics* (1911), etc. Meanwhile, the Diplomat was being shown several score volumes, said to be from King Farouk's library, though no one knew how they got to Sohag. Piled willy-nilly in an uncatalogued heap were five complete volumes of Roberts prints. The Dean groaned when the Diplomat pointed out the great commercial value of the Roberts books, and said he would try to have them locked away that afternoon. "You have no idea how difficult it is," he said, not for the first time.

From the university, sirens again in full voice, we went to call on the Governor. A large gentleman in fashionable Italian pumps and a tailored safari suit that was a size or two too small, the governor was at ease with his subordinates, and very positive. Sohag governorate is the same size and has the same resources as Assyut, he said, but we are totally different. There is no nonsense here of firing on cruise boats. Qena to the south and Assyut to the north, yes these have many problems. But Sohag is peaceful, for we give recreational outlets to youth, and solve police problems at an early stage. Returning somewhat later to the theme, the Dean suggested privately that Sohag serves a valuable function as a place of refuge from troubles with the police. The Diplomat and I began to understand that the more we saw, the less we knew.

Outside the governmental offices, shouting heralded the arrival of a group of theological students and workers, come to demonstrate support for Mubarak's third term as President of Egypt. The governor joined the chanting, banner waving crowd, as he escorted us out of the building.

"They say they are willing to sacrifice Mubarak," the Inspector of English told me with great sincerity. To this I expressed great joy, admonishing myself to keep a straight face, and congratulated him on his command of English. After all, his English was much better than my Arabic. Out then, into the desert, to see the wonders the Governor had wrought. Our first stop was the fourth century Monastery of the Archangel Michael, which had reopened in 1980.

"A monk lives here with four nuns," explained the Inspector of English, later referring to one monk and six novices currently in residence. The nearby land grab on traditional monastery property had the small religious community worried: weavers from Akhmim, it seemed, were already moving in next door, where a smart new village was under construction.

Eighteen months ago, there was nothing but desert around the monastery, we were told. But trim pink brick cottages had been erected and some were already occupied. We descended the hill and had another look at weaving on ancient handlooms. A short drive away, wells were pumping water from underground aquifers for a new 150-feddan plantation of Japanese mulberry trees, intended to feed silkworms for a new sericulture industry.

We drove on, visiting a nearly completed hilltop rest house, flanked by a spectacular mosque with twin minarets. An enormous vase-shaped fountain was turned on for our benefit. The monk, who had attached himself to our group, was silent as we admired the view over the valley and his once secluded monastery. The obligatory cold drink signaled our departure for a holiday camp of colorful tents in the valley below. There, in a circus tent with a tiled floor, we drank tea in praise of the Governor. It was 4 p.m. before we reached the Sohag police club and lunch.

That night, we dined at the Meryt Amun Hotel, again on plenty of cold meat. But first and afterwards we sat in the hotel's overgrown garden and smoked shisha after shisha as the Inspector of English expounded on his need for VSOs to teach proper English, and the Dean informed me about his membership in the Helwatia Sufi order.

"Do you remember the picture in my office?" he asked. "He is my guide. Do you understand what the *mutasawif* means?"

Power, I said. Divine power flowing through you. But, thinking of the Archangel Michael, who seemed to have a special presence in the area, I asked the Dean if he had a nonhuman guide as well. The Dean was shocked.

"We have no such thing in Islam," he said. And then our private conversation was interrupted by the others.

After a final call next morning on the University Vice President, we began our journey back to Cairo. The police escort crowded other traffic off the road, once stopping to seize the license of a taxi driver who refused to yield right of way. The escort accompanied us to the ruined White Monastery, established in the fourth century, brought to fame by St. Shenouda, and rebuilt in the tenth century.

Stones with pharaonic inscriptions and friezes, and Greco-Roman capitals from Atubis some ten kilometers away, are incorporated into the enormous basilica, only a portion of which retains its roof. Twenty acres are all that remain of the once vast monastic properties, and only five monks and several novices exist at the White Monastery in uneasy alliance with government authorities. With the exception of the church, the original monastic buildings lie unexcavated under the sand. A faded fresco of the Messiah enthroned adorns the church's remaining central dome.

Everyone took off their shoes to enter the church; but outside, in the main part of the original church, Coptic families picnicked and Muslim visitors smoked cigarettes. Up a stairway is the entrance to the ancient well, still providing drinking water, and a wall behind which visitors urinate.

A young novice in a white robe and black shawl was in charge of a small book and souvenir shop, and I asked him about the Archangel whose icon was displayed in the church. But the novice was uninformed or perhaps intimidated by the throng of officials.

The nearby Red Monastery, once home to 1,800 monks, is associated with the memory of Anba Bishoi. There are no monks there now, only a caretaker who led us into the tiny, thick-walled chapel of the Virgin, its outer walls painted pink. In the keep are fine grape leaf and acanthus stone carvings, and the main church has damaged, but still beautiful, frescos in its three remaining domes. Niches for long removed statues help support the domes, and there are traces of yellow, green, and red on the pillars.

But here, too, decay is far advanced. The iconostasis is of crude wood and has only five remaining icons, all in poor condition. There has been no restoration other than a tentative shoring up of the remaining part of the once great edifice. The Archangel hides his face. Still, in the courtyard, a blind man sings softly, smiling to himself.

Our guards accompanied us for about one hundred kilometers as Ahmed headed back towards Minya. There we overnighted at a four-star hotel, devoid of tourists. Our late afternoon stroll along the corniche was shadowed by a plainclothes guard, who drove off curious children. Next morning, the Governor of Minya received us cordially. But he had heard nothing of attacks on Sufis by radical elements, and wished only to reassure us that everyone in Egypt supports Mubarak for a third term. Later, on the outskirts of Minya, we drove through expansive and ancient Muslim and Christian cemeteries before heading north once again on the desert road. The same forlorn women and children, perhaps offering the same cucumbers, appeared.

The Governor of Beni Suef was not interested in us, and we stopped only briefly with him before going on, again under armed guard, to the village of Fashn some forty kilometers distant. Are the guards for honor or security? No one was saying. The road along the canal parallels the railroad line with its many colonial era stations, most with broken roofs.

Father Raphael of St. Mark's School collected us from the mayor's office, and we toured the installation where he intends, with British money, to start a training program for the physically and mentally handicapped. A small new photocopier, still in its container, was produced as earnest of his determination. In his eagerness to show it to us, the assistant dropped the fragile equipment.

It was late afternoon. Our entourage, including the National Democratic Party's local youth representative who is about 45, gathered for orange soda and chocolate biscuits in Father Raphael's office. Then, still under police escort, we exited Fashn with great flourish and even greater speed. With Ahmad at the wheel, it would take only two hours to reach Cairo, even on the agricultural road. "Michael row the boat ashore," I sang.

Icon of the Archangel Michael, church of St Mary the Virgin,
Al Muallaqat, Old Cairo (image provided by the church authorities).

45

Siwa: Escape from a Dying Oasis

12 November 1993

Alexander the Great visited Siwa, and Herodotus described the renowned oracle that first brought fame to the oasis. But those were the days of glory. The modern Siwa oasis is a place of mudbrick medinas, endless palm groves against desert sky, and sullen people hanging on to the end of a rope of violent history. Their salt-sodden world has been joined to the rest of Egypt, and the splendid isolation, which was Siwa's protection, is no more. Only the violence seems not to have ended. There is still power in Siwa, but it is of the sort that stalks.

The six-hour drive from Cairo to Mersa Matrouh bypasses Alexandria, crosses the battlefield of El Alamein, and continues along the northern coast. In the year since last we visited, the northern coast has been deeply damaged by strip cutting of limestone. Entire hillsides for mile after mile were cut away, and mountains of limestone bricks litter the verges, sometimes spilling over onto the highway. The monotonous destruction of the left of the highway was in keeping with the construction of rows of ugly villas and resort hotels on the seaward side of the road.

The Diplomat and I spent the night at the once isolated Beau Site Hotel, now surrounded by unattractive high-rise buildings. There were few other guests as it was October, and we were able to swim alone in the last afternoon in an aquamarine sea. Libya lay 130 kilometers to the West, and the Siwa oasis some three hundred kilometers almost straight south.

The town of Mersa Matrouh is a pathetically cruel place where hundreds of donkeys are worked to death each year, pulling heavy carts and overloaded "traps" which serve as taxis. Unshod, beaten with clubs, and many covered with terrible sores, few of the donkeys survive past five years. As we left town early the next morning, a military truck careened by us, and nearly collided with a donkey cart. Irate soldiers piled off the truck.

"Donkey," they brayed at the cart driver while the little gray slave, cruelly twisted in his traces, stood trembling.

We could have approached Siwa from the Baharia oasis, the route chosen in 524 B.C. by the army of Cambyses of Persia who hoped to destroy the Siwan oracle. However, his entire army of 50,000 was said to have vanished beneath the sand, after which the oracle spoke on for several hundred more years. The second approach is from the Libyan oasis of Jaghbub. But only smugglers use that route today, although there are rumors of a plan to clear the World War II minefields and open the road officially. We chose the third way, speeding in comfort on the modern highway along the old caravan route from Mersa Matrouh.

Travelers still arrive in Siwa with relief after traversing miles of unrelenting and mainly flat desert. But the deep greens of Siwa are deceptive, for this is a dying oasis, salt choked and treacherous. Siwa is a place of dead villages, dead soil, dead lakes, pillaged antiquities, and endless desecrated graves whose scattered bones crunch accusingly underfoot. Anyone who says differently has a hidden agenda, or is not paying attention.

But Siwa has always been a place of death. For at least 2,500 years it has lured travelers, traders, and would-be conquerors to their death. Some visitors have perished en route, and others died in the oasis itself, at the hands of the Siwans or of their own travel companions. The natural dangers of malaria and thirst have collected still others, as have the hazards of crumbling tombs and dwellings. It is also possible that more visitors than we care to know have died of causes that defy ordinary explanation. According to the fifteenth century Arab writer Al-Maqrizi, the inhabitants of Siwa "suffer much from the 'Jinn' who take away whomsoever they find alone," adding ominously that "the inhabitants hear their murmuring."[1]

The central feature of Siwa town is the ruined medieval fortress of Shali, from which the population fled in 1926 during massive rains that dissolved the salt-impregnated mud bricks of which the medina was built. The only ancient structure that remains in use is the fourteenth century mosque, roofed with palm trunks. Inside, visitors wander dangerously over crumbling walls and up melted stairways.

Across from the ancient medina is the Jebel al Mawta, honeycombed with late Roman tombs and connected to Shali, according to legend, by an underground passageway. During World War II, the citizens of Siwa town fled to Jebel al Mawta, tossed out the bones of their ancestors, and settled down to wait out Italian air raids on resident British forces.

Not far from Shali, on a hilltop in the village of Aghurni, is the desecrated Temple of Jupiter Amun, which once housed the oracle. The medina that surrounds the temple was abandoned early this century, and even the mosque is now disused due to mud brick disintegration. Although views from the temple over the salt lakes and palm groves are spectacular, there is no apparent remaining power there. The oracle does not speak, and even its presence is difficult to imagine. Ahmed Fakhry carried out some restoration in 1970, but the back wall of the temple of the oracle "is now at the edge of the cracking rock and will fall down if any more slides occur."[2]

The Temple of Jupiter Amun was connected by a causeway to a second temple of Amun, now known as the Temple of Umm 'Ubayhad. Majestic among the date palms, only a single wall of this second temple remains because of an earthquake in 1811, as well as to reuse of stone by a governor of Siwa in 1897. Nearby is the Jebel Dahrour, filled with tombs of the thirtieth dynasty and later. The whole is laced together by date palm groves dripping late autumn fruit. Innumerable springs feed the salt marshes.

We began our visit at Birket Siwa, west of Shali. Here, as everywhere in the oasis, people are constructing houses of limestone bricks from the Mediterranean coast. The skeletal white contrasts with the muted earth colors of the surroundings; and although the new dwellings are not susceptible to rainfall, they hold the cold of winter and heat of summer. In a palm grove, we heated coffee and a pot of stew, recuperating from the heat of the desert drive to the oasis. A foraging lizard arrived to investigate but, unable to tolerate the attack of a marching army of enormous ants, quickly retreated into thick underbrush, filled with the scrabbling of unseen creatures. Two cranes lifted from the salt march and, far out, wintering flamingos waded.

The problem with Siwa is that there is no way out, at least for water. In modern times, authority has never been sufficiently in control to utilize water properly. Nor have they found a way to channel the spring water out of the depression. Salt marshes ring the area, and cultivated land soon becomes too saline for further use except by more palm groves. But even the salt is of such poor quality that it cannot be exported. We wondered if salt had not contributed to the Siwans' seemingly dull disinterest, and even aggressiveness, in contrast to the usual Egyptian courtesy and kindness to outsiders.

Rejecting the unfriendly and dirty Bride of the Oasis Hotel, we checked into the basic but fairly clean Cleopatra. When darkness fell, we watched from our tiny balcony as floodlights lit the ruined medina of Shali. In the road below, homeward-bound donkeys were hammered by their drivers, and chickens were carried by their wings in the so called "pharaonic mode" which, despite the name, is cruelly practiced from the Middle East through to Asia. Usually the birds hang in limp agony, though occasionally one cries hoarsely "Rahma! Rahma!" In Siwa, however, there seems to be no such mercy.

At Abdo's café, we settled to watch the street scene. Men smoked shisha and played backgammon, some speaking in the Siwan language, a Berber dialect. According to our waiter, who wore blue bib overalls and a Palestinian headdress—but said he was a native of Siwa—the reason some donkeys' ears are cropped is punishment for biting. A nearby tethered donkey had evidently put up quite a struggle: both ears were cut and at different lengths. Perhaps his battle was not yet over, for his eyes were still alert. "Lord, in your rahma hear our prayer."

That night we slept poorly, battling dreams and swarms of mosquitoes attracted to our sweaty flesh. Until well after midnight, heavy goods trucks ground gears as they passed, heading out of the oasis towards the coast. At 2:30 a.m., lulled by the drone of mosquitoes, we were just dropping off to sleep when, inexplicably, cocks began to crow. It was the signal for the packs to assemble. As the barking of feral dogs grew louder, sleep fled. As dawn broke, I watched a white dog with twine deeply embedded in his neck, the ring of gore a mark of ownership gone rogue.

On the outskirts of town, we breakfasted beside a ruined mud dwelling on the edge of a salt lake before beginning a twenty-five-kilometer drive to the West. The track took us past the White and Red mountains to the Bilad al-Rum, where mud brick ruins of what some say was an early Christian church sit beneath a myriad of rock-hewn tombs. Further on towards Libya is the district of al-Maraqi, said to be probably the most fertile in the oasis, but capable of supporting only a fraction of the population of centuries past. And everywhere there are rock tombs, heavily damaged by centuries of treasure hunting. A Doric temple, still standing in 1869 and thought by the few outsiders who saw it to be the most beautiful temple in the oasis, had vanished completely.

In the early afternoon, back in the vicinity of the Temple of Jupiter Amun, we sought a quiet place where we could watch birds while eating lunch. But although there was limited shade on the border of a salt marsh, the spot was littered with the bones of abandoned donkeys, and there were no birds other than a soaring marsh harrier. The atmosphere was foul: dead lake and dead soil in a region encrusted with salt that sparkled in the fierce sunlight.

The Diplomat and I felt dull-witted, oppressed, and then urgently in need of leaving. We turned the Range Rover around to go and, though a moment earlier we had been completely alone, were halted by the appearance of two donkey carts approaching down the narrow marsh track. As we waited, the carts closed rapidly, then stopped. Without greeting, the driver of one cart said he wished to go left into the palm groves, and the second pointed aggressively straight into the marsh. It was apparent that the track was too narrow for either cart to continue until we moved out of the way.

I left the Range Rover to direct traffic, as the Diplomat began to maneuver onto the narrow bridge over a ditch. It didn't look like the carts could pass the Range Rover on the bridge, but as our vehicle pulled forward, the driver of the first cart suddenly beat his donkey, and cart and donkey then rushed forward from their side.

I was trapped between the car and the cart, with no space to open the door and get back into the Range Rover, even had there been time. Moreover, from the side of the donkey cart, there extended a long metal spike. I was, evidently, about to be either impaled on the spike or pushed beneath the wheels of the Range Rover. Frantic, I shouted to the Diplomat.

When I opened my eyes moments later, the two carts had passed over, as had the Range Rover. I stood alone on the small bridge.

"Drive! Drive!" I screamed, leaping into the car.

"Are you wounded?" cried the Diplomat. Possessed by fear, I could only shout at him again to drive on. In this place evil lurked, followed and, finding opportunity, struck. Although my flesh was unmarked, I felt than an enormous hole had been ripped in my auric shield. Who were these men with the donkey carts? How had they arrived just when they did, and how had the man with the steel spike known I would get out of the car, and thus positioned himself to such advantage? How had I survived? Was it all a fluke, a nightmare?

There were no rational answers to such questions, but energy gushed out where, so it seemed, the spike had passed through me. Apprehensive, unusually fearful, I rested eventually beside the ruins of Umm 'Ubaydah.

By late afternoon, we were once again far out in the desert, this time east of Siwa on the road which eventually peters out into a sandy track that continues to Baharia. Shaken and cautious, we did not stop to explore the temple in the village of Abu Shuruf, where children tried to detain us by jumping onto the Range Rover. But further on, in the ruined village of Al-Zaytoun, founded by freed slaves of the Grand Sanussi, we crawled through a still unexcavated stone temple of the Ptolemaic era. Rusting German jerry cans and fallen palm log roof beams represented the scattered hopes of people who, during the Nasser era, had been moved to Giza for easier surveillance.

The Diplomat emptied a modern jerry can of petrol into the empty tank of the Range Rover, and we headed back toward Siwa City. As darkness was not far off, we decided not to stop at an empty prison camp where Nasser's opponents had been detained. Then, a sudden puncture ensured that we did not make it back to

Siwa until after dark. Something seemed to be reaching out for us, trying to hold on. We both felt it and expressed foreboding.

That evening, the Anthropologist found us just as we entered the East-West Café. Overflowing with ideas about her projects and personal importance to the oasis, she attached herself to us as we ate. Behind the glitter in her eyes, staring from a face encased in the headdress of a Siwan woman of thirty years past, madness wavered. Her husband, likewise garbed in a flowing outfit, sat at a nearby table surrounded by fawning young Siwan men.

"I have many enemies," he told us, to which the Siwans responded that this could not be, so seeing how much they cared for him. "Oh, yes," the foreigner said, "I have many enemies."

When the Anthropologist, smiling with expressionless eyes, pressed me to go with her that evening to a Siwan home, I was momentarily tempted. But placing my hand over what felt like a still oozing spiritual wound, I decided going might be a very dangerous move. So did the Diplomat, a rational man, who knew nothing about my feeling of spiritual wounding, but also felt the danger.

"If you had gone," he told me as we drove back to the Cleopatra, "I didn't know if I would have seen you again."

The mosquitoes were fewer that night, the dogs farther away, and the roosters less vocal. But my dreams were all of leaving. In the morning, inexplicably, we found we had yet another flat tire, and while the Diplomat was changing it, the jack collapsed—delaying us by at least another hour. Then despite all promises, the petrol station still had nothing to sell.

The Diplomat emptied our last jerry can of petrol into the Range Rover. I took the wheel and did not relax until we had climbed out of the Siwan depression.

46

Sorting It Out with the Zebaleen

20 February 1994

Where the zebaleen live, few outsiders go, and fewer still are welcomed. In the rocky, rubbish filled space they call home, just outside Cairo, between the Moqattam Hills and the northern cemetery, hatred and animosities flare easily, for there is little margin against death, both physical and spiritual. See the scaling skin, the inflamed eyes, the filthy hands and clothes. Try not to stare at those whose faces are stretched tight and hard by burn scars.

No one here looks really clean, and the children are particularly begrimed. And as usual it is the weak—the women, the children, and the animals—who are most exploited. The flesh of the zebaleen is under assault, and also the spirit.

The Moqattam Hills, a rock quarry to the pharaohs, is these days home to some of their least fortunate heirs. The zebaleen are those who live by picking through that which even Cairo's other poor throw away. The narrow lanes of the trash pickers' village are sodden, awash with rubbish, garbage, children, and dogs. What others discard, the zebaleen take home. Piles of bottles, cans, plastic containers, metal, and cloth flow into the streets from their ramshackle and illegal houses. These items, and even the seemingly edible rubbish, are tipped into the ravine, from which smoke rises in clouds. The omnipresent putrid stench overwhelms visitors.

Behind the settlement rises a blackened rock face. Weakened by years of burning, the hillside recently split off an enormous section, which crashed down on the hovels, killing at least thirty people. The next day, an eyewitness reported, the area was also littered with the corpses of pigs, for the zebaleen are Christians, and allowed to raise pigs in the shadow of the City of a Thousand Minarets.[1]

"Such pork is dangerous," a Christian Egyptian, who is not one of the zebaleen, told me, recounting the story of her near death from trichinosis. Subsequently, she said, "I came to appreciate the Judaic and Islamic injunctions against eating pigs." Vaguely, I remembered eating dry, stringy, tasteless Egyptian pork years earlier, and wondering about the origin. That little piggy clearly had a miserable life before he was turned into pork. Rubbish in, rubbish out.

It would be difficult to find a spot in all Egypt where animals, donkeys in particular, are in worse shape than among the zebaleen. Their drivers are often reckless young boys, hungry, illiterate, absent-minded, and socially brutalized. All day, their small grey and white draft animals, locked in jerry-rigged harness, pull the heavy carts by twos and threes through Cairo's tangled traffic. Whipped and clubbed, their legs are lamed, their back and feet often bloody. Some fall and die on the way, or are smashed by motor traffic. Once, I saw a donkey being led away with a hunk of flesh as large as a great pot roast hanging off a back haunch. The living flesh bobbled as the stricken animal walked on.

"I first came here four years ago," Samira told me. "Leila brought me. I saw her hug these people and sit on the floor with them and I was amazed. Since then, I have learned to give and to receive love. But we don't give charity."

We stood on the second floor of the Association for Protection of the Environment's new center, overlooking the ravine. The girls, Samira said, are required to wash themselves and their hair and clothes before coming inside, before being taught to read, to sew, and to weave rag rugs. Earning power gives dignity, self-respect, even independence. Several teenage girls held out their work for our admiration.

In the ravine, the boys are emptying their carts. The load shifts on one foolishly parked cart, and it flips over, throwing the harnessed donkeys onto their sides. The boys shout angrily, and beat the donkeys back to their feet. The empty cart moves forward under the lash, pulled by staggering, limping little animals, tormented by boys who are likewise abused.

Now the sorters, whose parents have paid for this privilege, move forward to claim their rights. Broken glass, toxic chemicals, caustic substances, perhaps even explosive materials— all these must be sorted. The billowing smoke gathers in the hollows of the dump and curls into the lungs of the small zebaleen.

The girls trained at APE are wage earners and will, I tell myself, perhaps be more desirable as wives for the brutal young donkey drivers outside. But perhaps the girls' economic clout will help protect them from the lash, drudgery, and early death. Perhaps some of them will be able to read about birth control? Perhaps.

Certainly many other people also hope so. A French TV crew is rushing about, making a documentary, and downstairs two papermakers from the University of Minnesota are teaching a skill they hope will expand economic options for the zebaleen.

Leaving the Association for the Protection of the Environment, we are confronted by possibly the dirtiest 13-year-old boy in the world. He leans into the car, reaching for us, and one of my friends gives him a small baksheesh.

"Well, yes," she responds to my raised eyebrows. "I know they give no charity here. But he was watching the car, wasn't he? And… oh, bother! This *is* Egypt!" We drive slowly through the surrounding village on muddy, increasingly steep streets, until one of my fellow voyeurs loses her nerve, and orders the car to turn around. As we pass out of the zebaleen area, back onto the main road, donkey boys are beating their weary donkeys up the final, seemingly almost perpendicular, incline. The cart shudders, the donkeys heave, and a boy seated atop the cart brings down his club. He has been up since long before dawn; it is now nearly noon, and he is bringing the garbage home.

"What sort of husband, what sort of father will he become?" I asked myself.

47

Of Mud, Walls, and Women

31 March 1994

On the road to the delta, trucks, carts, and markets sprawl out into the road. Our bus threads its way through the maze of interlocking humanity, animals, vehicles, and vegetables. The towns are embolisms on the artery that leads to Tel Balamoun. We pass two large brick works. Despite official prohibition, Nile alluvium is still being baked into bricks.

Frankly, there isn't much left of Balamoun, a site occupied from at least the twentieth century B.C. until abandonment in the sixth century A.D. What remained of Balamoun's limestone temples and surrounding complexes was fed into nineteenth century kilns. Only a few scraps of white stone litter the salt mudflat, which stretches away to the surrounding hillsides. With other visiting members of the Egyptian Exploration Society, the Diplomat and I climb a hill and, thanks to vegetation patterns, trace the course of ancient foundation walls. The past is always with us, just beneath the surface of our physical and spiritual worlds.

"Howard Carter didn't pay much attention to mud brick," explains the British Archaeologist. He leads us past a gaggle of men who hack at the covering mud with short hoes. A line of brightly dressed young women in veils and straw hats are transporting the mud, dumping it a short distance away in "Howard Carter's Trench." Their posture is perfect, and the baskets ride securely on their heads. The women, teenagers really, and I grin at one another.

Too much of modern archaeology is actually this sort of rescue operation, the last encore for ancient worlds before the stage darkens forever. Got to get a fix of Memphis, before rising ground water dissolves it for all eternity. Rush to take photos of what's going to vanish beneath the Cairo ring road. Quickly examine the prehistoric graves at Pelusium, before farming canals cover the site. Dig up and reexamine the potsherds and mud bricks, hurled aside by earlier archaeologists and treasure hunters in their quest for statues and jewelry. Then, because we have forgotten who we are, we asphalt over the sites that could help us remember.

Modern Balamoun is a barren plain where even rescue archaeology seems impossibly late. Here the deluge has come and passed. On the surface, nothing survives and, subsurface, there are just mud brick walls. Only a blind lover could rejoice over Balamoun. Only the British archaeologist, who lovingly shows us the great wall built by Nectanebo I. More walls. More mud brick. Archaeology as necrophilia. And then we move on to nearby Beit el-Hagar.

Nectanebo built here as well, and his efforts are more evident. However, the immense temple to Isis, constructed in the thirtieth dynasty, is now a massive mound of jumbled stone. An earthquake, one of our fellow-travelling archaeologists ventures. The rest of us nod sagely, and scramble among the fallen granite blocks, many with fine carvings. Wait! I had seen that erect posture earlier in the day. And the two hands raised in greeting. Egypt lives, despite the jumble.

"Ah," says the Diplomat. "There's that one breasted woman again." On a broken block, square-shouldered Isis receives the homage of lesser gods. Queen of heaven and earth, life and death, she stands proud, maternal, serene. Rude little boys shout at us from the surrounding concrete block wall, throw a few pebbles, and are chased away by the custodian.

Later, en route home, I find myself chanting "unworthy custodians" in time with the churring of the tires. Not the specific custodians at Beit al-Hagar, of course, but all of us, foreigners as well as Egyptians, who have failed to protect important historical sites. Is there anyone other than archaeologists—because it's their job—who really cares about the past, except for monetary and other selfish purposes? Is there anyone who tries to connect past to present, other than to impress tourists? Is there really no connection between ancient history and present humanity, despite all our efforts to convince ourselves? Has the power of the ancient past entirely departed?

A few nights later, I attended an exhibition. "Transition" the Artist called it, choosing the medical term for that most painful period of labor, the interval when the child's head moves through the birth canal. The Artist, Nazli Madkour, has certainly labored in anguish, but although she had warned me that the paintings were filled with anger, I was not prepared for the depth of grief and fear that radiated from her latest work. Yet here at last, power, like a healing blessing, had come to rest between modernity and ancient Egypt.

"The Wailing" is perhaps too obvious. It centers on an enormous book, which belches fire and is clad in iron bars. Bearded men with red faces and bloody hands uphold the book, surrounded by pregnant, veiled, soul-drained women, mummy-form in their robes. The dancers look familiar to me, for I had seen these same lithe female figures only a few days earlier, carrying mud on their heads. Here they are faithfully reproduced as in the eighteenth dynasty tomb paintings, except for the tears they weep over their daughters.

"Look Forward in Anger," exhibited further down the wall, is the most violent pastel painting I have ever seen. Shagarat al-Dur, female ruler of the Islamic period, dominates one corner of the painting, sword in hand. Her posture is defensive, protective of the submissive women nearby. She is Isis reincarnate. But beside Shagarat al-Dur, the mummy form of an ominous green man is growing larger. As though this were not terrifying enough, Nazli's vision darkens further with the next painting.

"The Second Age of Chivalry" is explosive. Its central figure is a grotesque Anubis, the jackal god of death, presented here riding a donkey. Spears of lightning flash from the back of his head. Women, the living dead, stand motionless, mute with agony, in a molten landscape.

"I tell you, hopeless grief is passionless," Elizabeth Barrett Browning wrote. "If it could weep, it would arise and go." But although Nazli speaks with the voice of EBB, she is, I think, treading on the tail of Hieronymus Bosch.

I am annoyed by the jabbering crowd which jostles me, and amazed that people in this holy place keep wanting to chat about the dinner last night, the reception next. Inwardly I cringe, longing for shelter, for retreat from the scalding—fearful that I will weep openly. Until just before we leave, I ignore the Artist, fearful that I will not be able to endure her explanations. When Nazli finally finds me alone before one of her paintings, we weep together.

In the morning at the Gezira Club, the dogs and I stop beneath Mary's three trees, which tower like Graces over the golf course—weeping long branches, now bright green with tiny new leaves, and burnished orange with tassels. Soon, they will give birth to masses of yellow flowers. I pick up a large carob pod and break it open. Then stealthily, in the rich Nile alluvium, beneath the garden rubbish behind the tennis court wall, I plant three seeds.

Nazli's trees, I say to myself. May Isis water them with her tears.

Ancient and Modern: A woman at Tel Balamoun, March 1994

48

Serabit—the Place Where Moses Dwelt

14 April 1994

Serabit seems like the most remote place in Egypt. About forty kilometers north of Mount Sinai as the raven flies, the site is almost unknown to Egyptians as well as tourists. Entry from the main west coastal road to Sharm el-Sheikh is through a series of stunningly beautiful wadis, along the route Moses must have taken on his flight from Pharaoh. Our objective was possibly that of Moses as well: the mountaintop on which stands the Temple of Hathor, surely the highest pharaonic site.

Turning left into the desert at Abu Zeineima, we drove 38 kilometers along ruined asphalt, often dodging enormously overloaded trucks. Since ancient times, manganese has been mined here. It was Easter weekend, following a rainy winter, and thousands of long dormant desert plants were in bloom—carpeting the sand in purple, yellow, and white flowers: tiny, neat, perfect. The trucks became fewer, and finally the track burst out into the fabulous Wadi Humur.

Everywhere there were signs of seminomadic human society. Goats, scattered shacks with adjacent tents, a black bag hung in a larder tree, pickup trucks. Boys appeared from nowhere and ran beside the Range Rover.

"Serabit! Serabit!" they screeched into our faces, wild eyed, venal, and barbaric. There is one resource here and I, I, I *will* be the one to lead you there, and the one to collect the reward. The boys stood in the track, forcing us to stop. They leaped onto the vehicle, clinging to the sides, shouting and frightening.

The Diplomat lectured the boys about safety and eventually we drove on, at last leaving the boys—group after group—in their settlements. At dusk, alone at last, and near the entrance to a side wadi, we made camp under an acacia tree near an ancient well. As we sorted out our gear, two blackstarts, a scrub warbler, and a white-crowned black wheatear flew close to inspect us.

Night fell. Soon after, the Diplomat ventured beyond our fire to offer jumper cables to a driver far down the wadi, who was vainly turning over a nearly dead battery. The lights of the two vehicles drew close. Primordial memories, perhaps written in the ashes of ancient fires, warned me to withdraw beyond the firelight. There I waited until the Diplomat returned. To which cleft of the rock would I have fled if another had arrived in his stead?

But no one came to our fire, although it burned until dawn. We slept in the arms of the wadi, sheltered against the desert wind. I dozed fitfully, however, sleeping and waking, reluctant to lose a moment of the Big Dipper's journey. As darkness turned to dawn, the Dipper completed its turn until, with first light, the handle sank beneath the horizon. As bird calls began, shafts of light caressed the distant peaks. By eight a.m. we had received five visitors, one of them canine, who addressed himself with gusto to the washing up water.

Rabia came twice to our camp in his pickup truck, first to remove a teenage pest and then, with his elder brother, to announce himself our guide. Extremely thin, constantly smoking, weathered, and toothless, the Guide looked far older than the "about thirty" he claimed. His older brother was the businessman: married, garrulous, well connected. Rabia, an apparent also-ran, sat silently apart as we drank tea with the brother. But it didn't take long to recognize our guide as "a chosen one."

Leaving the Barakat camp, the Range Rover ground and skidded for twenty minutes through deep sand to the base of the jebel. Rabia, wedged in the back, had lost his lugubrious look. As we started on foot up the jebel, his intensity quickened. Confidence, even power, were expressed by his pace, his bearing, the tilt of his head. On the jebel, the Guide was at home. Contrary to the indifference of most bedu, he named the wadis, the flowering shrubs, the distant peaks, the various lizards that flickered in and out of the shade. There seemed nothing about this place which he did not know, not boastfully, but because he was, most evidently, a man well connected here.

Dressed in a white galabiyah and white headdress, the Guide's thin figure floated up the path before us. Mostly we walked in silence through a wilderness of broken walls, tumbled stones, and scree, on a winding path that quickly steepened. Sometimes, we scrambled. Frequently, Rabia stopped to let us rest, though he himself did not seem to be even breathing, much less breathless. Once he reprimanded us obliquely.

"The people in Cairo don't know how to walk anymore. They can hardly walk down the street! We of the desert can only stand the noise for one day, then we have to leave Cairo and come back here!" He laughed at his own joke, borrowed the Diplomat's binoculars, and squatted at the end of a precipice. For ten minutes he swept the boundaries of this kingdom of ruined jebels, not once lowering the glasses. We had to call to him to start the final ascent.

First excavated in 1906, the temple at Sarabit was further restored in the 1970s during the Israeli occupation of Sinai. Rabia told us about the twenty-five Israeli experts who hired the Barakat truck and did several years' work. Although the Serabit temple is not massive or beautiful, it must once have been imposing. Unusual sandstone formations, dedicated by Middle and New Kingdom officials, have been re-erected into a giant stone library.

An ancient cistern was still in use, judging by nearby plastic jerry cans. But Rabia turned aside our question about who uses the formations and the larvae infested water, and for what purpose.

"No one," he said abruptly. The sacred cave dedicated to Hathor is in dangerous condition, and a sign placed by the Egyptian Antiquities Organization warns visitors to keep out.

"There is no problem here," Rabia said firmly and led us into the cave. Wooden braces, unconvincingly supporting tons of rock, argued otherwise, and we backed out quickly, leaving Rabia standing meditatively within, his hand placed lovingly on the rock face.

Next to the cave is the Hall of Sopdu, a rock cut sanctuary where, according to our guidebook, the god of the Eastern Desert was adored. It was evident that Sopdu, Hathor, or some unannounced deity, still has devotees at Serabit. Though the sanctuary was well lit by natural light, there were traces of candle wax before the altar. Rabia, looking surprised when I pointed this out, shook his head and denied knowledge.

"No, no. Nothing here," he said. Feeling it would be wise to do so, I turned away to avoid his searching eyes.

Before we began the descent, the Guide squatted for a while above the jumble of dressed stones, surveying the yellow, maroon, red, and black of the surrounding jebels. His gaze was sweeping, powerful, soothing. The last High Priest of Hathor—or Sopdu himself—could not have looked more satisfied.

Lillian at Serabit, Sinai, April 1994

49

St. Catherine's Mountain

15 May 1994

It was 10:30 p.m. when we reached St. Catherine's monastery. Father George had been waiting for several hours, and our accompanying friend, an Egyptian engineer, apologized for the unintended delay. Only thirty minutes remained before the generator went down, and the old Arab servant, roused from his bed to help George show us to our rooms, was not pleased. Irritated at having been awakened, to our astonishment he raised his voice against the monk who asked why the wrong keys had been supplied. In that small sign came a hint of the enormous conflict that surrounds the monastery at this time of great crisis, perhaps the greatest this ancient orthodox community has faced.

For almost a millennium and a half the monastery has survived attack by pagans, Muslims, and fellow Christians. It has never been overrun, ravaged, or looted. Modern circumstances are more subtle but no less dangerous. St. Catherine's priceless library is now inadequately maintained due to bureaucratic obfuscation and historically well-founded monkish suspicions. Once there were hundreds of monks at St. Catherine's monastery, but numbers had dwindled greatly—even before the onslaughts of secularism, modern tourism, and an Egyptian government uninterested in preservation of the monastery other than as a tourist attraction.

Monastic life is constantly disrupted by demands for official visits. George sighs. Recently, they were forced to open up during prayer time for a visit by "the King of France," who turned out to be an Air France representative with good connections in Cairo. In such circumstances, he said, good monks will not stay. Forty years ago, there were eighty monks at St. Catherine's. Today, only fifty have permission to live there. Less than twenty actually do so, and these include the young, immature, and inept, who, as George describes it, "need to be ripened."

The next day, Father George leads us along the rocky path that passes by the Garden of the Forty Martyrs. Earlier, a monastery jeep had hurried the four of us around a corner of the jebel to conceal us from prying official eyes. We are headed into a "military area," and have no permission. The monks, of course, consider the area theirs and, when possible, do as they please when access is needed to various parts of their historical domain.

We must reach the summit of Jebel Katrin before dark, and we need a donkey to carry our water and sleeping bags at least part of the way. But it is still mid-afternoon, and there is time to stop off at the Forty Martyrs, the early Christians of Cappadocia whose memory is perpetuated here. Bedouin boys scamper about, sons of the tribe that has served the monks for centuries. We wander among the olive and fruit trees.

"You do not understand!" George turns fiercely on us. "We have not just abandoned this place." He swings his arms as though to embrace the lovely garden. "There were two monks, living here two years ago. But they were seduced by Bedouin women who just kept appearing in their cells. One left the monastery. One now lives in the monastery under discipline." The words are wrenched from him. The monastery is desperate for recruits—and this is what has happened!

Earlier in the day, seated in the monastery's reception area, we met seven monks in search of a monastery. Victims of a capricious bishop, they had left Greece, taken up residence in one of St. Catherine's nearby dependencies, and hoped for permission to remain. But monks cannot, by tradition and oath, simply move on if they don't like their bishop. "The Magnificent Seven" George calls them, shaking his head. Now we hurry on behind the donkey, passing two Russian monks resting beneath a wall. Are they, too, contemplating a move here?

"Abuna!" George hails them. Their wispy beards float in the slight breeze. George, hair and beard carefully trimmed as befits his usual work as a teacher in Cairo, strides on before us in his black robe. He is powerfully built, but now in his late fifties and suffering from back problems.

The Jebel Katrin rises 8,700 feet before us. Grander than Jebel Musa, it is the highest peak in the Sinai Peninsula and, like other high places against which God's prophets railed, must have been used as a site for human sacrifice. Would that explain the bones of a woman, found there by a monk in the seventh century, bones brought down to the monastery and today revered as those of a Fourth Century Alexandrine martyr? Maybe. Maybe not.

Still, the Sinai is a place of death, as well as of enormous life-giving power. As we mount steadily, the donkey plodding before us, George tells us about a monk named Anastasios who "just disappeared" in 1974 while walking back to the monastery from the Jebel Katrin. "No one knows why," George says "but there were rumors of spying for the Israelis." Forty days after he disappeared, Anastasios's bones, picked clean by the birds, were discovered in a wadi.

Resting often, trying to conserve the water we carry, fearful that we will not make the summit before dark, we labor on higher and higher in a rocky world, now patched by flowering bushes. It is spring, and the weather still mild, but the coming night will be very cold. Wind rises as, after four hours, the snaking track brings us to the base of the holy mountain. There, the donkey can go no further, and our goods are handed over to us by his owner. We four pilgrims, now burdened by our few worldly belongings, stagger on up an even more difficult path.

Enormous and uneven steps lead to the pinnacle, where a small building appears to grow out of the rock. With stiff fingers, George finally opens two padlocks. The wind is rising, we are wet with perspiration, trembling with fatigue, and nervous of what we may find in this seldom visited place. Inside the building are a small chapel, a monk's cell, a kitchen with an enormous fireplace and a "guest room" with four wooden planks. There are candles in the chapel, and we light several against the thick darkness that fills the structure.

George prays in the chapel and then, exhausted, we eat our cold supper in the guest quarters. Not long thereafter, the Diplomat and

I retire to the monk's cell with our candle. I try to convince myself that I do not feel a dark spirit hovering here, despite the large cross painted on the wall of our cell. Dreams, aspirations, spiritual longings, and negative energy seem to float in this place, and it seems quite unlikely that any of us will sleep well, despite our fatigue.

The Engineer leaves his candle lit all night for both prayer and comfort. In the morning, he will admit that he hardly slept, and recount how he called out to George, offering assistance as the monk moaned painfully throughout the night. In our dark and dusty cell, the Diplomat and I heard nothing of this, curled in sleeping bags toe to toe on the plank. But I, too, spent the night waking, and then sleeping again, turning painfully, half expecting a visitation of—I knew not what. Once, the Diplomat awakened us both, crying out for help in his nightmare. In the early morning, exhausted, we both fell into a deep sleep, and because no light can penetrate the cell through its one blocked window, we lay in the dust, sleeping deeply until almost nine o'clock.

In the morning light, we see that a precipice extends down one side of the chapel. But we clamber around another wall and look across the valleys and peaks towards Mt. Sinai, on whose summit we can just make out a tiny chapel. Amazingly, there are no tourists there. Jagged mountains surround. Behind us and far, far away, we see the Red Sea.

Before we leave, we all enter the chapel and light candles. George lights the sacred oil, and prays silently before the few and poorly preserved icons. We leave him alone with St. Catherine and hear, from outside, his lonely voice chanting an ancient prayer in Greek.

"Is there a tradition or a special position for the Archangel Michael at St. Catherine's Monastery?" I ask George as we descend the Jebel Katrin. No, he says. Yet the day before, I had noticed, for the first time despite several visits to the monastery, the large number of Michael icons in the main church.

Travels into the Heart of Egypt   263

Ready for the climb? Pilgrims preparing to ascend Jebel Katrin, May 1994

Pilgrims at the summit of Jebel Katrin, May 1994

St Catherine's chapel atop Jebel Katrin, May 1994

Prayer on Jebel Katrin, May 1994

50

Questions on the River

July 1994

The good ship *Hotp*—possibly named after the famed Fourth Dynasty pyramid architect Imhotep—carries us on an overnight voyage to the pollution of Helwan (affectionately known as Hell) and back the following afternoon. You get on about noon, sail after lunch and, if you wish, party all night. Bored by Cairo's social life, bothered by his ambassador, and broiled by July weather, the Diplomat decided we should give the *Hotp* a try. Those at least were the reasons he gave.

However, two weeks earlier, fourteen British women, including several wives of British diplomats, had taken the voyage to Hell and back. Every one of them was said to have been as well provisioned as the lady who later told me that she took along a case of wine. Not surprisingly, there were subsequent questions concerning their deportment. None of the women would speak plainly about what happened—or not—on the *Hotp*, and some of them were no longer speaking to one another. Nonetheless, rumors abounded through the diplomatic community of lithe, dark young men, of orgy and of debauchery.

"Most unsuitable," said the Diplomat, clearly thinking that the overnight trip would be a welcome break in the diplomatic life style. I suspected that the embassy wives who were not speaking to one another had all cried on his shoulder, and now he wanted to see for himself. With enormous effort, he extracted two tickets from the Misr travel office in Tahrir Square. Thus, on a clear summer afternoon, we boarded the *Hotp* at its central Cairo mooring next to the Meridien Hotel. The great river was high, and it was time to party.

As soon as the *Hotp* headed up river, the crew began to collapse the upper deck canopy to allow unscathed passage beneath the many bridges that cross the Nile at Cairo. By then, most passengers had gone below to the bar or to their cabins, and it was already clear that women do seem to favor the *Hotp*. Our cruise had two or three groups of Arab women, each chaperoned by a lone man. But there was also a delegation of seven aging TWA air hostesses. Interesting, I thought, that the latter were enthusiastically applauded by the former during after-dinner games in the bar. But I'm getting ahead of myself.

As we moved swiftly towards the first bridge, the head deckhand—lithe, dark— ordered all who remained on deck to crouch. The span of Qasr Al Aini loomed before us, and clearance would be less than two feet. The boat's engines, bearing us rapidly toward the bridge, pulsated against the strength of the River. Following the example of the deck hand, all of us who remained on deck hunkered down. Except for one middle-aged American.

I couldn't see his face but thought I knew what would be expressed there. He stood rigidly upright until it was almost too late. Then, as though against his will, the American dropped down just before the boat passed under the great bridge. No one spoke. Perhaps, I pondered, no one but the American and I realized what had almost happened.

Later I approached him in case he needed to talk. It was, I felt, my duty as director of Befrienders Cairo, a listening service for distressed and suicidal people, to encourage people to talk if they wished to do so.

"You thought about it," I said, touching his arm.

"What?" His face revealed nothing.

"The bridge," I said. "You thought about it then."

"The bridge," he replied. "It would knock you over." His voice was dreamy. He turned away my offer to listen, his question of whether to be or not unanswered.

At lunch, two young foreign fellow travelers—male, lithe, light—asked if they could join us at a table we had selected near a window. Through the meal, they spoke cryptically to one another, carefully ignoring us. I decided they had met only recently, had basic disagreements in style and philosophy, and were undecided about becoming lovers. When the verbal sparring took on an unpleasant edge, we finished our coffee and returned to the top deck.

That afternoon, I sat on deck reading Runciman's *History of the Crusades* as we passed village after village, and a two-man band with a synthesizer disturbed the tranquility of the great river. The shouted statements of shore bound youths were unclear. Were they jeering because the Hotp carried the idle and enviable rich? Were we, a ship of fools, likely to be fired on by some blunderbuss-wielding fellah? Rather than an indication of contempt, did the whistling and shouting express a desire to join us? Or was this outcry merely expression of young Egyptian men's persistent need to be noticed?

In late afternoon, death tried again. One of the many children on board fell into the small unattended pool on the fan deck, and was pulled out by another passenger. Much rushing and wailing ensued, followed by the hysterical collapse of the child's inattentive mother. Caught from behind by her husband, she was hauled back upright by her large breasts. All the women who saw, including me, automatically put our hands protectively over our breasts.

As some wailed and some prayed, an Egyptian surgeon and an American with CPR training assaulted the small body, pummeling her abdomen, massaging her chest, breathing into her lungs, and rolling her about so that finally she choked, coughed, and started to breathe, and then to regain color. Those who had watched the drama returned to their deck chairs. Briefly then, we put into the former resort town of Helwan, for the child to be taken to hospital.

Village after village swept by, swarming with people—both in and out of the water. Rubbish tips peppered with dogs, goats, and children flowed down to the river. A Middle Eastern myth holds that moving water is pure. Several days earlier, the Egyptian government had been called on to announce itself satisfied that the Egyptian Nile had not been polluted by the hundreds of bodies being dumped into the great river in Rwanda.

"Is that a naked man?" asked one of the airhostesses hopefully. She took my binoculars and trained them on a man who stood unclothed save for the Nile, which reached like stockings to his knees. Surrounded by children, most of whom seemed to be girls, he waved and then jiggled his member for our benefit.

"Most unsuitable," said the Diplomat.

The chimneys of cement factories and brickyards belched on both shores as we pushed against the weight of the great river, which seemed determined to escape us by rushing down to the Mediterranean. The brilliant green of fields, splashed with the orange of ripe dates, was marred by black, white, and russet smoke from factories and refineries. The three pyramids of Dashour were barely visible through the haze of windborne pollution. We rubbed our burning eyes, and the band played on.

Day was coming to an end. Black palm trees, fronds silhouetted like fingers, helped hold up a red sky. On shore, many fires glowed, some large and some small. Rubbish burning? Weed clearance? Supper on the stove? Another woman who had poured kerosene on herself, and even now is escaping an unbearable life by means of an excruciating death?

Not far south of Dashour, the *Hotp* pulled in towards shore. On a track parallel to the River, the headlamps of a parked car flashed. As the car began to follow, the ship's spotlight trapped it in a brilliant beam. Terrorists? Security agents? No, just our lost passengers, returning for the evening entertainment—the small daughter restored to health, none the worse for the afternoon's seeming disaster.

Shamefully, at dinner we avoided the young men who had lunched with us, enjoying our wedding anniversary in peace at a private table. By the time we entered the *Hotp*'s lounge afterwards, it was already quite full. Music played, and only children were dancing under the gaze of their proud mothers. But the fun was about to begin.

The Hopt's after-dinner games are from one aspect very Egyptian, a family affair geared to include everyone. Watching, declining to play, I was charmed by one father who made certain that not only his own children but everyone else's also had a chance to win.

But the games themselves were quite Western—the teasing teenage games that made our blood race in the 1950s. Passing an orange from neck to neck with no hands allowed to assist; dancing solo until called into a group by the master of ceremonies, who stopped the music and shouted a number so you had to hug your entire group; balancing with your partner on a sheet of paper folded smaller each time the music stops. None of this was possible for the veiled women, but they watched with joy—even those with no children.

The hour grew late, the cognac we had brought was finished, and the Nile lapped around the floating hotel, moored between a field of sorghum and a brick kiln. On the dance floor, a British woman in her fifties leaped into the arms of an Egyptian in his twenties. Both smiled blissfully, and the veiled women applauded. Around them the children boogied on, asking no questions, understanding all.

"Most unsuitable," said the Diplomat.

51

Along North Road

Early November 1994

North Road is an area of picture-book sand dunes sprouting palm trees. But this area of the Sinai is also a showcase of greed, short-sightedness, and environmental disregard—with endless mounds of rubbish, proliferating villas, nets to catch migratory birds, and grandiose agricultural and industrial schemes. These will undermine archaeological sites and benefit the wealthy, while further displacing the Bedouin who have lived here for centuries. North Road leads through a paradise turned sour. This part of north Sinai even made me sorry the Israelis had left.

Human existence in Sinai has always been transient and precarious, and it seemed appropriate that most of the modern construction seems so shoddy. Buildings only a few years old were already peeling concrete from cracked walls. Caught between desert heat and winter Mediterranean, man's handiwork is kneaded mercilessly. Along North Road, the mud flats, now riven by roads to mines and salt works, encase remains of settlements thousands of years old.

But we didn't begin on the North Road, choosing rather to enter the Sinai further south. Having spent the night at Ismailia, we crossed the canal on the ferry and set off northeast through an area of Sinai we knew to be restricted—although the Ministry of Defense never ceases to declare that there are no longer any restricted roads in Sinai. Approximately a year earlier, the British defense attaché had been greatly annoyed to miss a dignitary arriving from Israel when the Egyptians turned him back after he had reached to within a few miles of El Arish on the coast.

We were more fortunate. Our first find was the museum at Tabil el Shagara. There, bunkers that once served as headquarters for a section of the Bar Lev line are among the sturdiest manmade structures in Sinai. They are also a monument to Egyptian self-congratulation. However, the museum is not precise, containing as it does the manikin of a surgeon in the former operating theater with binoculars around his neck. But we got the point. Earlier, when we were walked around the site, led by an unusually articulate guide, a sizeable explosion occurred in the near distance.

"Bomb," said the guide. "A camel or a Bedouin. It happens all the time." He seemed disinterested. But we were grateful for an additional reason not to drive off-road in the area.

From Tabit el Shagara we drove the few kilometers to Bir Gifgafa, and took the forbidden road to El Arish. The usual mixture of self-confidence, tipping the guards, and keeping the engine running helped us through several checkpoints. Then, at Bir el Abd, we were told that the road we wanted was blocked by sand, forcing us to turn toward El Arish on a road that passed the Magarah Coal Mine. British funded over several years, the recently opened mine is now an embarrassment. Wait until the British press wakes up to the fact that a government that is closing mines at home has just financed one in Sinai—and soft coal at that!

In the end, on the outskirts of El Arish, an astonished colonel asked how we had come so far through restricted territory. Briefly, he deliberated about sending us back the way we had come, then waved us through with a warning. We concluded that, rather than military operations (too dangerous in such heavily mined territory), the restriction was more likely due to bureaucratic feuding between two generals, departments, or ministries.

Seeking relief from Cairo, the city of a thousand muezzins and ten thousand responsibilities, the Diplomat and I had visited El Arish three months earlier. In August, at the height of the tourist season, we spend three nights at the self-styled four-star Egoth Oberoi. Then, in November, tracking migratory birds, we returned to the now deserted hotel for one night. The two tiny Bedouin boys, who in August had prepared coffee in the hotel lobby, were gone, hopefully to school, but probably not, and the room attendant, who in August ran his hand across my backside, was nowhere evident. But the towels were still grey, and food was stuck to the wall above the sink, perhaps the result of outrage over hotel food, room service or, more likely, both.

In August, we had watched the antics of three fat and pasty white brothers in the saltwater swimming pool. As their veiled wives cuddled infants at poolside, the brothers showed off, playing breath-holding games, shouting, and thrashing like children. But in November the pool was empty, and we swam leisurely in the tepid water despite the recent storm that had filled the pool to overflow and left lakes along North Road.

In August, we had eaten at an El Arish tourist restaurant with a friend from the Multinational Force in Sinai. In November, we ate spaghetti on the veranda of our room and watched the lightning flicker across the dark Mediterranean. Winter had come. The camel races were over, and thousands of birds were passing through, many of their historic places of sanctuary now under threat of development.

But there seemed to be no such danger at Zaraniq wildlife sanctuary, where we saw flights of cranes. To get there, we had to bully our way past young soldiers, who demanded permits from military intelligence sources in El Arish, as well as an escort from the environmental protection agency. Our declarations that authorities in Cairo had assured us that formalities would not be necessary for a visit to the sanctuary were ignored.

Arrogantly, we fulminated over how difficult it is to deal with ignorant young men. Only their superior firepower kept us calm. The area is forbidden, they said. Why, we asked. Because it is protected, they replied. That actually made sense. The only way to avoid allowing just about any Egyptian area being trashed is to put it off limits to everyone. We almost gave in but, having come thus far, simply drove around the guards and continued on our way. It was an arrogant and dangerous thing to do, and I'm not proud of it. But, being foreigners, we got away with it.

Ancient Palusium, thirty kilometers from Kantara on the Suez Canal, is under great threat. The town ceased to exist, probably in the eighth century, when the Palusium branch of the Nile silted up. Now "emergency archaeologists" labor to map its outlines before the planned new canal brings farms and settlements, which will sweep away the earlier traces of human activity here. At Palusium, the ground was very soft from the rains, but recently exposed ancient bricks still flaked in the sun. A few more winters, and all would be mud. The site guard shadowed us, lest we carry away any antiquities and then, in a gesture of self-help goodwill, offered to sell us a few coins he had pilfered.

As we continued along North Road towards Kantara, I thought about the town of Yamit, an Israeli agricultural settlement whose inhabitants blew up their town in 1982, when ordered to leave it and return to Israel. Collapsed homes, a supermarket, and other buildings were still to be seen beyond El Arish near the other end of North Road.

The area around Yamit is fertile, and the rolling dunes are covered with date palms. Settled Bedouin, who work on the irrigated land that surrounds Yamit, have hedged the fields with brushwood and plastic sacks. Thinking of Yamit, I felt sorry that the Israelis had left, and suspected that the Bedouin, seeing their land now eaten up at an ever-faster rate by Egyptian immigrants and new construction, feel the same. But what does a government do with so many more people every year?

52
Missionaries in Minya

19 November 1994

"It's an Egyptian secret," the Doctor said. He joined his hands firmly over his ample abdomen and sighed, his tone betraying a rather macabre glee that we had unwittingly risked ourselves. He was extremely pleased, he said, that we had come at last to Minya, and in doing so all of us had survived. My companions—Soad 16, Said 70, and Seham 31—frowned.

We had just spent four and a half lovely hours considering how to present the value of listening therapy, also known as befriending, to people to whom the idea would be entirely new. Gazing out the window as the slow train from Cairo crawled past fields, villages, and canals, we had balanced dirty glasses of scalding tea and had not for a moment seriously considered that fanatics in galabiyahs might rush from the fields, firing upon us with blunderbusses.

"Oh, yes" the Doctor said. "It is an Egyptian secret. "Ten days ago when I took this train from Cairo, we were fired on just after Beni Suef. Though wounded, the engineer managed to halt the train at the next station, the one into which the attackers hoped the train would crash. But he throttled the train down before he died. The assistant was dead already, of course. Things were so messed up that we even had to wait while they brought another engine. Ya salaam! But I didn't want to tell you."

The Doctor sighed happily and motioned us to cram into his small car. As always, it seemed, he was entirely in charge. In retrospect, I realize that he had invited the Befrienders to visit in an effort to use us for his own ends, which included both recognition and riches. But as yet, none of us understood that. Docile as sheep, we allowed him to drive us through the congested streets to his small flat. His wife, who met us at the door, issued assurances of undying love for us and all Befrienders, no matter who or where they are.

Minya, city of at least one million people, is actually a large village. It features a university, one decent hotel, and several modern buildings. But all these are on the corniche, where green gardens border the Nile. Behind this is the urban village where chickens, goats, and horse carts compete with wildly hooting cars and trucks in the crooked, unpaved streets. There are no sidewalks, and houses and shops open directly onto streets filled with jostling, shouting pedestrians, trying not to be run over. Four days ago, two policemen were murdered in Minya by armed men, who fired and then escaped back into the crowd. Minyans, of course, hate the police. This at least we knew. Perhaps we should have asked ourselves what that meant. But the people of Cairo hate the police, too, and so...off we had gone to Minya.

Our host maneuvered the car haphazardly through the chaos, talking endlessly, and all the while gesturing and swiveling back and forth in his seat to better shower me with compliments. The sycophantic and unctuous patter continued over lunch, and the Three S's and I began to yearn for the time when all this blatant flattery would cease and we would actually be introduced to "my group who want to start befriending here." After all, we needed to get on with it, as we had no intention to spend the night in Minya.

"We want you to increase our love," the Doctor intoned. Then, urging us to eat more, he seized an enormous chunk of greasy chicken he lifted to his lips, kissed loudly, and handed to Said, who accepted the unwanted meat, kissed it himself, and replaced it in the dish. Finally it was time to go spread the word about befriending.

A short drive brought us to the corniche and a permanently moored Nile steamer, on whose awning covered deck the meeting would be held. No videos, the steamer's manager told us. This rule had come about, it seemed, because video-wielding foreigners were well known to deal in pornography, and we were thus well warned not to try. I put away our introductory film, and we turned to greet the collection of veterinarians, secretaries, chemical engineers, psychologists, veiled ladies, Christians, Muslims, and assorted hangers on, all gathered by the Doctor.

It was four p.m. We had their attention, or at least their presence, until 7:30. As I stood to open the meeting, the *Nile Queen*, a tourist cruiser, passed closely alongside our ship, choosing the deepest channel on this wide but shallow stretch of river. The vessel carried no tourists, at least none we could see. Instead, several soldiers with automatic rifles glowered down on us from the Queen's upper deck. Seeing a crowd, they directed their weapons at us for good measure. For a few moments, like the Minyans, I lapsed into silent resentment against thoughtless tourists, government officials and, especially, arrogant young men with automatic weapons. Then the *Nile Queen* passed, and it was time for me and the team to speak.

Immediately it became clear that Dr. Sobhi and his attendants, despite several trips to Cairo, had made no discernible progress in explaining what Befriending is about, i.e. simple listening in confidence to people who are suicidal and/or despairing, and helping them hold on to life. Moreover, it was soon apparent that the people invited to the meeting by the Doctor had come expecting to learn how to do counseling, find employment, make business contacts, meet foreigners, get rich, preach the Word (topics not entirely precise), meet important people in Cairo, and in other ways please our host. We had hardly begun before the arguments started.

"You are quite wrong," I was told before I was ten minutes into the usual Befriending presentation, before my colleagues were even allowed to speak. The attendees then took over the meeting in order to inform their visitors from Cairo there is "no suicide" in Egypt and, in fact, asking about suicidal feelings encourages people to kill themselves. The Doctor smiled beatifically as we were informed that what desperate people need is religious help. Moreover, only professionals can help the despairing, and people like the Befrienders need to get out of the way. After all, advice is what unhappy people need, not some sort of "emotional support," whatever that is. And then the questions began: Why can't we start with a counseling service? Then what about a befriending center and a finance cooperative and we'll run the befriender aspects off the interest? How come we can't be a branch of Cairo center and have some of your money? Then how much money *can* you send us?

Through it all, our host said nothing, sitting near the back of the deck and occasionally smiling gently or nodding in agreement. Perhaps his love was growing. Certainly he seemed at peace, and apparently even his chronic colitis was quiescent. Even better, he had stopped talking (for the first and last time during our visit, as we later realized). Toward the end of the meeting, after we had been given a short time in which to explain the principles and practices of befriending, done two role plays, discussed how befriending works in Cairo, why it is needed in Egypt as it is in other countries, and explained who should consider volunteering and who not, Sobhi said it was time to take a picture. Soad, whose relatives came from Minya, told me later how appalling it was that one of the young men was "disrespectful." Not aware of local mores, I had only noticed a young man maneuvering to get next to the foreigner in the picture.

Finally, the meeting ended, but our attempts to walk from the cornice to the train station were thwarted by the Doctor. Colitis now in full spate and swigging a "bebs" as he drove, our host decided to take us on a tour of the city, ignoring our pleas that the train was scheduled to leave in fifteen minutes.

"You must stay longer. Three or four days," he declared firmly, and headed onto the Nile bridge that connects with the road to Assyut. His wife, who had squeezed in beside me in the back seat, exuded holy joy. But an Egyptian, no matter how used to working with strange people, can be goaded only so far. The Three S's erupted at this point into a flurry of flowery Arabic expressions of gratitude for all the Doctor had already done for us, and protests against further inroads on his time. Eventually, reluctantly, Sobhi executed a U turn in the middle of the bridge and took us to the train station.

On the train back to Cairo, my three outraged Befriender colleagues exploded. Said declared that no more than ten people even tried to understand what we were on about, and whether they were potential callers or potential volunteers, he was never given the opportunity to work out. The other two told him this figure was far too high. Seham claimed that the veiled woman Sobhi invited along had no interest in befriending, and came only for the opportunity of an evening out. Soad, outraged by the Doctor's efforts to use us for his own ends, was scathing about the high percentage of Christian "fanatics" on the list of names that we had managed, with difficulty, to extract from Sobhi.

"And did you see the tattoos inside their wrists?" she cried, forgetting—to my glee—my own spiritual ties. "Crosses! I need befriending!" All three of my companions were adamantly anti-Sobhi, declaring the man a venal, dishonorable hypocrite. Perhaps, I said contritely, I have been blinded by my great hope for a center in Minya.

"We've got to get past that man," Said said, trying to console us all.

So we travelled back to Cairo, discussing how we might gently move Sobhi aside in order to find the treasure we sought, that as yet unnamed person we hoped would become the first director of Befrienders Minya. Meanwhile, somehow, we had to stop Sobhi—who had already applied to register "my society" with the Ministry of Social Affairs—from using our name without applying our principles. Without saying so, I doubted he would try to set something up when we sent no funding. As it turned out, that was the one thing I got right.

Later, as the fast train to Cairo thundered past Beni Suef, the Three S's and I ate handfuls of peanuts and chortled over the look on Sobhi's face when Said kissed off the chicken. We were too relieved by our escape from the "Mad Christian" to reflect on whether this train, too, might not be fired upon. Instead, we joked about the Fretful Psychiatrist, Soad's husband, who was waiting for us in Cairo and—as we were to discover—matching whisky for whisky with the Fretful Diplomat at his home in Zamalek.

Privately, I treasured one scene from that evening on the river. As I talked to Sobhi's ragtag group about how those who despair may be helped to release their pain, a full moon, bright and orange, rose from the black escarpment on the other side of the Nile. Then on the faces of two or three listeners I saw that beautiful expression of hope and vulnerability, which comes from understanding that "listening therapy" does often hold suicidal people back from death, whereas telling suicidal people to trust in God and stop being so feeble about life usually just makes matters worse. This renewed my hope that someday there would be a befriending center in Minya.

53

Humming from Western Desert to Eastern Desert

18 December 1994

I could tell by the persistence of his tuneless humming that the Diplomat was not entirely convinced of our safety as we pulled away from the New Kharga Oasis Hotel and found the road towards Dush. If, without being shot, we made it from the New Valley across the Nile, and then through the Eastern Desert to the Red Sea before nightfall, there was still no guarantee of a hotel in Qusair, and we would most likely have to camp in the December desert without tent or camp beds—which we had thoughtlessly left in Cairo. We conjectured on whether the pontoon bridge at Luxor would still be in place and then fell silent, both of us keeping to ourselves the long list of difficulties we were likely to encounter on the road to Luxor. The most critical was whether the temporary bridge across the Nile would still be in place.[1]

At 75 kilometers from Kharga, shortly before we reached the fourth century church at Baris, we turned left onto the new desert road to Luxor. The terrain was flat, unvaried by dunes or yardangs,[2] the escarpment a distinct mirage, the morning bright and still cool. Another three kilometers, and soldiers waved us through a checkpoint. It would be a full day.

The ten-year-old Range Rover also hummed. At fifty kilometers we climbed onto the escarpment, where another checkpoint translated us into a world of rolling, yellow, orange, and blue-gray hills. There followed several kilometers of narrow winding road between giant, jagged boulders before a long stretch of flat desert took us toward the river. Here and there, the recent rains had coaxed clumps of bright green plants out of the sand.

At just over 312 kilometers from Kharga, and having crossed another barrier of rocky hills, we reached the outskirts of Armant. The Diplomat was humming again. Official travel advice from London is to avoid this area of the Nile Valley. We are fifty kilometers south of Naqadah, a village which contains the ruins of four ancient monasteries and a large Christian population and where, in October, a British tourist was shot dead. Luxor, where we hoped to cross the Nile, is halfway between Armant and Naqadah. We turned north.

But first, having emerged into the town just before the much-restored monastery of St. George, we decided to break the journey. Alerted to our arrival, soldiers spoke into radios and then led us to the monastery gate. The surrounding green area was festooned with rubbish, but also with migrating white wagtails. A round, rather sour faced monk greeted us, but did not offer his name.

There was a pre-Christmas service in process and, contrary to usual Coptic hospitality and lack of formality, the monk was reluctant to show us the church or anything else in the monastery. Impassive peasants in galabiyahs stare, as we are quickly hustled in and out of the church. No one returns our greetings. No one smiles. Exactly why are Upper Egyptian Christians in this area so abnormally unfriendly? Is the fear I suddenly feel mine or theirs?

I ask about the chapel of the Archangel Michael, but the monk waves aside the request. In the guest reception room, where we drink tea with the mostly silent monk and two lounging soldiers, I ponder my sense of unease, even of imprisonment. A wagtail flits from corner to corner of the high ceiling, beating frantically against the closed windows. We are relieved when the soldiers signal that it is time to go.

Sandwiched between two pickup trucks filled with soldiers, we head north at great speed on a road bordered by canals and cane fields. It is from these fields that men have recently emerged to fire on police and foreigners alike, and into which they afterwards retreated. There is talk in Cairo, Assyut, and Luxor of burning down the cane fields and planting sugar beet instead. But sugar beet suits neither the soil nor the culture. The men we see bending now to harvest surely mutter resentfully, perhaps fearfully, among themselves.

The area is extremely poor. Among the fields and spilling onto the road and into the canals are mud brick houses, donkeys, dogs, water buffalos, palm groves and, as always, children and more children. Our escorts in the vehicle ahead fix both their steady gaze and their weapons directly upon us. I wonder who they will shoot first should there be an attack by the so-called terrorists.

Mercifully, our tandem journey is brief. At the left turning to the Valley of the Kings, the police escort leaves us without farewell. Descending to the river, we find that the pontoon bridge, erected to convey dignitaries from their East Bank hotels to a recent extravaganza production of *Aida* at the Temple of Hatshepsut, is still in place. We cross on the clanking, swaying bridge to find Luxor as crowded as always, although this time there seem to be few tourists.

Having with some relief crossed over the great river, we find the streets thronged with crowds of school children, buses and, as always, carriages pulled by skinny horses. We pass the museum, the Luxor Temple, lines of moored cruise boats and then, treading back through the city, find the airport road from which we turn towards Qena. Again the road runs between canals, and again the Diplomat is humming.

"We'll turn east onto the desert road at Qift, this side of Qena," he says. "A policeman was killed at that checkpoint two weeks ago. But before Qift we pass through Qus where, in September, gunmen killed a UNICEF cameraman and four police escorts."

At roadside between the canals, kestrels each guard their own patch of field. We speculate about the lizards and small mammals that live in the cane break, and the Diplomat waves cheerfully at harvesters who stare back stony faced. Children, at least respond, shouting unintelligibly.

The Qift checkpoint is unmanned. On the bridge crossing the canal, we stop to ask directions of two men squatting beside a shisha just off the road. The men grin, affirmatively showing brown teeth and then one, leering, lumbers towards my open window. Quickly the Diplomat accelerates. The paved road continues through the narrow green belt pasting ugly new high-rise housing, as yet unoccupied, on the town's outskirts. Then, once more, the desert embraces us.

The Eastern Desert has its own bloodthirsty stories of habitat and highway reaching back into prehistory. Until the tenth century, Quseir was the most important Egyptian port on the Red Sea. At Quseir, ships from the Indian Ocean offloaded their goods, making this route between Quseir and the Nile a link on the Silk Road. At Legeita, 145 kilometers from Quseir, we pass the first in a series of Roman wells.

The land is flat and framed by distant purple, orange, yellow, and brown hills. Near at hand, the Range Rover flushes flocks of sand grouse. Soon the road deteriorates, its edges chewed by recent flood waters. Further still and great chunks of the road have been washed away. Finally, long stretches of pavement are missing altogether. Other vehicles are not numerous, and those we pass are heavily overloaded. When traffic slows, we maneuver among heavy goods vehicles pulling wagons and Peugeots stuffed with far too many fellahin, their worldly goods piled high above the cars. It is late afternoon, and with the sun behind us, the light is perfect. Roman watchtowers on hill tops guard the road. Occasionally we pass a ruined fortress, the Roman bricks still solid. Our road descends towards the coast in a fairyland of light and color as night falls.

We reach Quseir in the dark and gratefully check into the Sea Princess Hotel, the only available hotel, and I the only woman in it. The rooms are partitioned cubicles, and the inhabitants young men traveling for whatever unidentified purposes propel them. Exhausted, we retire early.

For half the night, the man in the cubicle across from us sits, door open, rustling plastic sacks. At first I think he is eating, then decide he is mad, and finally conclude that he is homesick and seeks to simulate the sound of cane fields in the wind. At intervals until well after midnight, other inmates flap up and down the hall, slamming doors, shouting.

Finally I doze, but am awakened at midnight and again at two a.m. by a screaming puppy beneath the window. Toward morning, the coughing and hacking of our fellow sleepers grows more intense. We arise with the second call to prayer.

Travels into the Heart of Egypt 285

The Diplomat at the Temple of Hatshepsut near Luxor, December 1994

Humming through the Eastern Desert, passing a Roman tower on the road to Quseir, December 1994

54

In Search of an Angel

19 December 1994

Quseir, on the Red Sea coast, fell into disrepair in the tenth century, but was revived two centuries later by the Ottoman Turks. Today, the Fortress of Sultan Selim is unremarkable, as is the much later Church of the Virgin that we found among the yellow plaster colonial buildings of the phosphate works. Both church and phosphate plant show, once again, how Egypt evolves, era by era.

A Coptic priest who described himself as "married, not a monk" showed us through the church, explaining that it had originally been the Italian Church of St. Barbara. Presumably, then, the Italians built the phosphate works as well. See how history runs unwritten through our fingers! When I examined the icons, looking for angels, the priest remarked unnecessarily that all the icons except that of St. Barbara were new. Why, I asked myself, are our souls more comforted by the candle smoke patinas of the past than by the vibrant colors of today?

On the outskirts of Quseir is the still incomplete Movenpick Hotel where rooms will go for 300 LE a night. But will tourists really come here in such numbers as the size of the hotel indicates? Will the locals find work at the Movenpick? Will the Sea Princess close? Unlikely, so long as there are backpackers. But there are also, from time to time, terrified escapees from the cane break, men sought rightly or wrongly by the authorities, who emerge toting their meager possessions in plastic bags and seeking shelter elsewhere.

The road north traverses a flat coastline between sea and distant hills. Occasionally rusting notices warn of uncleared mines on beaches. That, too, is Egyptian. Bad news is understated, talked around, expressed euphemistically. Danger does not come stridently, obviously, as in New York City, but creeping unawares—in dreams, perhaps, or disguised as the Prince of Light. The Shining Serpent is clasped to the bosom in order to deliver his fatal sting. Nonetheless, we are alert—but mainly for another reason: a Goliath heron was recently seen south of Safaga, our next destination.

Twenty-five kilometers further north, Safaga is the ferry embarkation point for pilgrims heading to Jeddah for the hajj. A long main street is lined with shops and booths selling inexpensive clothing, sandals, sunglasses, bread, fruit, vegetables, and baskets. Goats and dogs are on their breakfast stroll. Large ships—merchantmen and ferries—rest at dock, and helmeted riot police with see-through plastic shields guard the entrance to a factory. We feel no threat here. But Safaga is not our final destination, only the place where we turn left once more, into the desert on a road that roughly parallels the Qift/Quseir road.

Unlike the more southern road, the 157 kilometers between Safaga and Qena seem undamaged by recent flooding. And although this road lacks the Roman watch towers and forts of yesterday, today we shall drive through the rust brown hills with enormous anticipation. Inexplicably, Egyptian indifference to Roman Egypt is underscored by the Blue Guide's failure to mention either Mons Claudianus or Mons Porphyrites, Eastern Desert sites where early Christians died in their hundreds, possibly thousands, cutting granite, porphyry, and other rock for Roman monuments and temples.

After some 37 kilometers, we stop at a roadside hut and ask directions. A teenage tire repairman leans into my side of the car and suddenly runs his hand along my leg. I shout for the Diplomat to drive on and we do—along the wrong track so that we have eventually to retrace our way until we find the unmarked and broken tarmac road which leads—after another 18 desolate kilometers—to a truncated Roman watch tower. The paving ends four kilometers further at a small Bedouin settlement and then, after three final kilometers, we are at Mons Claudianus.

The walls and arches of the ruined fortress are cradled by the cliffs, where enormous column drums and dressed granite blocks lie as they were abandoned 1700 years ago. Roman numerals had been chiseled into several of the drums. What happened here to cause the sudden shut down? Plague? Rebellion? Fall of the empire? And what happened to the people who last worked here? We wander among the ruins and scuffle through mounds of broken pottery shards already worked over by centuries of wondering travelers.

The sense of anticipation is much stronger now, and after lunch I settle in a sunny spot to wait. The wadi is enclosed by red, yellow, and brown rock and scree walls. There are no signs of life other than a few scattered desert scrub plants. Bones of a large animal are scattered about, some with traces of tissues still attached.

Michael, I ask, is there a message for me here in this place of sorrow, this place of exit only by death?

Yes, my child. Listen for my voice...There are many voices which would deceive...I will not allow you to be in danger...The work of Michael in Egypt will continue...The Lord has done much healing in this place in past centuries...

Across the ridge a blue light plays. Interspersed with it is a pattern of dancing pinprick lights. Angels, I think to myself. But what do I know about angels? A splendid raven, kin no doubt of she who fed Elijah, St. Paul, and St. Anthony, settles on the highest point of the jebel.

It is mid-afternoon, and we must leave if we are to spend the night at St. Paul's monastery. Back to the main road, back to Safaga and then on for sixty kilometers to Hurghada. Some fifteen kilometers from Hurghada, the town begins to announce itself by a sprawl of hotels, many of them still incomplete. Where will it end? Who will heal the fettered earth, the poisoned sea?

"In Hurghada," the Diplomat says, "two Germans were killed by gunfire in September."

We take the bypass. On then 110 kilometers to Ras Gherib by which time it is dark. The Diplomat drives 25 slow kilometers north towards Zafaranah and at last turns left for the final 13 kilometers to St. Paul's monastery, an outpost that is no longer a remote desert retreat. The monk who opens the gate and gets out the guest register seems to be expecting us.

Brother Yusuf, summoned from prayer, makes us an omelet, and then settles in to practice his English. He has been here for three months, his real name is Hisham, he is a teacher, he has never heard of Mons Claudianus. We are showed the separate men's and women's sleeping quarters outside the monastery and Brother Yusuf retreats within: first prayers will be at four a.m.

The Diplomat and I, reluctant to sleep separately, sit alone outside the protective walls drinking red wine beneath a sky filled with stars. Someone passes nearby, and we hide the bottle least a pilgrim stumble. Although it was the Diplomat who first suggested we spend the night at this monastery, he is suddenly troubled.

"Why did you want to come here?" he asks me. I know he has begun to experience the power of this place because earlier, as we waited for supper, once again he saw the colored lights around my head and shoulders. In his uncertainty, the Diplomat interprets the Presence as possibly evil.

I sleep fitfully in the women's quarter, where I am alone in a room with beds for five. But it is winter, and fewer pilgrims come to this cold place. From my sleeping bag I can look out a small window in the thick stone wall and see pinpricks of light in the night sky. Christmas soon. And angels made the first announcement.

The Diplomat, awakened by the four o'clock bells, then turned over and slept soundly until eight o'clock. He declared himself relieved that I have not been carried off by demons or monks. Then we wait, alone again in the VIP room, while a monk prepares us breakfast of bread, cheese, marmalade, and foul. We bury our noses in large mugs of coffee, our only contribution to the generous meal offered by the monastery.

It is to visit the Church of the Archangel Michael that I have come this time to St. Paul's monastery. Abuna Safirus sends us alone into the church where a service is in progress. Monks chant, triangle and cymbals sound, we all kneel. But I do not feel Michael here as at Claudianus. "I will lift up mine eyes unto the hills from whence cometh my help."

Abuna Safirus takes us to the Church of St. Paul pointing out the cave where the saint lived, invented monasticism, met St. Anthony and was buried by lions—who scraped a hole for him in the sand when St. Anthony proved too old and feeble for the task. The monk points out frescos of Michael, Gabriel, and Raphael, three archangels from the Coptic pantheon of seven. Suddenly he turns to me.

"What do you know about cherubim and seraphim?" he asks, and then answers when I hesitate. "They are higher than the archangels who are meant to help men, for the cherubim and seraphim serve God alone. The cherubim have six wings: two to cover the face, two to cover the feet and two to fly with. The seraphim have only four wings but have also four faces: human, lion, ox, and eagle. Before his fall, the Devil was a cherub." Beside me, the Diplomat sighs.

We do a little gentle birding on the three-hour journey back to Cairo. Until we turn inland towards Ma'adi on the southern outskirts of Cairo, the road closely follows the sea, where white-eyed gulls with strangely alert serpentine faces gather on the rocks.

"Michael!" I muse. "Here I thought I was meant to serve you, and now it seems that you wish to help me. I certainly don't know much about angels. Well, row the boat ashore….And teach me about healing."

Icon of Archangel Michael, Abu Seifein, Old Cairo, December 1994

55

Moulid of Al-Sayeda Zeinab

27 December 1994

"Whose idea was it to come here?" Ashraf asked plaintively. Solidly middle class, he was finding his first experience of a moulid nearly overwhelming, as did the Diplomat and I and my friend Siham. It was the worst crowd I'd ever been in, and each surge of bodies, coming from several sides simultaneously, nearly lifted us off the ground. I felt fear begin to rise in my chest. From behind me the Diplomat barked, "Keep on your feet."

Ahead stood the mosque of Al-Sayeda Zeinab, granddaughter of the Prophet and heroine of the Battle of Karbala, who had died in Egyptian exile. Wreathed in multicolored fairy lights, the shrine breathed blessing upon us. Within, we hoped, there would be relative calm as Quranic recitations continued through the night, and devotees thronged in to pray for healing, birth of a son, abundant crops, a job, or examination success.

Novelist Yehya Haqqi described a country child kneeling at the entrance of the shrine and covering the marble doorstep with kisses: "If any of the pedantic theologians happened to see him and his family, he would turn his face away from them in disgust, condemning the evil times and invoking the aid of God against such idolatry, heresy, and ignorance. The majority of the people, however, used to smile benignly at the naiveté of such peasants in their clothes smelling of earth, milk, and fenugreek."[1]

There might well have been tranquility within the famous mosque on this leila al kabira, the Great Night, which concludes a weeklong celebration of Al-Sayeda Zeinab's birthday, but we were not destined to find out. There was clearly no way to get inside the mosque. Tens of thousands of worshippers, merrymakers, dervishes, merchants, carnival barkers, and the simply curious congregated around the sixteenth century mosque, built over the saint's tomb in the Ibn Tulun quarter of Cairo. Women in black. Women in bright colors. Dervishes all in white. Dervishes in colored turbans. Farm boys in galabiyahs. City boys in slacks and stylish sweaters. Children with tall shiny hats and whistles. A legless man risking his life to ask for alms.

The crowd would, perhaps, have been bearable except for the "streamers." As they do in carnivals around the world, teams of young men forced their way through the crowds, pushing, jerking, thrusting. At least they weren't grabbing and smashing. Yet. The mob surged over the beggar. As the crush increased, voices began to admonish.

"Foreigners should not come here! Turn around! Turn around!" The words were urgent, well-meaning. Linked hand to hand, we four had foolishly moved into the two-block area around the mosque where thousands reveled and sought admission to the shrine. We needed to retreat fast—if that was possible.

Hands began to grab at us, pinching, pulling, shoving. I remembered a recent *Middle East Times* article about the moulid of Hussein, held a few weeks earlier.[2] At that birthday celebration, two young foreign women were rescued by heroes from the crowd who, having formed a protective circle around the women, used belts to beat back scores of other men who seemed intent on tearing off the women's clothing.

In retreat at last and still linked, we four fought our way out of the vortex to an eddy behind a giant swing overloaded with children. En route, Siham, headscarf flying, delivered several amazing body blocks, one of which almost lifted a particularly aggressive young fellow off the ground. Still, she later told me ruefully, "I, too, was touched."

"Fatimid idea, these moulids," Ashraf muttered apologetically. "Not really Islamic. Shia stuff practiced by uneducated country people." Still embarrassed at what he had led us into, he ushered us out from under the rocketing swing, whose cars were crammed with shouting children. We followed him down a side street filled with portable shooting galleries, freak shows ("Come see the flying lady!"), food stands, and tea houses. The crowd parted and remerged again around an exhausted donkey, which stood, apparently dying, in its traces. Three men passed, surveying the scene from camel back.

The air was thick with odors: incense, manure, garbage, sweat, and gunpowder mingled with the odor of water buffalos recently killed, and now hung on hooks above the street, as well as the aroma of hashish from nargilehs in the makeshift tea shops. The moulid is a time of license, when men and women sit openly together smoking and sipping tea. We are nearly decapitated by a heavy swing, driven, it seemed, from nowhere, by a very fat woman exuberantly reliving her childhood. A youth leaped from the crowd and slams his fist into the back of a passing policeman. Astonished, the policeman turns, and then embraced his assailant with joyful cries of recognition.

"The government sends along a few policemen armed with long sticks as a gesture towards keeping order at the moulids," Ashraf says, "but by and large these birthday festivals of saints belong to the dervishes." Colorful makeshift tents lined the alleys, each tent temporary home to members of a Sufi tariqa. Outside each tent a large banner announces the order's name, while inside the dervishes dance to flute and drum, working themselves into spiritual ecstasy. As there is no more room in any of the tents, we join people already peeking through the holes in the tent material.

There are at least sixty-eight Sufi brotherhoods in Egypt,[3] and at any time somewhere in Egypt a moulid, probably several, is being attended by these gentle people. The Sufis seem, in fact, to be the exact opposites of the fundamentalists, which goes far towards explaining why the orders, once persecuted by the government, are now officially protected. Today some moulids are even opened by government officials in a show of common cause against religious extremism.

"Walk towards God," the Sufis say, "and He will run towards you." The way to walk is a personal decision. However, the veneration the Sufis accord their saints, the miracles they claim, and the self-mortification that a few orders encourage, make the Sufis anathema to the stern intellectualizers of religion. Whereas the

Allah of the fundamentalists is remote, stern, and judgmental, the Lord of the Sufis is omnipresent light and power, and so intensely intimate that union with Him is celebrated in erotic allegory. This, however, has aroused charges of shirk[4] from the religious purists and, occasionally, physical attack on Sufis.

Down one small alley nearly blocked by heaps of garbage, we find room under the tent of a group performing zikr, the dance of "remembrance" in which the Sufi seeks union with the divine. Oscillating violently from right to left and back, the devotees aspirate hu, meaning HE, the syllable bursting from their months in devotional fervor. The cadence is increased by a leader wielding a microphone, until one devotee, overcome by emotion and heat, falls and is helped out. His coveted place in the line is quickly taken by another. People smile a welcome, and motion us to stand on nearby house stairs the better to see. At the end of the large tent, women are cooking supper while their babies sleep.

Back on the main street, the streamers have become more numerous and bolder as the evening grows late. A desperate farmer with a wagon load of cauliflowers to deliver pleads with the crowd to let his panicking horse pass. We stand undecided in the street, buffeted by merrymakers, torn between desire and sanity. The Sufis, it seems, have us where we ought to be.

Meanwhile, Ashraf had told his driver to meet us in the square in front of the mosque, but there is no power in all Egypt that could get us there tonight. Or is there? The wail of the flute pulls us. Instead we lock hands once again and walk with resolve until we reach the outskirts of the sprawling festival and, at length, find a taxi.

Later, scoffing kushari in the Omda Restaurant in Mohandiseen, Siham promises to take me to a zar. She figures the two of us are equal to any afrit[5] going. Although the Diplomat looks dubious, I remember the body blocks administered earlier by Siham and decide she may be at least half right.

56

A Monastery Too Far

17 January 1995

We had spent the night above the monastery, arriving in three vehicles on the rim of the escarpment just before darkness fell. I was surprised in the morning when our friends, sitting in camp chairs drinking coffee, waved us off. Descent was not for them. The dramatic scenery, the difficult geography, intrigued them, not the black-robed men below, their strange and antiquated Christian beliefs, or their sprawling compound known as Deir Anba Samwil.

The descent was rapid as the Diplomat and I slid through soft sand, and then slowed down as we jarred step by step over sharp, flinty stones. Hurrying to keep pace with him, I leaned backwards, trying not to fall. The silver Ethiopian cross banged heavily against my chest, and already the day was very hot. For many months I had felt compelled towards this Coptic monastery and as we approached, a sense of being pulled in grew stronger.

The day before, driving around the rim, we had seen from above the hermit cave of Samwil, a sixth century saint. One week earlier the two of us had visited another monastery in the Fayoum from which Samwil had set out seeking greater silence and austerity. Although I had visited Deir El Malak three years earlier, the Monastery of the Angel had not impressed me. But, knowing we would leave Egypt in a few weeks, we decided to return.

The Church of the Angel is dedicated to Gabriel, not Michael. But as soon as I entered the church, I felt an enormous joy, combined with a frisson of inexplicable expectation. The monk guiding us began to explain that the monastery is a place of special reverence, not only for Gabriel but also for the Archangel Michael. In the modern Michael chapel I knelt, as the monk did, before the altar.

Exiting the church, we were approached by an old monk, who had kept the monastery alive by living here alone in the days before the Egyptian monastic revival began. The old man brought consecrated bread, broke a loaf and, uncharacteristically, gave me the center bit with the cross, the part other priests had always been careful to give to the Diplomat.

Today, we were told, there are five monks at Deir el Malak, four or five novices, and five "dead saints." Some two years ago, five desiccated human bodies were found near the monastery and labeled "martyrs." The long beard of one identified him as a monk, but the smallest body is that of a child, his robes neatly arranged to show that he had not been circumcised. The monk who guided us gave his name as Salim Muhurrak, and did not know how long the martyrs had been buried or anything else about them.

Deir Samwil, further on, is both more remote and more flourishing, and we were told that it held fifteen monks and six novices in 1985. But it was clear from the number of buildings that many more have been added since then. A long sturdy fence was being constructed in the desert some distance from the monastery. Security against extremists? Boundary demarcation against land-grab opportunists as in Wadi Natrun? Perhaps both.

We entered the monastery compound through an open back gate, passing dormitories where black robes hung drying in the cold morning sunlight. Down a long sandy path, past a plantation of eucalyptus trees, we came to the gate of the original enclosure and passed through to find two young monks playfully ribbing one another. One of them took us into the Church of the Virgin, replete with modern icons, while the other went to fetch a more senior monk.

Ten minutes later, Father Isaiah, a swarthy, heavily bearded man in his late thirties, took over our initiation. We followed almost timidly as he described the history of the monastery and its churches, moving next to the meaning of the icons. One icon depicted St. Macarius, founder of the Wadi Natrun monastery of that name, and beside him a man with several wings.

"He was given a cherub as his angel," Father Isaiah explained, "because he was special." Next, the monk told us the story of the monks who went forth to a promised meeting with Jesus, but missed him, not recognizing as their Lord the old man who accosted them on the way up the mountain to the rendezvous.

"I follow Michael," I had said earlier when the younger monk, now vanished, asked about my religion. So difficult to explain, even to try to explain. The Diplomat was silent until just before we left the church, then as I walked back to the altar of the Archangel Michael to place a donation in the box there, I heard him answering several questions from Father Isaiah.

"Why did she choose Michael?" he asked.

"She did not choose him," said the Diplomat. "He chose her." There was silence in which I turned awkwardly towards them, embarrassed. How do you tell a fellow human being you believe that an angel has revealed himself to be your mentor and guardian? How can anyone claim such connections without appearing preposterous and probably mad?

Isaiah waited at the church door and did not let me pass without his question. "How? Can you tell me?" Then he caught himself, eager but cautious. "Only if you can, of course." It was a statement of faith. So I spoke briefly of the opening on the Nile, the surge of joy and wonder, the fear of possession and madness, the response to my question with the name Michael, the promise of strength for work to come.

I could see hope bursting through the young monk's eyes, the same longing I had felt, the same thirst. We walked through other parts of the monastery, mindful of those waiting atop the plateau and the steep climb awaiting us.

In the small room that enshrines the remains of St. Andraus the Blind, who died here after more than ninety years in the monastery, Isaiah grew animated. Yes, he had known Andraus, but only briefly, as the saint died so soon after his own arrival. There was pain in the way he said this, a longing for the blessing that, alighting on others, seemed so far to have passed him by.

"I was a dentist," he told me. "A monk puts on black clothes to show that he has died to the world. But here I care for the teeth of the monks." Evidently, there was plenty for him to do. Although only ten new monks had been allowed to join during the past decade, there are at present over a hundred desert fathers at Anba Samwil, making this out-of-the-way and little-known monastery one of the largest in Egypt. But there are no true hermits here, Isaiah said in answer to our question, only two or three who are allowed to practice asceticism "at the first stage" of retreat from the community.

We refused tea due to the press of time and, leaving the sanctuary, began our long ascent back to where our friends awaited us. Father Isaiah came with us, at first only to the end of the garden area, then to the base of the cliff, and finally up the ragged, rocky slope. I remembered the story of the monks who failed to recognize Jesus and wondered if Isaiah, being uncertain, was determined to avoid the same mistake. Or did he wish to make certain we left the premises? By the time we reached the lip of the escarpment, the monk's green plastic sandals had been ruined.

The kettle was on beside the Range Rover. As we drank tea, one of the others, a journalist who hoped to write about Deir Samwil, plied the monk with questions. Though she seemed intent on making him confess that the new fence was for protection against Muslim extremists, Father Isaiah would not be drawn.

While the others loaded the chairs, cups, and kettle into the car, I walked Isaiah to the end of the escarpment. He hesitated briefly, before beginning the descent in his tattered sandals. Then he spoke urgently.

"If there is a message from Michael for me..."
Early 1995

Deir Anba Samwil—Anba Samuel's monastery south of Fayoum, January 1995

57

Trouble at Abu Seifein

"Come now," Karim said urgently. "You must come *now*. There are a few people here with the Abuna, some for and some against, but he refuses to leave the church, and Pope Shenouda's[1] office has informed us that the Pope is on the way to arrest him. Perhaps you can convince him to give in."

"Why me?" I asked. "Can't you talk to the Abuna, help him understand that if the Pope wants to remove him, there's no sensible solution other than submission? How can he defy the Pope?"

"But he does defy," Karim insisted, "and the situation has become dangerous. I've been here with other Christians for several hours, and despite trying everything we can think of, Abuna will not be moved. But you know him. Maybe he'll listen to you."

Working together at Befrienders Cairo, Karim and I had listened to and supported many unhappy, desperate and even suicidal people but this was something quite different. How could I, a foreign woman, dare to intervene in a dispute between Coptic clerics? The Abuna surely already knew that resistance was futile and could easily lead to violence. But Karim's demand didn't seem to leave me an option. Anyway, I was a former journalist as well as a befriender and, like the old fire horse who picked up speed when he heard bells ringing, I couldn't help myself.

"I'm on my way," I told Karim. Before leaving Zamalek, I asked dear old Nur to tell Alan where I was when he came home. Then I got into my clapped-out little car, which no one would ever have thought to steal, and set off for old Cairo. It should take about thirty minutes to get there, depending on traffic.

During the previous two years, I had spent many hours in the ancient church of Abu Seifein—the Father of Two Swords—a place of palpable holiness, adorned with icons, relics, and incense and filled with The Presence. I went there often to show visitors around, but I also went alone to pray, to listen, and to sit in silence. In time, I had met the Abuna, discussed Coptic theology and the use of icons, and learned how he had been at the helm during several years restoration of the essentially fourteenth century church, the origins of which date back to the late fifth or early sixth century.[3] In that holy place I had, after long loneliness, heard again the Voice which calls us to love God and to sacrifice for the sake of others. But on the day Karim called me, I had to bang on the door and shout several times before a small door opened in the large door and I was allowed to creep through.

There were some twenty-five Copts, mainly men, and all very tense, pacing around in the ancient church. Karim knew as well as I that there was little hope the Abuna would yield to my importuning any more than to his. But he was relieved to see me and took me straight to the priest, who was wearing his usual long black robe and, today, sitting on a simple, armless chair at the back of the church with a frown on his face. The usually half-dark church was alight with scores of candles, carrying the prayers of those who had locked themselves in the church with their priest.

What, I wondered, had brought the Abuna to his disobedient, almost suicidal, action? As a trained engineer he had been instrumental in generating both architectural and artistic restoration of this ancient holy place. Restoration was not yet complete, and perhaps never would be, but Abu Seifein belonged to God, as did the Abuna himself by his vows. What was going on here? Was he having a breakdown?

I knelt beside the angry and stricken priest, pleading that he submit in order to prevent violence in a holy place, to remain true to his vows, to protect those who cared for him. But the Abuna remained unmoved. I understood eventually that all the people who had gathered in the church were on the Abuna's side, and thus possibly willing to help resist his removal. Surely there was a lot going on here that I knew nothing about.

"Please," I told the Abuna. "Can you not submit? Violence in the church would be profane." But although he spoke to me as a friend, Abuna was as stubborn as a two-year-old, and unhappy that I could not support his protest. God has given me this church, he said, and I have been God's servant in bringing it back to life. There is more work needed here, and I will not leave and go back to a monastery in the desert.[2] My pleas that he submit to the Pope before there was a riot, people were injured, and the church which he loved was damaged or destroyed were useless.

By this time every candle in the old wooden church had been lit, and all the hanging oil lamps glowed, reflecting the prayers of the Abuna's agonized supporters. His handful of followers were as vulnerable as he, their courage remarkable. They sought God's mercy on their abuna, they told me, and a change of mind and of heart by the Pope. As we spoke, others came up again and again to ask Abuna to find a compromise so that he would not be taken away from them by Pope Shenouda.

It seemed to me that the Abuna was doing what most of us do when we can see no way forward, yet believe we cannot back out. We sit still then, and pray for miracles, throwing our future into God's face while forgetting that God our loving Mother doesn't respond positively to tantrums. Abuna had overseen the architectural and artistic restoration of Abu Seifein. He had taken on the preservation of icons and pillars, had the roof recovered and renovated the chapel of Mari-Jacob el-Mokatha. He had even been able to see to the sealing and restoration of the Cave of Anba Barsoum El Eryan, now a shocking three meters below the water level. But for reasons I did not know, his achievements had not prevented the Pope's order for him to move on. Something had happened, of course, but no one was telling me what it was.

After a long while, having made no advances whatsoever towards compromise, Karim and I left the stubborn priest, who refused to come with us, and walked with others to the area beneath the altar. There, raising our hands in supplication, we asked God to bring peace between the Abuna and the Coptic Pope and to protect Abu Seifein church from violence. It seemed fairly clear to me by this stage that God was not going to send angels to sort out the difficulties. What was needed, it seemed, was repentance and, as my mother used to say, "Sometimes you just have to do it!"

It was during these prayers that a sudden cry of "Fire!" rang out.

Although this was a false alarm, it was another sign of our precarious emotional as well as physical state. The doors were locked, and small oil and candle fires were burning all over an ancient building filled with wooden, paper, and cloth objects. Meanwhile, fear was mounting collectively. The Pope might arrive at any time, but if he didn't do so soon, it was possible he might find nothing but ashes.

Realizing there was little, if anything more I could do after two hours of alternate kneeling at the altar and kneeling beside the Abuna, I decided it was best that I leave. With considerable difficulty and some opposition, Karim arranged that the small door to the outside be reopened. I fled, then, in my impotence, wondering whether I would see Karim or the Abuna again and beseeching the Lord of Life to save both His church and His people.

Perhaps I should not have gone to Abu Seifein on that day. As it turned out, Pope Shenouda and his entourage did not arrive for several more hours, thus giving Abuna as much time as possible to repent and submit. But eventually the Coptic pope got there, and his disobedient priest was carried off to a monastery. Whether the Abuna's departure was in acceptance or in chains, no one could tell me for Karim, too, had wisely left before the end.

As members of one the oldest Christian churches in the world, Copts greatly value submission to God's representative. Thus I was relieved not to have been there when the Pope arrived, having been told on several occasions how severely disobedient Coptic monks may in some circumstances be treated. Their fate is entirely, it would seem, in the hands of authorities in the Coptic Church. Egyptian government authorities are, therefore, most unlikely to intervene if the Coptic pope decides to have a priest severely punished. Or perhaps even put to death? I never saw the Abuna again, although I continued to take visitors to Abu Seifein.

While living in Sudan some two or three years later, I heard that the Abuna was back in Cairo and, even more amazing, that he was still a monk, but not at Abu Seifein. I hope this information was true because the Abuna was a good man, spiritually open, inclined to mysticism, eager to know God, forward looking, and a good administrator. Certainly there is much more to this story than I know. What is clear is that the Abuna lost his temper in a debate with authority. Here, I am greatly sympathetic. The Lord of Life knows how many times I've done that—and almost always to my detriment.

Inside the Church of Abu Seifein, Old Cairo, January 1995

Notes

13 In the Wadi of the King

1. Joseph J. Hobbs, *Bedouin Life in the Egyptian Wilderness* (The American University in Cairo Press, 1989), p. 21.

16 With Florence Nightingale in Upper Egypt

1. Florence Nightingale, *Letters from Egypt: A Journey on the Nile, 1849–1950* (London: Barrie and Jenkins, 1987), p. 157.
2. Max Rodenbeck, "Draconian Powers," *Middle East International* 24 July 1992, p. 11.
3. Jonathan Cott, *The Search for Omm Sety* (London: Arrow Books, 1989), p.127.

17 Qanatar Prison

1. I never knew the teenager's name or what happened to her.
2. The Girlfriend was released from Qanatar Prison and returned to the United Kingdom before the end of 1992.

20 Faith and Solitude at the Monasteries of St. Anthony and St. Paul

1. Kenneth Scott Latourette, *A History of Christianity* (New York: Harper and Brothers, 1953), p. 225.
2. These words were prophetic. Twenty years after the monk said this to me, large numbers of Copts continue to leave Egypt for safer and more prosperous places to live. But the monasteries in Egypt's deserts are overflowing.

23 Aswan without Tourists

1. Amelia B. Edwards, *A Thousand Miles Up the Nile* (New York: St. Martin's Press, JP Tarcher Edition, 1983), p. 200.
2. Ibid., p. 168.

25 From Cairo to Kharga

1. R. A. Bagnold, *Libyan Sands: Travel in a Dead World* (London: Michael Haag, Ltd., 1987 [originally published in 1935]).

29 On Tour from Liberation Square

1. Cassandra Vivian, *Islands of the Blest: A Guide to the Oases and Western Desert of Egypt* (Maadi, Egypt: International Publications, 1990).

34 Alifa Rifaat's Vision

1. Quoted in Nevine Khalil, "More Violence or Just Different," *Al-Ahram*, Weekly, 17 March 1993. p. 2.
2. Brian Keenan, *An Evil Cradling* (London: Hutchinson, 1992).
3. Emily Nasrallah, *A House Not Her Own: Stories from Beirut* (Charlottetown, Prince Edward Island, Canada: Gynergy Books, 1992).
4. Alifa Rifaat, *Distant View of a Minaret* (Oxford: Heinemann, 1983), translated by Denys Johnson-Davies.

40 Befriending Cairo

1. Befrienders Cairo, a member of Befrienders International, the Samaritans abroad. Their message was: "Call now if you are facing a personal crisis. If you need someone to talk to. If you feel life is not worth living. Free and confidential. You will not be told what to do. And you will not be alone anymore. Arabic and English spoken. Tel. 344-8200. 3rd floor, 209, 26th July Street, Sphinx Square, Mohandiseen." Befrienders Cairo lasted for over ten years—a miracle in its own right—and long after I had left Egypt.

42 Mena House and Minor Pyramids

1. For a history of the Mena House, which became a hotel in the

1880s, see Nina Nelson, *Mena House Oberoi: A Short History of a Remarkable Hotel* (Cairo: Palm Press, 1987).
2. Richard Hoath, *Natural Selection: A Year of Egypt's Wildlife* (American University in Cairo Press, 1992).
3. I. E. S. Edwards, *The Pyramids of Egypt* (London: Penguin Books. Revised Edition, 1991), p 144.

43 Spiritual Journey on the River

1. Florence Nightingale, *Letters from Egypt: A Journey on the Nile, 1849–1850* (London: Barrie and Jenkins, 1987), p. 77.
2. Ibid., p. 74.
3. Ibid., p. 77.

44 Looking for Michael in Middle Egypt

1. The British Voluntary Service Overseas, established in 1958, is similar to the American Peace Corps.

45. Siwa: Escape from a Dying Oasis

1. Al-Maqrizi, *Al-Mawa'iz wa al-tibar fi dhikr al-Khitat wa al-Athar [Sermons and Learning on an Account of Settlements and Antiquities]*, cited in Ahmed Fakhry, *Siwa Oasis* (American University in Cairo Press, 1973), p. 95.
2. Fakhry, *Siwa Oasis*, p. 152.

46 Sorting It Out with the Zebaleen

1. Keeping of pigs was forbidden by the Egyptian authorities some years later following a widespread outbreak of trichinosis. I am not aware what further hardships the removal of this source of funding and of food, however tainted, placed on the zebaleen.

53 Humming from Western Desert to Eastern Desert

1. The Egyptian government, hoping to prove that Upper Egypt remained safe for tourism, staged an elaborate production of *Aida* in late November 1994 at the Temple of Hatshepsut in Deir el Bahri. Poor attendance brought cancellation of four of the seven planned performances and attendees embarrassed the government by telling the international press that they had seen more police than citizens.

Meanwhile, everyone complained of the bitter wind and the opposition press decried the arbitrary burning of west bank cane fields in order to prevent attacks on visitors by irate citizens. There were also claims that blankets donated by international agencies for victims of the disastrous October floods showed up around the shoulders of the wealthy at Deir el Bahri. But at least, some people said, there had been no "public" violence.
2. A yardang is a streamlined hill carved from the bedrock or any consolidated or semi-consolidated material by the dual action of wind and abrasion, dust and sand, and deflation.

55 Moulid of Al-Sayeda Zeinab

1. From Yehya Haqqi's novel *Qandil Umm Hashim*, translated by M. M. Badawi in the Arabic Translation Series of the *Journal of Arabic Literature* (Leiden: Brill, 1973). Reprinted in *Arab World Weekly*, "A Visit to the Shrine," 22–28 December 1994, p. 21
2. Elizabeth Pearson and Katie Walker, "Festival Exposure," *Middle East Times*, 23–29 October 1994, p. 9
3. Nicholaas H. Biegman, *Egypt: Moulids, Saints, Sufis* (The Hague: Gary Schwartz/SDU and Kegan Paul International Ltd., 1990), p. 13.
4. Shirk is the sin of equating someone or something with God.
5. A zar is a ceremony to exorcise afrit, or evil spirits. Clearly pagan in origin, it features dancing and music, usually involves only women, and sometimes includes animal sacrifice, usually of sheep or chickens.

57 Trouble at Abu Seifein

1. Coptic Pope Shenouda III, patriarch of the Coptic Orthodox Church died at the age of 88 in March 2012 after leading Egyptian Coptic Christians for forty years. He was imprisoned in 1981 after accusing President Sadat of failing to control Islamic militants and not released until 1985 by President Mubarak. Following the fall of Mubarak in 2011 tensions between Christians and Muslims accelerated and churches were attacked by mobs in several areas of Egypt. A Christian protest in October 2011 resulted in the killing of some two dozen people. Leaders of both the Muslim Brotherhood and the Egyptian army joined Pope Shenouda "in an unprecedented move aimed at showing unity" during Orthodox Christmas celebrations in 2011. See obituary of Pope Shenouda III in the 19 March 2012 edition of the *Washington Post*.
2. Abu Seifein, the Father of Two Swords, is among a handful of ancient Egyptian churches said to date from the end of the fifth and begin-

ning of the sixth centuries. It was turned into a sugar cane warehouse in the eighth century, rebuilt as a church in 970 and burned down in 1168. Restoration and reconstruction began around 1174 and Abu Seifein was eventually reopened for worship in 1313. (Amany Fouad, *The Restoration of Abu Seifein* [*Egypt Today*, Spring 1992]).
3. The modern church of Abu Seifein has been changed and repaired many times since the fourteenth century. But by the early 1990s it was greatly in need of additional refurbishing, including preservation of its icons and protection against continually rising groundwater in the Cairo area.

Glossary

'ursh	piasters; small Egyptian coins
a'outhu billah	I seek refuge in God
abuna	Father
afrit	mischievous spirit
aide memoire	a memory aid
ala toul	straight ahead
al hamdulillah	praise be to God
Allah	God
Anba	Father: used of a senior Coptic clergyman or saint
araq	an aniseed-based liquor
as salam aleikum	peace be with you
ba	part of the soul that could travel between the worlds of the living and the dead, according to ancient Egyptians
babaghanouj	an eggplant dip
baksheesh	gratuity; tip
baraka	blessing
bedu/Bedouin	nomadic desert-dweller(s)
beps	Pepsi
berseem	clover; animal fodder
birket	small lake
bish'a	ordeal
boab	doorman
darb el arba'in	forty days' road
effendi	Sir; an Ottoman dignity
falafel	a dish of beans and herbs fried as croquettes

Glossary

faseekh	pickled fish
fasit afreet	a breath of air (literally, a spirit's fart)
fatwa	a formal legal opinion under Islamic law
feddan	an area of land slightly larger than an acre
fellah(in)	peasant(s)
feluccas	sailing boats
firman	Ottoman decree, edict
foul	beans
galabiyah	a loose shirt-like garment: common dress of males in Egypt
Guftis	laborers on an archaeological dig
Hajj	Pilgrimage
hajjis	pilgrims
hashish	cannabis
henna	a reddish-orange cosmetic
iftar	the meal to break the fast in Ramadan
inshallah	if God wills
jebel(s)	hill(s); mountain(s)
jihad	struggle; effort
jinn	genie
ka	part of the soul which ancient Egyptians believed to require sustenance in the afterlife, hence provisions provided in tombs
kebab hala	a dish of stewed beef
kerkadeh	drink made from hibiscus flowers
khawaga(s)	foreigner(s)
kohl	preparation used for darkening the eyelids
kushari	dish of rice, macaroni, and lentils
kwayisa	nice; good
LE	Egyptian pounds (from the French *livres égyptiennes*)
mabsouta	happy; content
madrasa	school
majlis	meeting room; council

Glossary

malesh	never mind
mamluke	Mameluke; Ottoman soldier; (originally slave)
mastaba	ancient Egyptian tomb of mud brick, rectangular in form with sloping sides and a flat roof
medina	city, town center
mihrab	a recess in a mosque indicating the direction of prayer
moulid	birthday; anniversary
muezzin	announcer of the time for prayer
mukhabarat	security or intelligence services
mutasawif	a Sufi
nargilehs	water-pipe; hubble-bubble; shisha
natron	a salt formerly used in mummification
norias	waterwheels
qasr	fort; tower; castle
qubba(s)	literally, dome(s); tomb(s) of holy men
rahma	mercy
Sa'idi	a man from Upper Egypt
saida	happy
shabti	funerary figure representing a servant for the dead in the afterlife
shirk	polytheism; idolatry
shisha	waterpipe; hubble-bubble; nargilehs
suffragi	waiter; house servant
taftish	inspection; checkpoint
tariqa	a Sufi order
tasrih	permit; permission
wadi(s)	valley(s)
walad	boy; youth
witwat	bat
ya salaam	what a pity
yardangs	keel-shaped crests or ridges of rock, formed by action of the wind
yusif effendi	tangerine

zar	séance; exorcism of spirits
zebaleen	Cairo rubbish collectors and processors
zikr	remembrance
zirs	water jars

www.ingramcontent.com/pod-product-compliance
Lightning Source LLC
Chambersburg PA
CBHW071955220426
43662CB00009B/1144